Suicide in Prisons

Suicide in Prisons

*Edited by Graham Towl, Louisa Snow and
Martin McHugh*

BPS Blackwell

© 2002 by Blackwell Publishers Ltd
a Blackwell Publishing company

Editorial Offices:
108 Cowley Road, Oxford OX4 1JF, UK
 Tel: +44 (0)1865 791100
350 Main Street, Malden, MA 02148-5018, USA
 Tel: +1 781 388 8250

First published 2000 by The British Psychological Society
A BPS Blackwell book
Transferred to digital print 2004

Library of Congress Cataloging-in-Publication Data has been applied for

ISBN 1 85433 329 1

A catalogue record for this title is available from the British Library.

Set by Book Production Services, London

Printed and bound in Great Britain by
Marston Lindsay Ross International Ltd,
Oxfordshire

For further information on
Blackwell Publishers, visit our website:
www.blackwellpublishers.co.uk

Contents

List of tables and figures

Tables

Figures

Foreword

Since taking up the post of Director General of the Prison Service, I have made – and continue to make – reducing suicides in prison one of my main priorities. Providing a safe and decent environment for prisoners and looking after them with humanity are primary objectives for the Prison Service; the preservation of human life is fundamental to our duty of care. The number of people who have died in prison over the years is a terrible waste of life. Staff and prisoners are affected, more deeply than many of the public might imagine, but of course it is relatives and friends who bear the burden of each of these individual tragedies. I don't underestimate the challenges that we face in trying to reduce suicides. Nor would I wish to overlook the very good work that is already undertaken by staff, prisoners, and other agencies and volunteers, such as The Samaritans. I am pleased that the Prison Service has taken the important step of becoming more open with relatives through sharing the results of internal investigations into deaths. I am sure that there is more that we can do.

One important area is ensuring that we expand and share our knowledge of the causes of suicides in prison. This is a topic that is about more than just prison; it is about the relationship between prison and the community. I am pleased to endorse this publication as a very helpful endeavour in drawing together and consolidating our understanding. I hope that it will also stimulate debate and further research in this important and challenging area.

Martin Narey
Director General of the Prison Service, England and Wales
July 2000

Preface

Collectively, the authors of this collection of chapters on suicide in prisons have well over 30 recent years' experience in research and practice in that environment. It is from such a broad experience and knowledge base that the authors have distilled key themes in terms of policy, research and practice.

The book is divided into three broad sections. The first sets the context in terms of policy, practice and the research base. The second section has as its primary focus three key perspectives on addressing and structuring interventions with suicidal prisoners. The third section switches in focus to staff training needs and an exploration of the rarely discussed issue of the aftermath of suicides in prison, looking at all those affected. The final chapter of the book looks to the future in terms of some likely developments.

First, Martin McHugh and Louisa Snow put into historical perspective the policy developments that have occurred for the management of suicidal prisoners. Usefully, they tease out a number of recurrent themes that have been the antecedents to more recent developments in the way in which HM Prison Service, England and Wales has grappled with the issue and management of suicides in prisons. Chapter 2, by David Crighton, consists of a review of the evidence available on completed suicide in prisons, including a detailed analysis of six of the more influential studies. One pervasive theme in the chapter is a critical approach to the methodologies used, with a view to informing future research endeavours. Chapter 3, by David Crighton and Graham Towl, is entitled 'Intentional self-injury' (ISI). The term ISI is used in preference to the less precise and somewhat anachronistic term 'deliberate self-harm' (DSH). The literature on self-injury and its relationship to suicide is critically reviewed.

Continuing on from setting the scene in terms of policy, practice and research on suicide and self-injury, the second section of the book has a firm focus on interventions with prisoners. Three chapters are included, reflecting the importance of effective risk assessment and staff–prisoner relationships and prisoner–prisoner relationships. In Chapter 4, by Graham Towl and David Crighton, a framework for risk assessment and management is outlined (the Cambridge model), and this is applied to work with suicidal prisoners. In Chapter 5, Graham Towl and Danielle Forbes outline some basic counselling skills to assist in effective work with suicidal prisoners. In Chapter 6, Louisa Snow outlines the role of peer-group support for prisoners, emphasising the value of formalised peer support groups.

The third and final section of the book involves a shift in emphasis from the suicidal to those around them. Chapter 7, by Jo Bailey, Martin McHugh, Lisa Chisnall and Danielle Forbes, outlines staff training for those working with suicidal prisoners. Clearly, without effective and timely training, national strategies for helping suicidal prisoners will falter. The potential in terms of the impact on prisoners needing assistance is difficult to quantify but must surely be a necessary condition of the implementation of effective suicide awareness and prevention policies. In Chapter 8, Louisa Snow and Martin McHugh address some of the difficult and challenging areas associated with the aftermath of a suicide. They tackle this sensitive but important area with an approach previously notable for its absence in the literature on suicides in prisons. In the final chapter, the editors attempt to draw together some of the key issues with an eye to future directions for research, policy and practice.

We hope that this book will be of interest to a range of individuals in both academic and forensic institutions. Above all we hope that it will be a useful resource for all those with an interest in helping suicidal prisoners.

About the editors

Graham Towl is Head of Profession for Prison and Probation Psychology Services. He previously held the positions of Area Forensic Psychologist in Kent and East Anglia Prison Service areas. He has also worked in the NHS. He was formerly chair of the British Psychological Society's Division of Forensic Psychology. He has visiting academic positions at the Universities of Cambridge and Kent. He is co-founding editor of the *British Journal of Forensic Practice*. His publications include co-authorship of *The Handbook of Psychology for Forensic Practitioners* (1996, London, Routledge), and editorship of *Groupwork in Prisons* (1995, Leicester, BPS) and *Suicide and Self-injury in Prisons* (1997, Leicester, BPS)

Louisa Snow is jointly researcher with the Suicide Awareness Support Unit, Prison Service Headquarters, and the University of Kent, where she is undertaking doctorate research into attempted suicide and self-injury amongst prisoners. She has written a number of articles on self-injury and suicide in prisons.

Martin McHugh is currently Head of the Management Selection and Succession Unit, Prison Service Headquarters. He was previously Head of the Suicide Awareness Support Unit, Prison Service Headquarters. Previous positions include Principal Forensic Psychologist for recruitment and training of psychologists and Principal Forensic Psychologist in High Security Prisons. He has written a number of articles and papers on suicide and self-injury in prisons.

David Crighton is based at the Priory Healthcare NHS Trust in Sunderland.

Jo Bailey is based in the Prison Service Eastern Area Office.

Lisa Chisnall is based at HMP Bullwood Hall.

Danielle Forbes is based at HMP Highpoint.

Suicide prevention: policy and practice
Martin McHugh and Louisa Snow

Overview

This chapter describes the context within which current strategies on suicide prevention have been developed in prisons in England and Wales. Particular attention is given to the last 30 years, during which a number of guidance and instructional documents have been issued. These are explored in some detail. The chapter concludes with a consideration of some of the issues affecting the implementation of policy.

Context

The causes of an individual suicide (whether in prison or elsewhere) are rarely simple. It follows that preventive solutions are unlikely to be simple. This may seem an obvious statement, but the history of suicide prevention in organisations such as the Prison Service is often coloured by a search for the solution to the 'problem' of suicide. The reality is that suicide is a complex behaviour pattern, prompted by different factors and motivations according to differing circumstances.

In developing strategies for suicide prevention in prisons, account must be taken of factors external and internal to the prison, each of which may result in a heightened risk of suicide among prisoners. This differentiation between internal and external factors is nothing new. In his report for 1910–11, the Medical Inspector for prisons in England (Smalley, 1911) states of suicides that 'influences are operating in either the special characteristics of prisoners going to prison or in the special conditions that attach to imprisonment'. Further, the 'frequency [of crimes of passion] in the criminal record of these prisoners is an indication that the suicidal tendency is really related to the nature of the offence, and is not an effect of the known or anticipated severity of the punishment which the prisoner has to face'. These comments are quoted by Hobhouse and Brockway (1922) as evidence that prison administrators are likely to err towards regarding the causes of suicide as being within the individual prisoner rather than the prison environment, thereby diminishing the accountability of administrators.

The relative weighting of factors that are internal and external to the individual prisoner as causative of suicide has been a key issue in the development of suicide prevention strategies. It is now commonly – but by no means universally – accepted that prison suicides are as much a community as a prison problem (HM Chief Inspector of Prisons (HMCIP), 1999). In fact, it could be argued that to view prison suicides as an exclusively prison matter, i.e. solely a function of what imprisonment does to prisoners, will hinder the development of comprehensive suicide prevention strategies. This sharing of responsibility between prison and community should in no way be regarded as a diminution of responsibility on the part of prisons, but rather as a reflection of the reality of the situation and what needs to be addressed. Of course, the question of how much imprisonment *per se* has contributed to an individual suicide will always be a matter of debate.

In developing strategies for suicide prevention in prisons, as in other secure settings and within the community, a major problem facing policy makers is simply the magnitude of factors that have the potential for impacting upon suicide risk. By way of illustration, each of the following prison factors has been proposed as influencing the degree of risk:

- the overall quality of the prison regime and the opportunity afforded for meaningful activity for prisoners;
- the extent to which prisoners feel safe and protected from intimidation or bullying;
- the degree to which the physical environment is safe and restricts opportunities for self-injury;
- the availability of quality services for prisoners with mental health problems;
- the extent to which prisoners are able to maintain family ties;
- the extent to which prisoners are able to disclose and discuss their problems;
- the ability of staff to identify prisoners at heightened risk and to offer appropriate management and support.

This list is by no means comprehensive, but it illustrates that, for a suicide prevention programme to be totally effective, a large number of elements of prison policy would have to work in synchrony. In practice this is likely to be an elusive goal. First, there is an inherent tension within imprisonment between care and control (Towl and Fisher, 1992); secondly, there is the effect of unintended or unforeseen consequences.

Neither of these phenomena should appear as a surprise; in fact they have their parallels in suicide prevention within the community. As the introduction of new over-the-counter drugs helps to reduce pain and discomfort, so their availability opens up new avenues for self-overdose. In contrast, the introduction of non-toxic domestic North Sea gas in the 1970s had the unintended consequence of a significant reduction in suicides (Kreitman, 1976) – unintended because the change of production was guided by economic rather than philanthropic motives. Similarly, although on a much smaller scale, changes in Prison Service policies may impact upon suicide in unintended ways. Consider, for example, the following:

- Aiming to provide an individual cell for each prisoner is a fundamental goal of Prison Service policy in England and Wales. There is evidence (albeit limited) that sharing occupancy of a cell may reduce the risk of suicide for some prisoners. This may be a factor explaining the stabilising of the rate of suicides between 1994 and 1997, when overcrowding resulted from a dramatic rise in the prison population during this period.
- Maximising the time prisoners spend out of their cells is a Prison Service objective. However, increased time in association may lead to increased opportunities for intimidation or bullying by others, unless supervision is adequate.
- Introduction of in-cell televisions may be beneficial in keeping prisoners occupied and less prone to suicidal ruminations, but it may also increase the availability of potential ligatures and ligature points.
- The introduction of differential regimes based upon earned incentives and privileges provides a powerful mechanism for control and improved behaviour and is of benefit to those prisoners who conform and progress through the scheme, but such a system may result in reduced support for some vulnerable prisoners, putting them at increased risk of self-injury.

In summary, positive changes in one area may have quite unintended consequences in another. There is no easy solution to this dilemma, any more than there is in the community at large. Some have argued that the controlled, restrictive nature of prison confinement should make it easier to reduce suicides because of reduced opportunities for self-injury and greater levels of supervision and observation than are normally available in the community. This view is predicated upon a naïve, oversimplistic view of the nature and purpose of imprisonment. Although by its very nature imprisonment reduces an individual's sphere of influence, self-control is not eradicated – nor, arguably, should it be. The preservation of self-control and maintenance of opportunities for exercising choice are fundamental to reducing the pains of imprisonment (Sykes, 1958) and, as Liebling (1998) and others have argued, such preservation may be crucial in reducing the likelihood of suicidal behaviour.

One issue that is rarely discussed is the degree to which an individual prisoner is entitled to the choice to end life. This issue involves an ethical and philosophical debate that is beyond the scope of this book, but is fundamental to what staff and prisoners imagine is both achievable and desirable as a goal in suicide prevention. It is only for the last 40 years or so that suicide has ceased to be a criminal act in the community in England and Wales and, more recently, that self-injury has ceased to be an infringement against good order and discipline within a prison. There is clearly a very delicate balance to be preserved between correct exercise of the duty of care for those placed in state custody and the maintenance of individuality and the preservation of individual choice. In this important sense, prevention of suicides is quite different from prevention of escapes, which must arguably be prevented at all costs. Put more starkly: attempting to escape is a punishable offence; attempting to complete suicide is not, although some responses to self-injury may be seen as punitive. Reducing suicide simply by reducing the means to self-injure is a sterile, artificial line of prevention (Stern, 1998: 133) which carries the risk of dehumanising, intrusive practices that are degrading and of dubious benefit, even in the short term (Dexter and Towl, 1995).

How, then, are policy makers to find a way through this minefield of causes and effects where so many factors may be in potential conflict? A pragmatic solution emerges if we view suicide prevention as operating on two levels: first, at a global level across the whole establishment where a variety of factors may impact and whose outcome, as indicated earlier, may not be foreseen; and, secondly, at a specialised level that facilitates the correct identification of prisoners at heightened risk and provides appropriate support. Unsurprisingly, policy makers have tended to focus on the latter approach. This is not simply because the global factors are complex and unpredictable, but rather because, however holistic and well integrated the regime, there will always be a need for a system of identifying and supporting those prisoners at heightened risk of self-injury or suicide.

An overview of how current Prison Service policy has developed now follows.

Development of Prison Service policies on suicide prevention up to the early 1990s

Although the roots of the current strategy for suicide prevention in prisons in England and Wales first appear in print in 1973, it would be quite misleading to imagine that there were no strategies in place prior to this. Lady Constance Lytton, a suffragette who spent many weeks in Holloway prison at the beginning of the twentieth century, bemoaned the reliance upon physical methods of suicide prevention, in this case the wire netting used to prevent prisoners jumping from the galleries (cited in Stern, 1998). The following quotation from Hobhouse and Brockway (1922: 550) reinforces this rather exclusively environmental approach to suicide prevention:

[O]ne of the features of the interior of an English prison ... is the elaborate nature of the precautions adopted against suicide. The cell furniture and utensils are so devised as to render extremely difficult even any attempt at self-destruction. The knife provided for the prisoners' meals is such as would make extremely slow and painful any suicide attempted by its means; cord and other articles which might be used for self-strangulation are kept as far as possible from the prisoner's possession. The artificial light in the cells is apt to be very defective largely on account of the arrangements adopted to prevent the inhalation of gas. This precaution ... ensures that one hundred thousand people are inconvenienced, in order that one may be prevented from ending his discomfort.

In contrast to this initial focus on environmental factors, Prison Service Standing Orders in use prior to the First World War emphasise a broadening of approaches to suicide prevention. The following factors are described as associated with heightened risk of suicide, again by Hobhouse and Brockway (1922: 317):

The attention of the governor and other responsible officers is directed to the following points relating to suicide. It appears that:-

- the tendency to commit suicide is greater during the first week of imprisonment than at any subsequent period.
- persons under remand or awaiting trial are more liable to commit suicide than those who have received sentence.
- prisoners in prison for the first time are more liable than others to commit suicide.

Precautions, therefore, are especially necessary during the earlier weeks of imprisonment, and those who are in prison for the first or second time are more likely to suffer from the state of mind which tends to suicide rather than those who have been many times in prison, and are hardened in crime.

The report of the Medical Inspector (Smalley, 1911), referred to earlier, states that, of 86 cases of suicide analysed, 36 committed suicide within a week of admission to prison and five on the day of reception. Although there are some differences, this overall profile for suicides in prisons bears a remarkable resemblance to prison suicides in the 1990s (see Chapter 2), in particular the heightened risk associated with the early stages after reception. This is a remarkably robust finding.

The early 1970s

The foundation stone for current strategies was laid with Circular Instruction (CI) 39/73, which summarised extant instructions. It is worth exploring a little of the instruction in detail to provide a flavour of the issues that crop up again and again through the last quarter of the twentieth century. The emphasis is less on formalised procedures or systems and more on increasing general awareness of the problem. It reminds staff of the measures that may prevent suicide in prisons, outlines a number of factors that may increase the likelihood of suicide, and describes the action to be taken when a suicide has occurred.

The importance of communication (between staff and prisoners, and between staff and other agencies) is emphasised, as is the need to deal effectively with any information received about prisoners by passing it directly to the medical officer who 'must necessarily take the lead in suicide prevention'. Despite this medical emphasis, it was acknowledged that other staff should be alert to any signs of suicidal inclination.

Attention is drawn to the specific periods in a term of imprisonment, which may pose the greatest risk of suicide:

- shortly after reception on remand;
- after reception on conviction awaiting sentence;
- after reception on sentence;
- immediately prior to release.

Note the similarities to those risk periods cited earlier from before the First World War.

The importance of continued support in the form of 'personal communication' during these periods is stressed, as is the importance of support from others in the establishment (e.g. a chaplain or welfare officer). It is stipulated that all new prisoners should be seen by the medical officer 'soon after arrival' (and by the morning after reception at the latest) and that long periods of waiting in reception should be avoided.

A number of factors (both individual and offence-related) associated with elevated risk of suicide are indicated:

- an offence likely to produce an 'abnormal level of remorse, fear or shame' (e.g. murder or sexual offence);
- a first offence, which will 'seriously undermine a man's self-esteem and his social position on release';
- a history of outbursts of aggressive behaviour, impulsiveness or hysterical temperament;
- 'mental disturbance' (particularly melancholic or depressive states, or anxiety);
- previous suicide attempts or threats, or previously self-inflicted injuries;
- drug abuse or alcoholism (especially during and immediately after withdrawal);
- no previous periods of custody.

Once a prisoner has been identified as potentially suicidal, it is recommended that the prisoner should be located in the prison hospital at night but, with the medical officer's agreement, should work as usual during the day. Any prisoner who attempts suicide should be located in the hospital for at least 24 hours and should not return to an ordinary location within the prison until after reassessment by the medical officer and after an effort has been made (in consultation with other staff) to 'probe the reasons behind the attempt and to deal with the underlying problems'. Prisoners should be returned to an ordinary location only on the written authority of the medical officer, who should 'advise staff how he[/she] should be treated'.

CI 39/73 introduced the use of an 'F' marking on the prisoner's record as providing an indication to the medical officer on reception that a prisoner had been known to be, or was considered as, potentially suicidal. The decision on the best location for such a prisoner was a matter for the medical officer. The marking was also intended to alert other staff on subsequent occasions, so that the reasons for 'depression, moodiness or attention-seeking behaviour' could be explored and a referral made to the medical officer. The existence of an 'F' marking would be communicated to other agencies within the penal system (i.e. police, courts). The 'F' marking registers a deep chord in Prison Service culture, and even in the twenty-first century its memory lingers on. It has its origins in a proper recognition of the importance of past history as a predictor of behaviour, but it fails to recognise the dynamic elements of changing risk over time.

The 1980s

The 1970s and 1980s saw a steady increase in the number of suicides in prison and an associated growth in political, public and media interest in the issue. In 1982, an 18-year-old remand prisoner died at Ashford

Remand Centre. The inquest verdict of a 'lack of care' on the part of the Prison Service prompted a review by HM Chief Inspector of Prisons of suicide prevention procedures. The review was completed and published in 1984 (Home Office, 1984).

The report was based on consultation with a number of professional and other interested bodies, establishment visits, a literature review, analysis of Prison Service suicide records and statistics, and a re-examination of Prison Service instructions. The report analysed current procedures, highlighting limitations and suggesting that, although no single or simple approach existed, the following factors were likely to be beneficial:

- General preventive measures. Improving regimes and staff/prisoner ratios; fostering prisoners' social contacts; and providing counselling services will decrease the likelihood of prisoners becoming suicidal.
- Implementing strategies to identify and manage 'high-risk' prisoners. Suicide prevention arrangements for some prisoners are necessary in most prisons, but limited resources must be concentrated on those most at risk. Such measures need not be incompatible with the general preventive measures outlined above.
- Staff training/education. It was reported that very few prison staff (of any discipline) received any training or education relating to suicide prevention; therefore training should be included in local/central educational programmes to familiarise staff with suicide prevention measures, to encourage understanding and caring, and to 'dispel simplistic thinking and misguided beliefs' (p. 47).
- Investigation of suicides in order that lessons may be learned. Monitoring of completed and attempted suicides (by Prison Service Headquarters) is criticised on the grounds that it is inconsistent and lacks detailed information. It is suggested that a valuable body of data should be gathered in order that more can be learned about suicidal behaviour, which would be aided by the introduction of a clear definition of what constitutes an attempt at suicide or episode of self-injury.

The 1984 report reinforces the view that the main responsibility for suicide prevention in prisons lies with the medical officer. Whilst officers and other staff can help with the implementation of treatment prescribed by the medical officer, all should refer prisoners to the medical officer where there are concerns; at which point of referral their responsibility ends.

The report criticised circular instruction 39/73 as being too vague; in particular, the roles played by particular members of staff lack explicit detail. The 'F' marking system is criticised: criteria for its use results in a large proportion of the prison population being labelled as suicidal;

once identified as at elevated risk, prisoners retain that status despite any changes in their circumstances or mental state. The system leads to a vicious circle:

> Prison staff doubt the value of the marker system, they begin to neglect the bureaucratic procedures ... necessary to keep the system running ... [T]he value of the marker is thus further undermined, faith in it is reduced even more, and so on.'
>
> (p. 44)

To summarise, the report recommends general improvements in the conditions for all prisoners, although it acknowledges that this type of global approach is unlikely to prevent all suicides and that therefore alternative strategies are necessary. Besides improving screening, referral and treatment procedures, it is maintained that an improvement would involve placing 'greater personal responsibility for taking action onto the shoulders of prison medical staff' (p. 48).

Another influential report around this time was the Chiswick Report (1985), which had been prompted by the spate of suicides at the Glenochil Institution in Scotland. This report had particular comments to make on the phenomenon of apparent clusters or spates of suicides.

The mid to late 1980s

Following publication of the Chief Inspector's review in 1984, the Home Secretary established a Working Group on Suicide Prevention which reported in 1986 (Home Office, 1986). This resulted in the issuing of Circular Instruction (CI) 3/1987 on the management of suicide prevention, which covered staff awareness; reception and referral procedures; medical assessment and documentation; support for prisoners; and the formation of Suicide Prevention Management Groups (SPMGs) at each establishment. The Circular discontinued the 'F' marking system primarily because the risk indicators upon which the system was founded were so weak that, if strictly applied, they resulted in a number of false positives and false negatives so large as to render the system ineffective.

Following the recommendations of the Working Group the new instruction stresses the need to identify the actual onset and development of suicidal crisis, rather than attempting to identify the type of prisoner who may become suicidal; and to ensure that an appropriate and timely intervention is made. The revised strategy sows the seeds of a multi-disciplinary approach. Although the medical officer retains responsibility for the management and treatment of those identified at elevated risk, the roles of other staff are more explicitly prescribed. The main elements of the new preventive strategy were thus:

- Management: to ensure a clear, co-ordinated and continuing lead in implementing the strategy and regular review of its effectiveness.
- Staff: to increase staff understanding of suicide and their responsibilities in dealing with it.
- Reception: to provide for the systematic screening of suicide risk on reception; for interim precautions to be taken on the first night in custody and support in the period immediately following reception (particularly for remands).
- Referral: to provide a clear system by which prisoners who show signs of heightened risk may be referred to the medical officer for assessment by any member of staff (via the unit manager) – a system that also provides for systematic communication of the medical officer's assessment and instructions to other staff.
- Preventive measures: to give the medical officer clear responsibility for deciding upon preventive measures, while encouraging more active involvement of both hospital and discipline staff in the management, support and monitoring of those at elevated risk, and providing for other supportive action to be co-ordinated by the wing manager.
- Documentation: to provide a single system of documentation to assist staff in the performance of their tasks, to warn staff when an actively suicidal prisoner is transferred, and to act as a long-term record of assessments made and action taken.
- Monitoring suicide prevention: to ensure that the prevention strategy is understood by all concerned and that the appropriate lessons are drawn from the management of suicidal prisoners.

The introduction of a Suicide Prevention Management Group in each prison is recommended for four reasons:

- to ensure a high level of staff awareness of their responsibilities;
- to ensure co-operation and communication between medical/discipline/other staff;
- to review regularly the effectiveness of local strategies;
- to consider aspects of the general regime that may be relevant.

Initial reception screening is undertaken by medical staff but with greater role definition. A new standardised system of documentation for the management of suicidal prisoners is introduced through Forms F1996 and F1997. Form F1996 allows reception hospital officers or nurses to record their assessment of prisoners and requires placement of them into one of three categories of risk: (1) strong indications of risk; (2) no immediate indications of risk, but some indications that require careful assessment; and (3) no risk indicated at that time. The prisoner

10

is then assessed by the medical officer who decides what, if any, preventive measures should be taken.

A system for staff referrals to the medical officer is outlined. It is nevertheless emphasised that, when making a referral, staff are not required to assess the significance of prisoners' behaviour but should act quickly and effectively on any sign or development that may indicate suicidal ideation. Referrals to the medical officer are made on the new form F1997, on which reasons for concern are recorded.

It is stressed that there can be no standard, centrally imposed procedure in dealing with prisoners identified as at heightened risk; rather, 'the professional judgement of the Medical Officer will determine the treatment adopted in each case, and this Instruction in no way derogates from his responsibility' (p. 14). Policy is outlined on the use of special supervision procedures (continual and intermittent), the location of potentially suicidal prisoners or those who have attempted suicide (which remains unchanged from the previous Instruction), immediate action to be taken in cases of hanging, and the use of shared, protective and stripped accommodation.

Circular Instruction 3/87 was soon superseded by CI 20/1989, which made some modifications to procedures. The revised guidance introduces streamlined reception procedures and makes mandatory the requirement for an SPMG in each prison. The primary responsibility for suicide prevention still rests with the medical officer, but the responsibility of other staff to prisoners, particularly in terms of the identification of those who may be at heightened risk, is repeated. Indeed, CI 20/1989 gives more detailed guidance on the respective responsibilities of staff, the reception process, and the functioning of the SPMG.

The main elements of this modified strategy are:

- the identification of prisoners who may be suicidal by means of systematic assessment by the Medical Officer on reception (assisted by other medical staff) and vigilance on the part of all staff throughout the prisoner's time in custody;
- helping suicidal prisoners to recover from crisis by appropriate location (in the hospital or elsewhere) and through sympathetic and supportive contact with other prisoners, people outside the establishment and, above all, staff;
- reducing the opportunities for suicide without reducing the quality of life for prisoners;
- ensuring that all staff are aware of the problem of suicide and how to prevent it, by regular overviews by senior management, through the SPMG and its annual review; good communication between staff; and training.

Further guidance was issued in the form of an addendum to CI 20/1989, introducing a document to assist managers in monitoring the continuing implementation of the suicide prevention strategy. The document was essentially a checklist, or (as it describes itself) 'an agenda of issues which will need to be addressed' by SPMGs periodically but certainly following a completed or a spate of attempted suicides. The addendum contains the new requirement that the SPMG meets at least quarterly.

Another addendum to CI 20/1989 was issued in 1990, bringing arrangements following deaths in custody up to date with organisational changes and focusing on the management of suicide prevention. The importance of creating a climate in which suicidal thoughts and feelings are less likely to take root is emphasised – for example, where:

> regimes are full, varied and relevant; where staff morale is high and relationships with inmates are positive; where inmates are treated fairly and as individuals; where good basic living conditions are provided; where every effort is made to encourage contact with family and the community.
>
> (p. 1)

The responsibility of managers is also highlighted:

> [I]t is the continuing responsibility of managers at all levels to ensure that the efforts to put [the strategy] into practice are thoroughgoing; that sufficient resources are available to make this possible; and that understanding of the procedures – and general awareness – is sustained by regular reviews and staff training.
>
> (p. 2)

The 1990s

Continuing concern over the steady increase in the number of self-inflicted deaths in the 1980s led to the setting up of the first full Thematic Review by HM Chief Inspector of Prisons (commonly referred to as the Tumim report) which reported in 1990. Public and media concern was aroused by the tragic death that year of Phillip Knight, a 15-year-old remanded to HMP Swansea. The thematic review of suicide and self-harm made a large number of recommendations (123 in total), which were wide-ranging and fundamentally challenging to the culture and ethos of the Prison Service.

The review criticised the foundation of the strategy for the management of the suicidal, as embodied in CI 20/1989, because of its focus on a medical approach to the problem, ignoring the social and environmental elements of the behaviours and failing to stress the importance of regimes and of positive relationships between staff and prisoners.

The need for an integrated approach was emphasised, as in the following excerpt:

> Current Prison Service policy fails to communicate the social dimensions to self-harm and self-inflicted death. It does not stress sufficiently the significance of the environment in which prisoners and staff are expected to live and work, or the importance of constructive activities in helping inmates to cope with anxiety and stress. Above all, it fails to give weight to the need to sustain people during their time in custody, the importance of relationships between inmates and between staff and inmates in providing that support. The danger of targeting suicide prevention as primarily a medical problem is that the Service may have become conditioned to the view that all the answers lie with the doctors. This is not the case. Prisoners, staff, families, visitors, the regime, the environment all have parts to play and management must stress and encourage progress on all these fronts if it is to affect the way staff behave and the attitudes they display.
>
> (HM Chief Inspector of Prisons, 1990: p. 7)

In addition to the perceived flaws in the strategy, the consistency of its implementation was also questioned. For example, it was found that doctors had insufficient time, accommodation or resources to carry out their tasks as prescribed within CI 20/1989. Similarly, it was found that the degree to which hospital officers conducted their prescribed duties varied: some were able to interview prisoners on reception and make preliminary assessments as to their state of mind when they could not be seen by a doctor on the same day; others were unable to because of staffing pressures. Further, it was not normal practice (as was required under the CI) for hospital officers to interview prisoners before they were seen by the doctor.

Moreover, certain aspects of the role of governors were questioned, including the lack of requirement that they be concerned with the quality of service provided, the absence of guidance about what the quality of that service should be, and the lack of a requirement to ensure that suicide prevention training is given to staff. The review questioned the extent to which SPMGs were integrated into the management structures within establishments, the frequency with which they met, and the difference they made to the strategy.

It was reported that wing managers who were instructed to use Form F1997 to inform medical officers of prisoners about whom they were concerned were fulfilling their duties. However, it was argued that discipline officers were constrained from providing adequate support to those at heightened risk for a number of reasons, including the large numbers of prisoners; a lack of staff continuity; deficiency of an active regime; and lack of training.

As indicated above, the recommendations of the Tumim report were broad-based, wide-ranging and challenging. They focus on general aspects of the quality of life for prisoners and suggest changes to various general aspects of imprisonment, the regime, employment and education, reception/induction procedures, staffing levels and staff/prisoner relationships, as well as more specific recommendations relating to the identification and management of suicidal prisoners that should be integrated within the whole establishment.

Amongst the more fundamental recommendations were the following:

7.10   Management training should give a higher priority to the prevention of suicide and self-harm.

7.25   Governors must ensure that suicide prevention is accorded a high priority and that there is an integrated approach to the issue.

7.28   Wing officers should promote an atmosphere and culture in which inmates and staff can relate positively to each other.

7.38   A constructive prison experience should promote personal responsibility in every prisoner.

7.39   Staff should be trained in giving counselling and support.

7.109   Staff training should recognise various specialisms within the inmate population.

7.104   Regimes and out-of-cell activities should be structured and properly staffed and resourced.

The Prison Service response to the Tumim Review: the development of the revised 1994 strategy

The publication of the Tumim review in 1990 prompted a fundamental re-examination of existing strategies on suicide prevention, in particular a re-appraisal of the predominantly medical approach to suicide prevention.

Following publication of the Tumim review, a dedicated unit, the Suicide Awareness Support Unit (SASU), was established in Prison Service Headquarters, tasked with providing support to establishments and examining good practice both within the Prison Service and outside, with the aim of drawing up a revised strategy on suicide prevention. A Prison Service paper, *The Way Forward* (unpublished, 1992), outlined the foundation for a revised strategy. Its development into a workable process, and the early work of SASU, is chronicled by Neal (1996), who provides a useful summary of it. One feature of the work at that time is of particular note: the partnership between policy and research. In developing a revised strategy, policy makers were able to draw upon research work then being conducted by the Institute of Criminology, Cambridge. This proved a model example of collaboration, resulting in policy and practice development being informed, and underpinned, by current research.

The newly revised strategy was drawn together in a new Instruction to Governors (IG) 1/94, entitled 'Caring for the Suicidal in Custody', which superseded existing instructions and circulars and was issued for implementation in April 1994. The overall aim of the revised strategy, as stated in that Instruction, is to 'identify and provide special care for prisoners in distress and despair and so reduce the risk of suicide and self-harm'. The strategy is based on the principles of primary, special and aftercare. The most significant change in direction is the emphasis the revised strategy gives to *all staff* as having a responsibility in the identification of suicide risk and in provision of support. The focus of the strategy is upon individual care. A distinction is made between primary and special care.

Primary care relates to all prisoners, whereby the aim is to create a safe environment and to help prisoners cope with custody by:

- creating a safe, humane and positive environment for prisoners and staff;
- encouraging supportive and trusting relationships within the prison community;
- relieving the fears of new prisoners and helping them to settle;
- helping prisoners to see ways of better coping with their problems;
- providing activities and choices that reduce isolation and depression and build self-esteem;
- enabling prisoners to maintain home and community ties and to prepare for release.

Special care is provided for prisoners who express suicidal feelings or are otherwise identified as suicidal by:

- treating those prisoners with compassion and preserving their individual dignity;
- allowing them opportunities to talk about suicidal feelings and encouraging positive choices;
- providing supportive human contact and supervision;
- protecting them as far as possible from harming themselves.

The revised strategy emphasises the need for a broad climate of care for prisoners that will enable them to cope better with problems, thus reducing the likelihood of suicidal thoughts developing. The responsibility for care for suicidal prisoners is achieved by:

- providing staff with support and training;
- encouraging prisoners to take a share of responsibility for others as well as themselves;
- working in partnership with prisoners' families and with statutory and voluntary agencies in the community;
- ensuring good communication and co-operation between all disciplines and agencies that work with prisoners.

Central to the working of the revised strategy was the introduction of a new form, F2052SH (Self-Harm At Risk), which replaced existing forms F1996 and F1997. The new F2052SH process can be activated by any member of staff who has concerns about a prisoner. It is not a medical form and thus does not attract medical-in-confidence constraints; hence, it is available for all staff to see and use. Form 2052SH acts as a vehicle for conducting and recording a case review and the development of a support plan for an individual prisoner. This was seen as an important step in facilitating better communication between staff.

The other crucial change introduced by the strategy was removing the automatic requirement that a prisoner identified as at elevated risk must be placed in the healthcare centre (hospital). Instead, the F2052SH process requires staff to consider whether the individual may be best managed by remaining within the residential unit, as appropriate.

The revised strategy was underpinned by a modular 'Guidance Pack on Caring for the Suicidal' (HM Prison Service 1994). This pack covers: Prison Service policy; the role of the Suicide Awareness Team (see below); auditing primary and special care; identifying and supporting prisoners at heightened risk; managing the F2052SH system; the role of The Samaritans; and the involvement of prisoners. In addition to the guidance pack, a new modular staff training programme was drawn up covering: understanding suicide and self-harm; identifying stress and despair in custody; listening and supporting; the management of at-risk prisoners; appearing at an inquest; and basic suicide awareness for prisoners. The training programme was introduced service-wide through local delivery using trained trainers.

To supplement IG 1/94, two further instructions were issued: IG 79/94 contained instructions on the use of observation and shared/supervised accommodation; and Prison Service Instruction (PSI) 32/97 provided detailed advice on the important role that The Samaritans have to play in suicide prevention.

Several features of the revised 1994 strategy warrant further comment:

- The strategy focuses upon suicide awareness rather than prevention. In fact, the prison Suicide Prevention Management Group is explicitly redesignated as the Suicide Awareness Team. This change of emphasis was deliberate. The former focus on prevention was thought to encourage staff to concentrate too heavily on environmental aspects, whereas the need was for greater awareness and understanding of the range of factors precipitating suicide.

- The strategy has at its heart the concept of multidisciplinary working. This is a concept that has been open to much misinterpretation. To work as intended requires a genuine partnership where the decision on provision of support is dictated by individual prisoners' need. There is always the risk that shared responsibility equates to diminished responsibility. It needs to be remembered that this concept of multidisciplinary working presented – certainly in 1994 – a very different approach to the management of the suicidal, overturning a long tradition that viewed the medical profession as having the prime responsibility in this area. It was unlikely that the cultural shift would be changed overnight. Some observers have used the phrase 'de-medicalising' to describe this cultural shift. It is debatable how useful this term is. It risks the implication that healthcare staff have a diminished role to play in the care of the suicidal, which is certainly not what was intended. The causes of suicide are complex, and some suicides will have resulted from mental ill-health. The multidisciplinary approach emphasises that staff from all backgrounds have a part to play, where the depth of that role will be determined by each individual prisoner's particular needs as a support plan is drawn up.

- Another key concept within the strategy is multi-agency working. The strongest manifestation of this has been in the development of a joint partnership with The Samaritans, whose involvement has developed on a substantial scale since the late 1980s. The great merit in the partnership is that The Samaritans are uniquely placed in both resources and experience to provide large-scale support to the Prison Service. The involvement of The Samaritans focuses mainly on individual befriending of prisoners and the training and supporting of selected prisoners as 'Listeners'. As would be expected between two organisations with a quite different ethos, the developing partnership is not without its tensions, which are for the most part entirely healthy. The principle of total confidentiality, central to The Samaritans' work, is quite alien to normal prison working and its acceptance requires tolerance and understanding on both sides.

- The formalisation of peer-group support through listener/buddy schemes provides an innovative and important contribution to the strategy (see Chapter 6 for a more detailed account). These schemes build upon the positive contribution that prisoners may have towards their peers and are predicated upon the active involvement of prisoners as responsible individuals, as opposed to passive recipients of care.

- In pinpointing the quality of relationships between staff and prisoners as central to effective suicide prevention, the strategy discourages over reliance on environmental factors, in particular the use of 'stripped cell' conditions. The guidance pack issued in conjuction with IG 1/94 advises:

> The use of unfurnished or protected accommodation is inappropriate for suicidal prisoners. It takes away the prisoners' dignity and control, and is often felt to be punitive. The trust of prisoners in staff will be undermined. They will be less likely to admit distress in future, and may even see suicide as a way of reasserting control of their destiny.

The effectiveness of current strategies

The 1994 strategy has outlived previous strategies and although further refinements are planned (see below), the underlying philosophy of a multidisciplinary/multi-agency approach has stood the test of time.

Sadly, as shown in Table 1.1, self-inflicted deaths have continued to increase during the 1990s. The increase has in fact been remarkably steady since the early 1980s and the precise reasons behind the rise are unknown. It seems reasonable to assume that some of the increase reflects the increasing rates of suicides amongst the groups of individuals who are at elevated risk of entering custody but, in the absence of reliable data on suicide rates amongst such groups, we do not have the evidence that would allow meaningful comparisons to be made. As can be seen from Table 1.1, the rate of self-inflicted deaths steadied for the three years between 1994 and 1997 (at around 115 per 100,000). It is entirely speculative whether this was connected with the introduction of the new strategy in 1994. The same period saw a dramatic increase in the prison population, which resulted in considerable displacement of prisoners away from their home area which, in turn, might be expected to increase the incidence of suicide. There are no simple explanations. However, the continuing increase in the number of deaths has attracted public attention and criticism as well as political interest.

It is difficult to evaluate the effectiveness of strategies with great confidence. We have no way of knowing what the number of self-inflicted deaths would have been had there been no revision to the strategy; nor is there any simple measurement of success. This fact is a source of continual frustration to prison staff, who invariably receive a bad press with little credit for their conduct in a difficult area of work. There are, however, some indicators that demonstrate the scale of the intervention work undertaken. On a typical day during the late 1990s, around 1,000 prisoners will have been identified at sufficient risk to warrant management on open F2052SHs (out of an average daily prison population of 65,500). Virtually all of these prisoners will be supported successfully through their crises and difficulties; but of course they will not attract any particular public or media interest. The scale of the Samaritan-supported prisoner 'listener' schemes is demonstrated in the following statistic: between January and March 1999 there were 26,600 contacts made of over 10 minutes' duration between prisoner listeners and fellow prisoners in distress. These figures give some indication of the level of work that goes on daily, unreported and that needs to be considered when judgements are being made about success and failure.

Table 1.1 Self-inflicted deaths in HM prisons in England and Wales

Year	Number of self -inflicted deaths	Average annual population (thousands)	Rate per 100,000 population
1983	27	43.5	62
1984	26	43.3	60
1985	27	46.2	58
1986	21	46.8	45
1987	46	48.4	95
1988	37	48.9	76
1989	48	48.5	99
1990	50	45.6	110
1991	42	45.9	92
1992	41	45.8	90
1993	47	44.6	105
1994	62	48.8	127
1995	59	51.0	116
1996	64	55.3	116
1997	68	61.1	111
1998	82	65.5	125
1999	91	64.8	140

Self-inflicted death in prison remains a very rare event and thus is a poor outcome measure. The level of self-injury is probably a better measure, for its relative frequency is such that meaningful before-and-after comparisons can be conducted. The problem here is the absence of reliable, standardised measures of self-injury, which would permit valid comparisons across prisons and over time (The Howard League, 1999a).

One method through which the Prison Service appraises and develops strategies is through investigations into completed suicides and near-fatal attempts, to examine whether there are lessons to be learned. The focus of internal investigations is properly on operational matters and compliance with procedures; this is quite different from the psychological autopsy. Such investigations have traditionally been conducted internally in confidence, although with recent developments on greater access and increased openness (see Chapters 8 and 9) it is to be hoped that more reviews will be available for public scrutiny.

An unpublished review of 60 self-inflicted deaths that occurred between 1 January 1994 and 30 September 1995 produced the following main findings:

- Basic circumstances of the deaths (matching previous reviews): for example, 95 per cent died through hanging; 98 per cent were alone at the time of death (although 27 per cent were in cells designated for sharing); 45 per cent were unsentenced; and 35 per cent were within their first month at the establishment.
- Main features of personal history: 48 per cent reported drug/alcohol problems; 26 per cent reported relationship problems; 45 per cent were reported as having major difficulties in adjusting to imprisonment; and 17 per cent were reported as acting in an aggressive manner.
- Risk assessment: 22 per cent were identified as at elevated risk of self-injury/suicide at the time of death; 33 per cent showed some evidence of forward planning, such as selecting times when staff were known not to be available or, alternatively, where the arrival of staff could be anticipated; 35 per cent had previously imposed self-injury earlier in that period of custody; 18 per cent had been showing noticeable improvement in mood prior to death; and in 18 per cent of cases very little was known about the prisoner (mostly due to recent arrival in custody).

In reviewing operational factors relating to the 60 deaths, communication issues emerged as a common theme:

- Information received after the event: in several cases relatives, friends or fellow prisoners declared concerns they had about the prisoner but had not passed on.
- Information known by external agencies: in 13 per cent of cases, risk information had not been effectively communicated to the establishment or had not been communicated within the establishment.
- Information between establishments: in 8 per cent cases, risk information was not communicated effectively between establishments on the transfer of a prisoner.

- Information within an establishment: in 13 per cent of cases, problems were reported in communication of information between reception units, residential units and healthcare centres.
- Shared accommodation: in 20 per cent of cases, prisoners had been designated as requiring shared accommodation but were alone at the time of death.

It is interesting to note that some of these critical points on transfer of information about risk are not unique to the prison setting and may be common across many institutions (Morgan *et al.*, 1998).

The findings from the above review give some pointers on where strategies might be strengthened. First, the review highlights the difficulty for staff when managing the small, but significant, number of overtly aggressive prisoners who also may be at risk of self-injury or suicide. Aggressive behaviour must be managed as a priority because of the risk to others, but there is a danger of over-concentration upon this aspect of behaviour, resulting in any subsequent suicidal tendencies being ignored once the violent episode has been managed successfully. Secondly, we naturally tend to interpret the appearance of improved mood as indicating a reduction in suicidal tendencies, but in some instances the reverse may be true: the improved mood may be a result of determination and resolve to carry out a planned suicide. This suggests a need for caution when an individual is taken off the at-risk register. Thirdly, identifying individuals as benefiting from shared cell accommodation needs more detailed operational definition. In particular, clarification is needed to distinguish between a requirement for continuous company rather than intermittent company, for instance during the night. This is an important issue because unless continuous company is specified and provided, there will be several points during the day when a prisoner can anticipate being alone; other prisoners sharing cells will have visits, go to work or education, and so on.

One issue of concern – one that has been proposed as evidence that the revised strategy is not working – is the number of prisoners who were not identified as at risk at the time of death. The review quoted above, consistent with later findings, shows that about 70 per cent are assessed as not at risk at the time of death. This finding should not surprise us, since we know that the prognosis for individual prediction on suicide at a particular point is poor, whether in prison or in the community. Thus the low proportion identified at risk at the time of death is not necessarily a cause for concern. It is possible to argue that a *reverse* finding would be cause for concern, for instance if 70 per cent of prisoners who died *had* been identified at risk at the time of death, for this would suggest that procedures for their management had been flawed.

Strategic factors in the late 1990s

The efficacy and implementation of the current strategy has recently received close scrutiny by HM Chief Inspector of Prisons in a thematic review entitled *Suicide is Everyone's Concern*, published in 1999. This thematic review involved a wide-ranging review of the strategy in operation, taking evidence from establishment visits, staff, prisoners and relatives of those who have died in prison custody, and a detailed survey of Boards of Visitors, an independent body involved at each establishment. The multidisciplinary foundation behind the strategy received broad endorsement in the review and in fact is reflected in the choice of title: *Suicide Is Everyone's Concern.*

This latest thematic review makes a number of recommendations for further strengthening and focusing for the strategy. Amongst the key points are:

* further developing strategies to meet the needs of women prisoners and young offenders/juveniles;
* developing the strategy in Local prisons (where a disproportionate number of deaths occur);
* developing a key performance indicator in relation to suicides in prison;
* aspiring to the concept of a 'healthy prison'.

Each of these areas is subject to work in progress, which is reported in the last chapter of this book.

A model of good practice in suicide prevention highlighted by the thematic review is that operating within New York City's Department of Corrections. During the 1980s a suicide prevention programme was introduced that saw the numbers of suicides reduce from over 30 per year to an average between two and six. These low numbers of suicides have been maintained in recent years: two (1993); four (1994); four (1995); six (1996); four (1997). This is within a prison population ranging between 18,000 and 20,000 prisoners, the majority of whom are housed on Rikers Island.

There are a number of factors that account for these impressive results. Essentially, suicide prevention within the New York Department operates within a comprehensive mental-health framework. The definition of 'mental health' is much broader than that traditionally used in the United Kingdom, and there are significant constitutional differences in the correctional model. In particular, the State Department of Health is responsible for the delivery of healthcare for prisoners through contracted-out services. The majority of 'general population' prisoners are held in dormitory-style accommodation, which reduces opportunities for self-injury. If a member of staff is in any way concerned about a prisoner (in terms of mental well-being or possible suicidal tendencies) that member of staff can recommend an immediate mental-health referral. This will result in the prisoner's transfer immediately to one of Rikers Island's Mental Observation Units, where almost constant supervision is provided by staff. The prisoner will remain under observation until it is felt that suitable recovery has occurred to allow a return to the general population or until that prisoner is released from custody. In addition to the support offered by staff, selected prisoners are trained as Inmate Observation Aides, whose task is to tour the wing or dormitory at regular intervals (at least every ten minutes) and keep a log of their observations. If they observe anything untoward, or are particularly concerned about a prisoner, they are obliged to report to the officer located on the wing. Inmate Observation Aides are paid, and it is one of the highest paid of all jobs in the prison. Finally, at a more cultural level, a further drive behind prevention of suicides is fear of litigation, which also acts as a powerful incentive for changes to be made to conditions and facilities if a death has occurred.

Transference of learning from the New York model is problematic; the model works as an integrated package. It would be difficult to extract individual elements to implement in isolation, and allowance must be made for constitutional and cultural differences between the United Kingdom and the United States. Of particular note, however, is the impressive amount of time – four days – that is devoted to mental-health issues in the initial training of staff. This is significantly more than that included in training for staff in England and Wales. For a fuller account of the New York model, see Snow (2000).

The 1999 thematic review proposes the concept of the 'healthy prison' as a goal for the Prison Service; it is a concept that has benefits for both prisoners and staff. The four main principles to test for a healthy prison from a *prisoner's* perspective are:

- the weakest prisoners feel safe;
- all prisoners are treated with respect as individuals;
- all prisoners are busily occupied, are expected to improve themselves, and are given the opportunity to do so;
- all prisoners can strengthen links with their families and prepare for release.

From a *staff* perspective the main principles are:

- staff feel safe;
- they are treated with respect as individuals;
- they are informed and consulted within their sphere of work;
- they have high expectations made of them;

- they are well led;
- they respect their own health.

As individual tests, these factors add up to a laudable objective. It must, of course, be emphasised that the link between the 'healthy prison' concept and a low suicide rate has yet to be demonstrated (or refuted). It will not be easy to establish a link, such is the comparative rarity of suicide; and, in fact, there are already examples of prisons that appear to be well on the way to meeting the criteria for a healthy prison and yet continue to experience self-inflicted deaths.

Summary and conclusions

As this chapter has shown, the development of policy and practice in suicide prevention in prisons and England and Wales is characterised by general shifts in emphasis, from physical prevention to greater staff involvement and from medical ownership of suicide to multidisciplinary ownership. To some extent these changes mirror approaches taken in the community; approaches to the phenomenon of suicide change as social and cultural values shift.

Policy and practice are also characterised by understandable anxiety over suicide as a symptom of underlying yet intractable problems. This anxiety is fuelled by media and political interest. There is a constant pressure for the organisation to be seen to be doing something to tackle 'the problem'. Whilst it is only right that the issue of prison suicides should remain under the public spotlight, it is also true that knee-jerk reactions and rapid changes of policy and practice are likely to erode staff confidence and thus be counterproductive.

A common criticism of suicide prevention strategies, both current and former, is that they fail in their implementation. This is a regular observation from internal reviews, as well as from external reviews such as HMCIP's establishment inspections and those conducted by organisations such as the Howard League (1999b). The most common failing is the inability to provide the amount of staff training required to implement programmes thoroughly. With hindsight, the modular staff-training programme developed in 1993 involved a method of delivery too complex to fit in with the foreseeable demands on the Prison Service in 1995 that followed the escapes from high security prisons HMP Parkhurst and HMP Whitemoor. Chapters 7 and 9 discuss this point and future developments in more depth. Another common criticism is inconsistency of practice across establishments. This reflects the differing relative starting positions of individual establishments. For some establishments, implementation of a new initiative may be straightforward and facilitated by existing arrangements; for others, a radical change may be needed and there may be other initiatives and priorities that have to be balanced. Rarely, with the exception of newly commissioned prisons, are establishments starting from a greenfield site.

One very interesting development in recent years has been the increased involvement of the private sector, extending to the running of whole establishments. Although the involvement of the private sector is not without controversy, the relative degree of freedom that contractors have in order to deliver the specification of the contract has led to some innovative approaches in extending the current suicide-prevention strategy beyond the level normally found in public-sector prisons. These new ways of working are having a positive impact upon the rest of the Prison Service. A helpful trade-off is emerging, in which both public- and private-sector services have much to offer each other from their respective cultures and ethos. Cultural change is a key issue in implementing effective suicide-awareness programmes. Although the private sector often starts from a position of advantage, profound cultural change can be achieved in the public sector, and a recent example of progress in a large Local prison can be read in *Changing a Culture* (Prison Service Journal, 1999).

Although a full review is beyond the remit of this chapter, the Suicide Awareness Support Unit at Prison Service Headquarters keeps a watchful eye on developments in suicide prevention in other prison systems. The Scottish Prison Service launched its revised programme in 1998, and the National Steering Group on Deaths in Prisons in Eire published a report in 1999. Perhaps the most striking feature that emerges across other countries is the robustness of the finding that the early stages of custody and arrival at a new establishment are associated with the period of greatest risk (Towl, 1999a). This has clear implications for the development of effective reception and induction processes.

To summarise, the development of an effective suicide-prevention programme in prison requires a carefully held degree of balance of care, control, and the creation of a safe environment. Each of these elements has a contribution to make. The relationship between the elements is complex, perhaps as complex as suicide itself. The key is in ensuring that a balance is maintained without undue emphasis on any single factor.

2

Suicide in prisons:
a critique of UK research

David Crighton

Overview

The aim of this chapter is to provide a critique of key research into suicide in prisons and to draw some preliminary conclusions from this research. For practical reasons the focus of the chapter is limited to studies carried out within the United Kingdom; references to international research base are therefore very limited. This is not to deny the importance of international research, but is rather an acknowledgement of the added complexity involved in making comparisons across different criminal and civil justice systems.

It must also be said at the outset that research into suicide in prisons is an area that causes considerable methodological problems. Studies of suicide by definition involve individuals who are dead. It is therefore impossible to ask individuals about why they took the actions they did. Researchers are, of necessity, forced to draw on secondary sources such as written records, and interviews with staff, relatives and friends. Such sources are imperfect, being subject to, for example, cognitive biases such as selective recall. It is entirely understandable that friends, relatives and staff will look for meanings and explanations for a suicide. All studies that involve retrospective analyses (sometimes called psychological autopsies) inevitably suffer from such methodological limitations.

As a result, a number of researchers have focused on individuals who have either attempted suicide or intentionally injured themselves. This approach is predicated on the notion that suicide represents the extreme end of a continuum of self-injurious behaviours, a view that has enjoyed growing empirical support. It is thus argued that, by studying individuals who engage in self-injurious behaviours, it may be possible to gain valuable insights into the processes involved in suicide. Here again there are some significant difficulties.

First, the notion that suicide is part of such a continuum of self-destructive behaviour is contested. Some researchers have argued for a very clear distinction between suicide and 'self-harm' (e.g. Kreitman, 1977). They see the two forms of behaviour as quite distinct in terms of epidemiology and phenomenology. If this position is accepted, then studies of individuals who engage in self-injurious behaviours, whilst being very valuable in their own terms, have little to tell us about suicide *per se*. Even if the notion of a continuum of self-injurious behaviours is accepted, it seems logically plausible that behaviours towards the extremes of the continuum will be markedly different in many respects. In turn, this raises the problem for researchers of determining at what point on a proposed continuum such comparisons between suicide and self-injury cease to have utility.

Secondly, there are substantial definitional problems relating to suicide, attempted suicide, self-harm and self-injury. For research purposes, defining attempted suicide as a distinct form of self-destructive behaviour raises considerable practical problems. Definitions of self-harm and self-injury are even more fraught (see Chapter 3).

Set out below are the major contributors to research in this field, and our comments on their work and conclusions.

Topp (1979)

Widely cited as the first empirical study into suicides in prisons is the research by Topp (1979). In his study, Topp began by discussing the earliest accounts of suicide in prisons in England and Wales, as documented by R.M. Gover a medical inspector for the board of prison commissioners (Board of Prison Commissioners, 1881). This was followed by a report by his successor Smalley in his report to the board (Board of Prison Commissioners, 1911), which analysed deaths in prisons for the preceding decade.

Topp went on to take a more empirical approach than Smalley by calculating overall trends in the rate of suicide in prisons. He did this on the basis of officially recorded suicide statistics from 1880 to 1971, subdividing this period into seven-year intervals. The total number of deaths recorded as suicide for this period was 775, and Topp reported that the rate varied from 28 to 60 per 100,000 (based on Average Daily Population per year (ADP)).

This research was followed by a more detailed analysis of the available written records on a smaller sample of '... all male prisoners who had certainly or probably committed suicide between 1958 and 1971...' (Topp, 1979: 24). This involved analysing a sample of 158 case records. Topp reported a mean of 13.3 deaths per year, and an overall rate of 42 per 100,000 ADP and 14 per 100,000 receptions, over the whole period. Of these 158 cases, Topp noted that 37 per cent were on remand and 63 per cent were sentenced. Of the sentenced group, 66 out of 117 were serving sentences of 18 months or longer, while the remainder were serving shorter sentences or were under borstal or detention orders.[1] Topp also reported that 77 of his sample had killed themselves within the first month of custody, a further 23 within the second month, 12 in the third month, eight in the fourth, with the numbers reducing to low levels from then on. He also noted that 90 per cent had previous convictions and 64 per cent had previously been in custody.

The study did not suggest any clear pattern in terms of the time or month of death, although it should be noted that the level of analysis used two broad time bands: 9 a.m. to 9 p.m. and 9 p.m. to 9 a.m. Saturday did, however, appear to be a more common day for deaths to occur. Topp went on to report, though, that 70 of the sample had a history of 'psychiatric treatment'[2] in the past, 56 as in-patients. Of these, he reported that 19 had a history of 'depressive episodes', while he states that another 79 had shown 'some tendency to depression in the past' (p. 25).[3] He also stated that 95 (51 per cent) had 'made previous suicidal threats or attempts, which had been multiple in 38 subjects' (p. 25). Topp also noted: 'The interval between the latest threat or attempt and the act which caused death was less than six months in 62 cases' (p. 25).

Topp went on to make a number of observations relating to what he termed 'social factors'. For example:

> In 153 cases (82 per cent) there were indications that emotional relationships had been unsatisfactory. Thus, 147 subjects (79 per cent) were single or separated; 100 (54 per cent) had been living in lodgings, alone or were vagrant, prior to their arrest; 83 (45 per cent) had no known contact with relatives or friends; 115 (62 per cent) had a history of social mobility; 71 (38 per cent) a history of parental deprivation before the age of 16; 96 (52 per cent) had shown some degree of aggression in their life style; 55 (30 per cent) had a drink problem and 21 (11 per cent) had a drug problem.
>
> (pp. 25–6)

He went on to argue that:

> in at least 50 per cent of cases ... the fatal act was performed ... on a sudden impulse ... [and] the suicidal act may have been part of a general display of attention-seeking behaviour.[4]
>
> (p. 26)

In discussing his results, Topp drew some tentative comparisons with deaths recorded as suicides in NHS psychiatric hospitals, noting a rate of 135 per 100,000 receptions at one NHS hospital in England.[5] Based on his analysis, Topp argued that the idea that death rates were particularly high during the initial stages of custody (Goring,

1913) was confirmed by his study. Those in the first month of their sentence appeared to be at particularly high risk of suicide. He also suggested that those serving longer sentences were more likely to complete suicide. Topp argued for the notion that a high proportion of prison suicides suffered from some form of 'psychiatric disorder' and suggested that a high proportion of such deaths:

> occurred partly as the result of demonstrative attention-seeking behaviour; 59 per cent could have had some expectation of being saved, at least 50 per cent seem to have acted on sudden impulse, 47.3 per cent committed the fatal act during daytime when staff availability could be anticipated, and 51 per cent had either made or threatened suicide attempts in the past. These factors suggest that a number of subjects may have been making attempts to elicit sympathetic attention, and when the desired response failed to occur they either escalated the attempts to a dangerous level or determinedly ended their lives.
>
> (p. 27)

This study has gone on to be widely cited and, in the words of the author in an addendum to the paper, the results 'were taken into account by a departmental working party in 1971 which initiated additional suicidal preventative measures in penal establishments' (p. 26). The study did, though, suffer from a number of basic methodological limitations. The most striking of these is perhaps a lack of operational definitions for the terms used. This makes replication of many aspects of the study impossible. Critically in this respect, the study involved an analysis of suicides and 'probable' suicides. The former group would appear to have comprised those prisoners for whom a coroner's court had returned a verdict of suicide, and this had been recorded by the Prison Service. The latter group appears to have been predominantly made up of those cases where a coroner's court had returned an open verdict, but where the author made a judgement that there was sufficient evidence that the death was a suicide.

The analysis of 'psychiatric history' suffers from similar difficulties with definition. Again, the ascription of a psychiatric history by Topp was based on subjective judgements, with little detail given on how these were made. The author's observations relating to 'social factors' are also problematic. For example, Topp reported that 38 per cent of his sample had a history of 'parental neglect'; it is difficult to interpret this in the absence of an operational definition of such neglect.

Analysis of Topp's discussion of his findings is further complicated by changes in both mental health practice and law, which have occurred since the research was undertaken.

With the benefit of hindsight, it nevertheless appears that Topp's research had three key effects on the area of prison suicides. First, it served as a stimulus to further research in this area. Second, it influenced the form of future research for many years. Thirdly, it can be argued that it had a key influence on policy and practice in the Prison Service from the 1970s until the early 1990s by giving broad endorsement to a predominantly medical approach.

Dooley (1990)

This study drew directly on the work of Topp. Dooley took all cases of unnatural death occurring in prisons in England and Wales between 1972 and 1987 (including remand centres and youth custody centres), comprising a sample of 295.[6] The written case records for those who had received a verdict of suicide in a coroner's court were analysed by Dooley, and the analysis was based on 'Prison Department personal (PDP) files.' (Dooley, 1990: 40). Dooley went on to describe the information available from these:

> These files ... contain information on the inmates' background, previous offences, previous periods in custody etc. They also contain accounts and statements from various members of the prison staff (governor, medical officer, chaplain, wing officers, etc.) and other inmates regarding the circumstances of the death. In most cases there is an account of the Coroner's inquest together with relevant media comments.
>
> (p.40)

Dooley stated that in assessing prisoners' motivations towards suicide, his main emphasis was on the content of the suicide note, if any. He suggested four categories of motivation toward suicide:

> For the purposes of analysis the motive for the suicide was recorded as being due to (a) factors relating to the prison situation; (b) outside pressures; (c) guilt for the offence; and (d) mental illness.
>
> (pp. 40–1)

In calculating rates of recorded suicide, Dooley divided the period under study into four-year intervals and calculated the suicide rate by average daily population (ADP) and also by receptions into prison. This led him to report a very marked increase in the number of suicides (121 per cent) between the 1972–75 period and the 1984–87 period. This compared with an increase in receptions of 23 per cent, and in ADP of 22 per cent. On the basis of his calculated rates, he reported an increase of 81 per cent in suicides per 100,000 ADP and of 80 per cent by receptions. Dooley's rationale for analysing his data in this way appears to have been largely pragmatic. Although this methodology did tend to obscure some marked variations within each four-year period, the range by ADP for 1972–75 was 16–38 while for 1984–87 it was 36–87. The overall upward trend in officially recorded suicides certainly seemed clear, but with significant variation within datasets.

In terms of demographic factors, Dooley reported that 98.3 per cent of his sample were men whilst 1.7 per cent were women. He noted that, relative to the proportion of women in the prison population (3 per cent), women appeared to be underrepresented in the suicide figures. However, he suggested that the women who received suicide verdicts did not differ significantly from the men in terms of demographic factors, although Dooley did not provide empirical evidence in support of this. On this basis, along with the small number of women recorded as suicides, a separate analysis by gender was not conducted.

The suicide group did not differ significantly from the general prison population in terms of ethnic origin:

Although not routinely recorded it was possible to establish ethnicity from a variety of sources including post-mortem and coroner's reports, media comments and various reports submitted by prison staff...

(p. 41)

On this basis, Dooley claimed that the representation of ethnic groups was in line with their numbers in the general prison population.

A breakdown of prisoners' pre-custodial living conditions was also provided. Over 26 per cent appeared to be of no fixed abode, or were living alone, whilst 61.7 per cent had some contact with others (living in lodgings, hostels etc.). Information on 12.2 per cent, Dooley reported, was not available.

An analysis of the timings of officially recorded suicide deaths in prison was also conducted. Here, the author noted a statistically significant excess of deaths in the third quarter of the year (July–September), with 98 (33.1 per cent) of deaths occurring during that quarter.[7] No differences were reported for an analysis by day of the week. However, almost 50 per cent of the deaths, Dooley argued, occurred between midnight and 8 a.m., with the remainder spread evenly throughout the day. These findings replicated those of Topp (1979) and of Hatty and Walker (1986) in relation to time in custody. Dooley noted that:

Fifty-one (17.3 per cent) of the suicides occurred within one week of reception into prison, 84 (28.5 per cent) within a month, 151 (51.2 per cent) within three months, and 227 (76.9 per cent) within a year of reception into prison. Sixty-eight (23.1 per cent) of the suicides had been in prison over a year when they killed themselves.

(p. 41)

In line with Topp's findings, Dooley reported hanging to be by far the most common method of suicide (90.2 per cent).

Dooley also went on to note that:

An average of 11 per cent of the people in custody were detained on remand. A significantly disproportionate number of those who killed themselves did so whilst on remand ...

(p. 41)[8]

Over 73 per cent of his sample had previous convictions recorded in their prison files. Similarly, 56.9 per cent had previous periods of custody recorded in these files. Dooley did not though provide comparison data on the prison population as a whole during this period, making the interpretation of these figures somewhat unclear. In terms of the sentenced group, Dooley reported that a significantly greater proportion were serving sentences of more than four years, with over 25 per cent being sentenced to life imprisonment.

He also went on to note that:

Almost a third (97) of the suicides had a history of psychiatric contact and over a quarter (80) had previous in-patient admissions; 85 (29 per cent) had a past record of alcohol abuse and 69 (23 per cent) of drug abuse. Sixty-seven (23 per cent) had received some form of psychotropic medication in the month before the suicide. In the 97 cases where a previous psychiatric history was established the primary diagnoses were as follows: psychotic illness (including drug-induced psychosis), 21 cases (22 per cent); depressive illness or reaction 22 cases (23 per cent); personality disorder, 25 cases (26 per cent); alcohol or drug addiction, 13 cases (13 per cent); other diagnoses or no diagnosis recorded, 16 cases (16 per cent).

(p. 42)

A high prevalence of self-injury prior to death was also observed, with 43 per cent having some record of self-injury on their Prison Service file and 22 per cent having a record of such injury during their current custody.

Dooley argued that 'the remand period is one of particular vulnerability for suicide' (p. 43) and he stressed the significance of a prior psychiatric history:

In the present study over 30 per cent of people in the suicide group had a history of previous psychiatric treatment, and this is greater than the 22 per cent in the sentenced population reported by Gunn *et al.* (1978).

(p. 43)

He then went on to hypothesise about the motivations of those who kill themselves in prison, based primarily on an analysis of the written records and any available suicide notes.

Dooley's study shares the methodological weaknesses common to such studies. First, it was based on a retrospective analysis of written records. As noted above, this raises a number of inherent difficulties for researchers. Additionally, he appears to have drawn on available written records in the Prison Service files. It seems likely that the reliability of such information will have been variable. In addition, information recorded in Prison Service files may be particularly limited for those recently received into prison, where the recorded information is based on often very brief interviews with prisoners.

The study was distinct from the earlier study by Topp (1979) in that it focused on cases that had received a verdict of suicide at a coroner's court. This is problematic in that the sample studied is derived from a legal decision-making process rather than being based on the cause of death or types of behaviour involved. The absence of information on self-inflicted deaths where verdicts other than suicide were recorded also complicates the interpretation of the results of the study. The apparently high numbers of those receiving official suicide verdicts with a 'psychiatric history' may simply be an artefact of the sampling.[9]

Liebling (1991)

This study was predicated on the hypothesis that suicidal behaviour is one extreme of a continuum of self-destructive behaviours. As such, the study primarily involved a series of interviews with 100 young offenders located in four young-offender institutions, 50 of whom had a recent history of intentional self-injury and 50 of whom were chosen at random from the remainder of the institutions' populations. There were 34 men and 16 women in each of the groups.

Liebling adopted a pragmatic approach to the selection of prisoners, choosing for inclusion in the research those who had any intentionally self-inflicted injury serious enough to result in treatment in the prison healthcare centre. The four young-offender institutions sampled for the study were, in turn, selected on the basis of practical considerations of suitability and convenience. Liebling went on to note that selecting inmates from a single establishment could have resulted in biased responses relating to the particular nature of that establishment or its population; the approach taken served to reduce this bias, by sampling a wider range of the Prison Service's young-offender institutions. The means of selecting a control or comparison group was methodologically straightforward, involving random selection from an alphabetical list of the establishment populations. No further selection, or matching of control subjects, was undertaken.

Semi-structured interviews were also conducted with a number of staff. Data from both groups of interviews were supplemented by an analysis of prison records and inmate medical records (for a subsample of 39 individuals).

The subject group tended to be serving longer sentences than the control group, and they had also received significantly fewer positive recommendations in 'Social Enquiry Reports' (SERs).[10] The fact that the members of this group were facing longer sentences, and had received less positive SERs, raises a number of interesting hypotheses. Further research, with a control group matched on sentence length, may be of value in separating out the possible contribution of this factor.

In an analysis of the family backgrounds of both groups, Liebling demonstrated that the control group showed slightly more unstable family backgrounds than the subject group. However, self-reported histories of mental health assessment/treatment and of familial histories of suicide and attempted suicide were reported to be higher for the subject group.

Somewhat at odds with the subject group showing more stable family backgrounds, was the finding that more of this group had experienced periods of local authority care. The subject group were also more likely to have received mental health treatment as either in- or out-patients. Liebling expressed caution in interpreting these results, though, noting that a significant proportion of such contact may have been simply for the production of routine psychiatric reports rather than being indicative of the presence of mental disorder.

The possible role of substance abuse in suicide and self-injury has been frequently mooted (e.g. Backett, 1987; Topp, 1979). Liebling found that her subject group had more major[11] alcohol-related problems before coming into custody and were more likely to have experimented with a wider range of illicit substances. She also reported that they were more likely to have a drug abuse-related index offence[12].

Self-injury was more common in the subject group before coming into prison. Members of the subject group were also more likely to report such behaviours as being 'suicide attempts'. Liebling reported nevertheless that a small number of those who repeatedly self-injured did not characterise their behaviour as suicidal. She went on to conclude, on the basis of her analysis, that a dimensional approach to problem characteristics may be a more useful way of comparing groups within the prison population, rather than looking for the presence or evidence of a range of events or attributes.

Both groups in this study reported experiencing difficulty in adjusting to imprisonment, with feelings of anxiety being common. Of the subject group, around a quarter were located in the healthcare centre, in itself a markedly different experience from the main residential 'wings' or 'units' in young offender institutions.

Significantly perhaps, more of the subject group preferred to share a cell – approximately one-half of the group compared with around one-third of the control group. Members of the subject group were also less likely to be involved in constructive activities in custody, although this may have been related to the high proportion located in the healthcare centre, where the availability of work and education are generally more limited. Even so, 60 per cent of the subject group were involved in education, but closure of these departments over the summer often meant that in reality these individuals faced long periods in their cells without constructive activity.

Other differences also emerged. A higher proportion of the subject group reported a dislike of physical education (30 per cent versus 4 per cent). The subject group also reported finding it more difficult to find constructive things to do when in their cells, with 33 per cent reporting that they could find nothing at all to do (compared with 4 per cent for the control group)[13]. Liebling noted that young male prisoners resorted to the notion of boredom to describe the feelings they had just prior to a 'suicide attempt', whereas young women prisoners tended to use the term 'depression' more readily.

There were clear differences between what Liebling termed 'copers' and 'poor-copers', suggesting that inmates with the fewest opportunities to occupy themselves (for whatever reason – some self-induced) were those least able to cope with isolation and boredom. The notion of such coping ability is used by Liebling to explain many of the observed differences between the subject and control groups in her study. She suggested that the interaction between the environment and the coping abilities of individuals might be used to differentiate young offenders. Based on the work by Williams and Scott (1988) on depression, she suggested that young prisoners who intentionally injured themselves, or attempted suicide during a sentence, would tend to demonstrate poorer coping skills than those inmates who did not engage in self-destructive behaviour.

A number of further observations were also drawn from the study. For example, a higher proportion of the subject group reported finding prison-based staff to be unhelpful (22 per cent versus 14 per cent). Perhaps the most striking thing here is that the proportions for both groups were quite low, whilst the difference between the groups was only 8 percentage points. The subject group was also reported to have had more complaints about the Prison Service disciplinary system and was more likely to have been given solitary confinement as a punishment. It is possible to speculate that these two findings were perhaps related.

More of the subject group had also been referred for a psychiatric assessment. Given the fact that the subject group was selected on the basis of contact with the healthcare centre, such a finding is unsurprising and a number of explanations are possible. These would include the possibility of higher levels of 'psychopathology' amongst the subject group. Alternatively, such referrals may simply have been a standard primary care response to self-injury.[14]

Visits from outside appeared to be significant, with both groups reporting marked anxiety in relation to visits. Only around one-third of either group reported receiving the maximum number of visits (one per fortnight at the time of the study), and both groups reported a number of problems with visits. Overall, though, the subject group reported receiving fewer visits and missing specific people more than the control group. They also reported writing fewer letters.

In summarising the differences between the subject and control groups, Liebling observed that the subject group were more likely to have had a history of psychiatric assessment or treatment. They were also more likely to have a history of serious alcohol abuse, to report witnessing parental violence, to have experimented with drugs, and to have spent more time in custody. However, the actual numbers reporting such experiences is often less than half of the subject group. Clearly, such individual correlates of self-injury have only limited explanatory power in isolation, with the interaction of multiple factors being involved.

As an explanatory concept, Liebling suggested that 'coping ability' might serve to account for the different reactions to custody of the subject and control groups. Thus those young offenders with poor coping ability will tend to resort to intentionally self-injurious behaviours more quickly than those with more developed coping skills. To date, there has been very little work done in terms of theoretical models of intentional self-injury, and this hypothesis is suggestive of a number of avenues of further research. It also raises additional questions. For example, it is possible that what is described as 'poor' coping may be a result of a number of other interacting and intervening variables.

Liebling's study also involved a number of interviews with Prison Service staff, as well as informal discussions. In terms of suicide and intentional self-injury, she noted that hospital officers and specialists saw some overlap or connection. Most, though, saw the two behaviours as distinct and different. This finding perhaps reflects the stress laid on the separation of suicide and self-injury as distinct phenomena in many specialists' training. The view was reflected in some of the attitudes expressed. Prison Service staff also tended to identify and stress the role of pre-existing vulnerability prior to reception. A number nevertheless recognised the role of the prison environment in increasing or decreasing the risk of self-injury.

Bullying was often cited by prisoners as a contributory factor in intentional self-injury, but staff were often reluctant to accept this explanation without qualification. Intentional self-injury was generally recognised by staff as a means by which young offenders could escape from difficult and/or threatening situations. What was termed 'minor' self-injury was often described by staff as 'attention seeking' or 'manipulative'. Overall, staff did not view intentional self-injury as an effective means of achieving goals. Furthermore, the vast majority of staff felt that there were constructive activities in which young offenders could participate; however almost two-thirds of the staff interviewed by Liebling did not feel that, on the whole, young offenders made constructive use of their time in custody.

In conclusion, Liebling stressed the historical isolation of prison suicide research from other suicide research. Certainly, when her study was undertaken this would seem to have had considerable veracity for studies of suicide and intentional self-injury. Earlier research studies were primarily based on psychiatric models. This had led to a number of methodological and theoretical limitations. Liebling went on to argue persuasively that the role of psychiatric illness as a factor in suicide and self-injury had been overstated in prison suicide research. She also went on to argue convincingly that suicide and self-injury are not primarily psychiatric problems and therefore do not require a primarily psychiatric response, but rather require a multidisciplinary approach.

There is some evidence from community-based studies to support the view that suicide and self-injury form part of a continuum of self-destructive behaviours. For example, Sletten *et al.* (1973) found that individuals who actually achieve suicide resemble attempters on a variety of diagnostic, family and demographic variables more than non-attempters. A later study by Pokorny (1983) of 5,000 patients found that:

> in most respects suicide attempters and suicide completers are similar, that is, they were mostly related to the same predictors and generally in the same direction.
>
> (Pokorny, 1983; as quoted in Botsis *et al.* (1997: 117))

Whilst research based on community studies suffers from a number of methodological weaknesses, and community studies cannot be uncritically applied to the prisons context, such research does give support to the notion of a behavioural continuum. Similar research within prisons, or indeed other forensic contexts, nevertheless remains very limited.

Bogue and Power (1995)

Bogue and Power's 1995 study was based on a sample of self-inflicted deaths that occurred in Scottish Prison Service establishments and that went on to be formally defined as suicide.[15] The study covered the period 1976–93 and involved an analysis of 83 deaths. The researchers reported that written prison records were available for 79 of these cases. Prisoner Central Records (PCRs) were used as the basis for gathering data, and these were described as including:

> reports by medical officers, prison nursing staff, psychiatrists and psychologists, plus details of the prisoners' forensic histories. Statements from discipline staff on duty, the medical officer, and the prison nursing officers concerning the circumstances of the prisoners death ...
>
> (Bogue and Power, 1995: 529)

A comparison was conducted across four-year periods within the overall period of the study. Bogue and Power concluded that there was an increase in suicides in excess of the increase in the prison population:

> For the 16-year period between the first 4-year segment, the mean annual ADP and the mean annual receptions to Scottish prisons increased by 1.6 per cent and 1.3 per cent respectively. However, for the same period, the suicide rate calculated on the basis of ADP and receptions increased by 40.4 per cent and 40.2 per cent respectively.
>
> (p. 530)

The researchers noted that, based on their sample, men were overrepresented and women underrepresented in the figures with only one woman appearing in their sample. Considerable caution is, however, needed in interpreting this finding (Towl and Fleming, 1997), given the small number of suicides by women prisoners included in the study.

The authors reported the mean age of their sample as 30.2 years. The mean age of the remanded suicides was not significantly different from that of the sentenced-prisoner suicides. However, for the period 1980–93 those aged over 30 years were significantly overrepresented.

The study replicated the earlier findings that remand prisoners completing suicide were significantly overrepresented as a proportion of average daily population (ADP). The authors are, though – in common with other researchers – critical of figures calculated on the basis of

ADP alone (Dexter and Towl, 1995). They reported that, when using reception figures as the basis for calculation of suicide rates, remand prisoners did not appear to be overrepresented in the suicide figures. Reception figures, they suggested, may in turn provide a much better estimate of the number of individuals placed 'at risk' in the prison environment.

Longer sentences did show evidence of being linked to higher rates of suicide:

> A significantly greater proportion of adult sentenced suicides were found to be serving sentences in excess of 18 months when compared with the general adult sentenced prison population based on ADP ($c^2 = 7.86$; df = -1; $p =< 0.01$).
>
> (p. 531)

The researchers also reported that a higher proportion of those completing suicide had been found guilty of, or been charged with, violent or sexual crimes, in comparison with the general prison population in Scotland.

In common with a number of other researchers, they found that hanging was by far the most common method used for suicide, with most reported as occurring between 9 p.m. and 6 a.m. Both these findings might reasonably be interpreted as largely a function of opportunity, in the context of prison.

One striking finding reported by Bogue and Power was that two-thirds of suicides occurred within three months of incarceration, and that over four-fifths of their sample killed themselves within one year of reception into prison. Even more striking, perhaps, was the finding that seven prisoners (9 per cent of the sample) killed themselves within 24 hours of reception into custody.

Based on their analysis, Bogue and Power also suggested that there was 'evidence of extensive psychiatric morbidity among the suicides' (p. 534). This comment was based upon a broad definition of 'psychiatric morbidity', that included drug abuse, alcohol abuse, personality disorder and 'depressive illness/reaction'. Only four people in the sample (5 per cent) were diagnosed as having a 'psychotic illness'. Such a finding is clearly greater than the population prevalence for such disorders but does not appear markedly higher than the prevalence of such disorders within the prison population (Gunn *et al.*, 1978).

In common with earlier studies, Bogue and Power reported finding high levels of previous 'deliberate self-injury', with 41 per cent of their sample having a recorded history of such behaviour. They also commented that '13 had made verbal threats or admitted to suicidal thoughts, whilst in custody' (p. 534). In turn, they observed that 29 prisoners were on some form of special observation at the time of their death, suggesting that there was some evidence of heightened risk of suicide in at least these cases. Of this group, 12 were on 'strict suicide observation', suggesting that these individuals had clearly been identified as at high risk. It seems clear from this result that observation and monitoring of the individuals were not an infallible safeguard against suicide and, as Bogue and Power note, such conditions can be 'extreme and potentially damaging' (p. 534). This, they suggested, had in turn led a number of medical officers to modify the nature of the supervision – by, for example, allowing prisoners some personal possessions.

Significantly, Bogue and Power drew attention to the role of methods of calculation of suicide rates in informing practice. They noted that:

> Remand prisoners have a high turn-over and spend less time in prison compared with their sentenced counterparts with the result that reception rates for prisoners on remand will be higher, and a greater number from this vulnerable group will be exposed to risk during what is widely regarded as being the most stressful phase of custody ...
>
> (p. 535–6)

There is evident validity in the point about the higher turnover of remand prisoners. However, the notion that remand is the most stressful period of custody can best be characterised as a hypothesis at this stage, although a number of earlier studies (e.g. Dooley, 1990 – see above) have used such notions to provide explanations of the higher rates of recorded suicide amongst remand prisoners, based on ADP.

Towl and Crighton (1998)

This study began by attempting to address some of the definitional problems that had bedevilled earlier research.[16] The Office of Population Censuses and Surveys (OPCS) publishes details of trends in suicide rates and methods in England and Wales (Charlton *et al.*, 1992). In their report on trends in suicide, Charlton and colleagues addressed the key issue of giving suicide researchers an operational definition. They provide two distinct operational definitions of suicide based on International Classification of Diseases (ICD) criteria.

   a) recorded suicides (World Health Organisation, 1948; 1955; 1965; 1977): 6th ICD E970–E979; 7th ICD E970–E979; 8th ICD E950–E959; 9th ICD E950–959 (as used in population trends 35[17]); and

b) suicides and undetermined (from 1968 onwards only): as (a) above plus E980–E989, excluding E988.8 after 1978.

In their study Towl and Crighton went on to conduct an analysis of written records and investigatory reports, based on operational definition (b). This approach differed from previous studies into prison suicides, where definitions similar to (a) have been adopted (Topp, 1979; Dooley, 1990; Bogue and Power, 1995). This involved the inclusion of all recorded[18] self-inflicted deaths in prisons, and Towl and Crighton noted that for the years 1988–1995 the proportion of such deaths that went on to be recorded as suicide verdicts ranged from 58 per cent to 84 per cent for men in prison (McHugh and Towl, 1997). For women from 1988–1996, the overall rate was 27 per cent (Towl and Fleming, 1997).

A number of researchers have identified background factors that may increase the risk of suicide – factors such as disrupted family backgrounds, familial histories of suicide, drug and alcohol abuse, poor school performance, unemployment, and depression (Diekstra and Hawton, 1987; Van Egmond and Diekstra, 1989). It is striking how closely such influences reflect many of the 'social factors' identified in studies of prospective criminal careers (e.g. Farrington, 1993). Such factors tend also to be associated with prisoner populations (Towl and Crighton, 1996). In this sense, prisoners may include a disproportionately large number of individuals who may be at a higher risk of suicide than average. Unemployment may be a particularly strong factor in increasing the risk of suicide (Platt and Kreitman, 1984; Moser *et al.*, 1984, 1990; Wilkinson, 1996). Interestingly, two recent studies indicate that the unemployment rates immediately prior to imprisonment are very high (Dexter and Towl, 1995; Jones, 1996), reporting rates of 77 per cent and 76 per cent respectively.

Two limitations to a number of these studies on suicide are striking. First, many are based upon small sample sizes (e.g. Dexter and Towl, 1995). Secondly, they are sometimes focused on one population, such as young offenders (e.g. Liebling, 1991) or one type of establishment (e.g. Jones, 1996). In both cases this serves to place limits on how far the results can be generalised. Towl and Crighton's 1998 study went some way to countering this by using a large sample (377 cases) and providing an analysis of all self-inflicted deaths across all parts of the prison system (i.e. among adults, young offenders and women prisoners).

The Towl and Crighton 1998 study also suffered from methodological limitations. So, although the authors were able to draw on a greater range and depth of written material than previous record-based studies, some of the difficulties inherent in analyses of this type remained. Thus, while the empirical data on many demographic variables can be assumed to be reliable (e.g. age, gender and so on), other types of information may be more problematic. Cause of death, for example, may be unclear. Attempts to gauge more qualitative information, such as the effect of prior events, pose even greater challenges for researchers.

Towl and Crighton have set out a number of findings from their research. Like Dooley, they suggested that the greater the sentence length the greater the risk of suicide. Life-sentenced prisoners in their study appeared, in particular, to be at an appreciably higher risk of suicide than determinate-sentenced prisoners. They also noted the powerful effects of the method of measurement used in calculating suicide rates amongst remand prisoners. When they calculated rates for remand prisoners using the Average Daily Population, the rate appeared high (238 per 100,000 per year); in marked contrast, when the rates were calculated using the number of deaths by remand reception numbers into prison, the rates were dramatically lower (39 per 100,000). This latter result compares with rates for determinate-sentenced prisoners of between 31 and 75 per 100,000 ADP. This led the authors to conclude that remand prisoners are at a similar risk of suicide to those given short determinate sentences (under 18 months) and are at a lower level of risk than those given longer or indeterminate sentences.[19]

The prison environment

Based on their analysis, Towl and Crighton have suggested that the different functions of prison establishments are reflected in their regimes. In particular, they suggested that in Local prisons there is a high 'throughput rate' amongst prisoners from, and to, the courts and to other prisons. Such throughput rates tend to be lower in other Prison Service establishments. They argued that this is likely to be an important factor in attempting to understand suicide in prisons. The majority of deaths (65 per cent) in their study occurred in Local prisons, with much lower rates being seen in Category C training prisons (10 per cent), youth custody centres (9 per cent) and dispersal and Category B training prisons (both 8 per cent). They did not, however, report this information in terms of rates. It is therefore possible that the preponderance of self-inflicted deaths in Local prisons is a result of the greater numbers of individuals being placed 'at risk' within that environment.

In 71 per cent of cases, death occurred while the individual was located in a single cell, compared with 23 per cent located in shared cells; in 7 per cent of cases the information was not recorded. Interestingly, there were no recorded cases during the period studied where death occurred while an individual was located in a 'ward' setting in prison.

The authors went on to test the hypothesis that younger age groups (i.e. 15–24 years) would be overrepresented in the figures for prison suicides. They argued that there appeared to be some evidence to support this hypothesis in the juvenile group (i.e. 15–17 years). With this exception, younger age groups did not appear to be overrepresented in the figures. This finding replicated earlier findings by the same authors based on smaller samples when examining self-inflicted deaths in prisons for the periods 1988–90 and 1994–95 (Crighton and Towl, 1997).

In their study, the authors replicated Topp's finding that the early period in prison appeared to be of particular significance. The importance of the early period of imprisonment appeared to be much more significant in individual cases than legal status (i.e. remand or sentenced). They observed that the risk of suicide was highest during the first week after reception into a new establishment.

The authors went on to discuss 'environmental factors', by which they meant aspects of the organisation of prison regimes. These were, they suggested, liable to have a significant impact on suicide rates in prisons. In support of this, they quoted the finding that approximately two-thirds of suicides for the period of study occurred in Local prisons. There is, they noted, a lack of research into the specific effects of high throughput rates in such regimes. However, they went on to suggest that a number of factors may be implicated, including the transience of the population being held. High throughput within an establishment is also likely to lead to a greater need to relocate individuals. This is liable to disrupt social contacts and increase uncertainty amongst both staff and prisoners. They also suggested:

> Perhaps most importantly, we suggest that as the transience of a population increases then the full development of positive staff–prisoner relationships will become progressively more difficult to develop and maintain.
>
> (Towl and Crighton, 1998: 189)

HM Chief Inspector of Prisons Thematic Review (1999)

In May 1999, HM Chief Inspector of Prisons published a thematic review of suicide and self-injury in prisons in England and Wales. To a large extent this followed on logically from the earlier thematic review by the Chief Inspector of Prisons in 1990. This more recent review focused primarily on the period 1988–98, during which there was a marked increase in the number and rate of self-inflicted deaths in prison in England and Wales.

The 1999 review reports a clear increase in the rate of suicide per 100,000 average annual population, from 54 in 1982 to 128 in 1998. The

Table 2.1   Rates of self-inflicted deaths per 100,000 average population[a] and per 100,000 receptions[b] for 1996–98

	Number of self-inflicted deaths in year	Average prison population in year	Rate of self-inflicted deaths per 100,000 average population in year	Receptions in year	Rate of self-inflicted deaths per 100,000 receptions in year
1996					
Sentenced	28	43,043	65	82,861	34
Remand (untried)	31	8,374	370	58,888	53
Convicted unsentenced	5	3,238	154	34,987	14
Total	64	54,655[c]			
1997					
Sentenced	34	48,412	70	87,168	39
Remand (untried)	26	8,453	308	62,066	42
Convicted unsentenced	8	3,678	218	36,424	22
Total	68	60,543 [d]			
1998					
Sentenced	27	52,176	52	86,800	31
Remand (untried)	40	8,157	490	64,600	62
Convicted unsentenced	15	4,411	340	42,400	36
Total	82	64,744 [e]			

Notes:
a) From records held by Suicide Awareness Support Unit, Prison Service HQ.
b) Data from Home Office Research Development and Statistics Directorate.
c) Figure of 54,655 does not include civil prisoners (55,300 average population).
d) Figure of 60,543 does not include civil prisoners (61,114 average population).
e) Figure of 64,744 does not include civil prisoners.

Source: Consolidated from *Suicide is Everyone's Concern* (HMCIP, 1999: 13)

report's authors also state that there was a 'marked increase between 1997 and 1998 which has taken place in the unsentenced prisoner population,' (HMCIP, 1999: 12). The authors go on to provide an analysis in terms of 'per 100,000 average population'[20] and per 100,000 receptions. In line with previous studies, they note that the rates for suicide in prison are very much higher than those seen in the community. They also note that:

the increase in the rate of suicide for unsentenced prisoners is larger than would be expected by the influence of population alone.

(p. 13)

The largest single rise in the rate for self-inflicted deaths per 100,000 receptions, between 1996 and 1998, is reported as being in the convicted/unsentenced population – with an average increase of 250 per cent reported. It is worth noting, however, that this result is based on relatively small numbers (samples of 5, 8 and 15 respectively for the three years). Conclusions based on changes in small numbers need, of necessity, to be made with considerable caution. A descriptive analysis of the legal status of prisoners for those who died by suicide during 1996, 1997 and 1998 was also undertaken. This data is reproduced in Table 2.1.

The report's authors also went on to analyse self-inflicted deaths by establishment type and offence type. They reached the conclusion that the rate of self-inflicted deaths amongst women prisoners was broadly in line with their representation in the prison population (for they represented 3.5 per cent of self-inflicted deaths and 4 per cent of the prison population). In contrast, they suggested that those charged with sexual or violent offences were overrepresented relative to their proportions in the general prison population.[21]

The authors also replicated a number of previous findings. First, they found that white prisoners tended to be overrepresented in the self-inflicted death figures (see Towl and Crighton, 1997). Secondly, they noted that younger age groups did not appear to be overrepresented. Indeed, they concluded that, overall, 'the age distribution of self-inflicted deaths is broadly in proportion with that of the prison population as a whole' (p. 16). They also report a similar pattern in terms of age for a sample of 'attempted suicides/incidents of deliberate self-harm' (p. 17) for the period 1996/7.[22] The one exception to this, they suggest, is the 21–29 age group, who appeared to be slightly overrepresented in the figures.

Using a sample of data provided by the Suicide Awareness Support Unit at Prison Service Headquarters, the authors also calculated the time from reception into prison to self-inflicted death. The results of their analysis paralleled earlier research, which suggested the initial period in custody was one of increased risk. In discussing their figures, the report's authors concluded that:

> These figures confirm that the first 24 hours is a very high risk time, that the whole of the first year is a medium risk time for suicide and that after the first year has past the risk of suicide is substantially reduced.
>
> (p. 17)

In fact, it could be argued that this is to somewhat oversimplify the situation. The initial 24 hours after reception are certainly a period of exceptionally high risk; however, the results of previous studies have suggested a gradual reduction in the level of risk, which continues to reduce from reception, levelling out after around three months from reception into an establishment (see Crighton and Towl, 1997; Towl and Crighton, 1998; Towl and Hudson, 1997; Towl, 1999b).

The authors also go on to look at the role of psychiatric disorder in suicide. They conclude that this whole area has been bedevilled by definitional problems that, in turn, have made any valid conclusions difficult to obtain. They suggest that high levels of psychiatric morbidity seen in prisons may in fact make this a less useful indicator of possible risk than in the community.[23]

Summary and conclusions

As noted at the beginning of this chapter, suicide in prisons presents researchers with some formidable difficulties. There are, to date, no methodologically ideal studies. The absence of carefully selected control groups limits interpretation of most studies, and this is a challenge for future researchers.

Despite the difficulties, however, there is a growing research base. In recent years the nature of research has also seen significant development. Early studies were primarily based on psychiatric models, and as such were largely concerned with identifying and describing correlates of suicide. Specifically, early studies stressed the role of mental disorders in mediating suicidal behaviours. Indeed, it has been argued that this has been greatly overemphasised at the expense of other factors involved in suicide in prisons.

Some clear themes have emerged from the research to date:

- The early stages of custody have emerged as a period of particularly high risk. From the time of reception into prison, the risk of suicide appears to decrease steadily over the first three to four months. There is also some evidence that the time spent at an establishment is significant and, to some extent at least, is independent of time in custody.

- For sentenced prisoners, risk of suicide appears to broadly increase in line with sentence length. Life-sentence prisoners appear to be at markedly greater risk than other long-term prisoners. Speculatively, the role of uncertainty in indeterminate sentences may be a contributory factor.
- There is some evidence that juvenile (15–17-year-old) prisoners are at marginally increased risk. With this possible exception, there is little evidence that younger age groups are at greater risk of suicide than older age groups of prisoners.
- The question as to whether the rates of suicide for women in prison are higher or lower than for men remains controversial. However, the balance of empirical evidence indicates that women have a lower risk of suicide than men.

Overall, there has been a significant development of the research into suicide in prisons. This has been reflected by a growth in the amount of research being undertaken. What are missing within the research base are explanatory theoretical models. Historically, the research has been primarily concerned with identifying correlates of suicide and intentional self-injury. Such models are, it may be argued, essential in guiding future research into suicide and suicide prevention in prisons.

3

Intentional self-injury (ISI)

David Crighton and Graham Towl

Overview

In this chapter we begin by exploring and examining the definitional and contextual issues associated with intentional self-injury (ISI). Next, we review the relevant literature in the area, focusing upon both the learning from existing knowledge and also some of the methodological limitations of the studies in question.

Logical and definitional issues

The legal systems in the United Kingdom have tended to shy away from attempting to define self-injury. Attempts at definition have come primarily from practitioners and researchers working with those who self-injure. This in turn has resulted in a great deal of variation in the definitions and terminology used, both in research and practice, with a plethora of terms being used to describe such behaviours.

Researchers have often sought to distinguish between different forms of 'self-harming' behaviours according to intent. Terms such as 'attempted suicide' have been used to describe self-harming behaviours where there is an expressed intention to die. 'Parasuicide' and 'deliberate self-harm syndrome' have been coined to describe self-injurious behaviours where there is, or is thought to be, little or no intention to die. A number of researchers have also drawn distinctions between self-mutilation and self-poisoning. The main terms used and the difficulties and advantages of these are discussed in more detail below.

Attempted suicide and parasuicide

Early researchers and practitioners often saw suicide and self-injury as being closely related behaviours. For example, Menninger (1938), drawing on psychoanalytic approaches, described self-injury as 'focal' suicide. Given the dominance of psychodynamic theories during this era, especially in North America, it is perhaps not surprising that most intentional self-injury was described as 'attempted suicide'.

Kreitman *et al.* (1969) questioned this view, coining the term 'parasuicide' to refer to acts of self-harm (including 'self-mutilation' and 'self-poisoning') where there appeared to be little or no intention to die. The term was therefore used to distinguish clearly suicide and attempted suicide, where the individual expressed a wish to die, from self-harm without suicidal intent. Indeed, it has been argued that acts such as self-mutilation and self-poisoning may be seen largely as antithetical to suicide (Babiker and Arnold, 1996). Similarly, Ross and McKay (1979) suggested that:

> There is in the action of the self-mutilator seldom an intent to die and often very little risk of dying. Although a self-mutilator could engender his own death by his behaviour, in the vast majority of cases this does not happen. His behaviour is actually counter-intentional to suicide rather than suicidal.
>
> (p.15)

In line with this view, it seems clear that the majority of authors since the 1960s have not accepted Menninger's view that self-injury was a form of suicide, serving instead as a psychological compromise that forestalled actual suicide. One key exception to this train of thought has been Shneidman (1985), who, although using the term parasuicide, stresses the continuity between self-injurious and suicidal processes.

It is also clear that the approach suggested by Ross and McKay is open to challenge on a number of logical grounds. To begin with, the notion of an individual being at little risk of dying is clearly a judgement; as is the ascribed intent of the person who self-injures. Even though there are clearly many cases where such an analysis may be accurate, and those who self-injure may have no intention of dying, it is open to question how far this can be generalised. Unclear or mixed intentions are often characteristic of both those who complete suicide and many of those who self-injure (Shneidman, 1985).

Categorisation of intentional self-injury

Many attempts have been made at constructing typologies of ISI. For example, Menninger (1938) suggested four factors in what he termed 'self-mutilation':

- the extent and type of psychological dysfunction of the mutilator;

- the subcultural context of the mutilator and the meaning of the acts within that context;
- the degree and localisation of the injury;
- the specific psychodynamic determinants of the behaviour.

A number of aspects of Menninger's approach have been subject to criticism. These include the suggestion from some that he was overinclusive in defining 'self-mutilation', with behaviours such as hair and nail cutting being considered alongside self-laceration, all within the term 'self-mutilation'. Conversely, Menninger's exclusion of self-mutilation among the mentally handicapped has also been criticised on logical grounds.

Ross and McKay (1979) adopted a markedly different approach of describing particular behaviours such as cutting, biting, abrading, ingesting and so on. They also went on to argue (as quoted in Walsh and Rosen, 1988) that three related dimensions were applicable to each of these specific behaviours:

- the severity of physical damage;
- the psychological state of the individual at the time of the self-altering act;
- the social acceptability of the behaviour.

Drawing on the ideas of Ross and McKay, Walsh and Rosen (1988) themselves outline four main types of intentional self-injury:

- ear piercing, nail biting and small professional tattoos;
- other piercing and ritualistic scarring (subculturally approved);
- mild-to-moderate damage occurring in a psychological state of crisis, and lacking in social approval except from similarly self-injuring individuals;
- severe physical damage, normally occurring in psychotic states and encountering no social approval.

Whilst most research has focused on the more physically damaging forms of self-injury, a number of writers have stressed the importance of seeing such behaviour within its broader social and historical context (Walsh and Rosen, 1988; Babiker and Arnold, 1996).

Deliberate self-harm syndrome

The notion of a 'deliberate self-harm (DSH) syndrome' is often attributed to Morgan (1979) and was, in turn, based on an epidemiological study conducted in the United Kingdom. The term DSH has been widely criticised on a number of grounds. The most serious of these is perhaps the lack of specificity of the term. The 1995 Concise Oxford Dictionary's definition of harm is 'hurt, damage' as both a noun and a verb. Thus 'harm' could include any behaviours that cause damage to the individual, either physically or psychologically. Very many behaviours would be harmful within these terms and such aspects of living such as substance abuse, smoking, overeating and tattooing could all certainly be described as 'harmful'.

Pattison and Kahan (1983) also advocated the notion of a DSH syndrome, but have adopted a markedly different definitional approach to that of Morgan (1979). They excluded all cases of drug and alcohol overdoses, along with all cases where the DSH seemed to be of high lethality. This difference of approach has, in turn, been reflected in the research into DSH; with studies in the United Kingdom tending to adopt the broad definition and those in the United States adopting the narrower definition. Although the notion of DSH has been the subject of increasing criticism, it has also greatly influenced the current research base. A number of authors (e.g. Walsh and Rosen, 1988; Towl, 1997) have argued that the term 'deliberate self-harm' is overinclusive and serves to blur the distinctions between behaviours that may have clearly distinct motivations and functions for individuals.

In addition, the use of the term 'deliberate', as a descriptor of self-injurious behaviours, is highly questionable (Towl, 2000). One dictionary definition of 'deliberate', again from the 1995 *Concise Oxford Dictionary*, may serve to illustrate:

> adj. and v. * adj. 1a Intentional (a deliberate foul). b. fully considered; not impulsive (made a deliberate choice). 2. Slow in deciding; cautious (a ponderous and deliberate mind). 3. (of movement etc.) leisurely and unhurried. * v. 1. Intr. think carefully, take counsel (the jury deliberated for an hour)...

In the context of self-injury, notions of carefulness, lack of hurry, careful thought and of cautious, leisurely and unhurried behaviours seem very poorly to characterise many of the behaviours subsumed within the DSH term.

The more general term 'intentional' would seem more accurate since it is defined in the same volume as 'adj. done on purpose'. This definition clearly does not make any assumptions about the level of planning or forethought or the structuring of the behaviours involved. It can therefore be argued that the term 'DSH' should be replaced by the more semantically accurate and more clearly defined notion of 'intentional self-injury' (ISI). This also has the important potential advantage of providing a clearer focus for research studies.

Nevertheless, despite our major reservations about the term DSH, for expository purposes below in describing some of the pertinent research we adopt the terms used by the authors of the studies.

Epidemiology

There are a number of epidemiological studies of self-injurious behaviours. However, interpretation of such studies is often complicated, as noted above, by wide variations in the definitions adopted. This often serves to make comparisons across different studies difficult.

Hawton *et al.* (1997) reported the findings of an epidemiological study in the Oxford area of the United Kingdom between 1985 and 1995. The authors state that they considered 'rates of self-harm (DSH) (self-poisoning and self-injury)' (Hawton *et al.*, 1997: 556). They noted a decline in the rates of DSH during the late 1970s and early 1980s, most particularly among adolescent girls. This was followed by a rise in the late 1980s (Hawton and Fagg, 1992). Multicentre studies (e.g. Schmidtke *et al.*, 1996 – see below) have also suggested that the United Kingdom has one of the highest rates of self-harm in Europe. Hawton *et al.* (1997) analysed 10,631 episodes of DSH between 1985 and 1995. During the period of the study they reported an average annual increase in the number of people self-harming of 4.6 per cent per annum.

In this study, the increase in DSH was most marked for men, with an increase of 5.8 per cent per annum in numbers of individuals self-harming, and a larger increase in the number of episodes, up by 7.9 per cent per annum during the period of review. These figures for males compare with increases for women of 3.8 per cent and 5.6 per cent respectively. Whilst women still self-harmed more than men, the gender ratio, in line with the findings above, decreased over the period of the study. Thus, in 1985, the rates of women-to-men self-harming was 1.43:1, and this reduced to 1.35:1 in 1990 and 1.23:1 in 1995.

Hawton *et al.* (1997) noted a very marked increase in the overall rate of DSH, with an increase of 62.1 per cent for men and 42.2 per cent for women over the period of the study. This increase was particularly marked in young men (aged 15–24 years), where the rate per 100,000 of population increased from 162 to 477 (an increase of 194 per cent). The pattern of increases in women was more marked in the 25–34 years age range (+35.6 per cent) and the 35–54 years age range (+67.7 per cent).

The authors also found an increase in repetition of DSH within one year of receiving medical treatment. For the period 1985–9, they reported that 13.1 per cent came to the attention of medical services for DSH within one year. Between 1990 and 1994, this increased to 16.1 per cent. The rate for repetition was also slightly higher for men, at 15.8 per cent, than for women, at 14 per cent, over the whole period of the study.

As with many community studies, caution is needed before applying the findings to forensic contexts. Within the study, as with other community studies, there was a high prevalence of self-poisoning. Hawton *et al.* reported that 89.7 per cent of cases that came to be included within their study involved self-poisoning, 8.3 per cent involved acts of self-injury, and 3.8 per cent both. This pattern is largely reversed in prisons, where acts of self-injury (primarily self-laceration and abrasion) are far more common than in community studies. Acts of self-poisoning, especially using prescribed medication, are much less frequent in prisons.

WHO European multicentre study on parasuicide

The World Health organisation conducted a multicentre European study of parasuicide (Schmidtke *et al.*, 1996). Data was provided and analysed from 16 centres in 13 European countries. In defining 'parasuicide', the authors of the study adopted the International Classification of Diseases (10th revision) definition (WHO, 1993). Parasuicide was defined as:

> an act with non-fatal outcome, in which an individual deliberately initiates a non-habitual behaviour that, without intervention from others, will cause self-harm, or deliberately ingests a substance in excess of the prescribed or generally recognised therapeutic dosage, and which is aimed at realising changes which the subject desired via the actual or expected physical consequences...
>
> (Schmidtke *et al.*, 1996: 328)

The authors also included acts that were interrupted before physical harm occurred, giving the example of people who were removed from railway tracks. The study excluded acts of 'self-harm' by people who 'do not understand the meaning or consequences of their own actions (for example, because of mental subnormality or insanity)' (p. 328).

For each of the 16 centres, available data from the period 1989–1992 was analysed in age bands of 15–24 years, 25–34 years, 35–44 years, 45–54 years and over 55 years. To take into account differences in population demographics, age-standardised rates were also calculated. In those terms for those aged 15 years and over, the highest male rate was found in Helsinki, Finland (327 per 100,000), followed by Oxford, United Kingdom (264 per 100,000). The lowest rate was reported by

Guipuzcoa in Spain (46 per 100,000). For women, the highest rate was recorded in Cergy-Pontoise in France (542 per 100,000), followed again by Oxford (368 per 100,000). The lowest rate was again Guipuzcoa (72 per 100,000) (Schmidtke *et al.*, 1996).

Two clear findings emerged from this study. First, the rates of recorded parasuicide varied dramatically across Europe during the period of the review. Secondly, with one exception the recorded rates of parasuicide were higher for women. The average ratio of male to female 'suicide attempts' for those aged over 15 years was reported as 1:1.5 (Schmidtke *et al.*, 1996 p. 330).

The highest rates of parasuicide were generally found in the 15–24 years age group for women and the 25–34 years age group for men. This confirmed, to some extent, the notion that younger age groups are at higher risk. However, the authors suggest that 'this simple inverse relationship between age and suicide attempts appears to be less valid for male subjects' (Schmidtke *et al.*, 1996: 337). The findings also contrast with those of Hawton *et al.* (1997) in the United Kingdom, who found that men in the younger age group (15–24 years) were at greater risk of DSH.

There are a number of methodological issues, common to many multicentre studies of this type, that need to be considered (see Leenars, 1994). For example, it is clear that full datasets were not available for all centres, and this makes comparisons between centres more difficult. Another issue is the variations between European centres in the definition of parasuicide. Making due allowance for such methodological problems, the study nevertheless serves to give a useful epidemiological picture of 'parasuicide' across the European Union.

Definitional issues in prisons

There has been a similar diversity in terms of definitions and terminology used in prison-based studies of self-injurious behaviours as has been the case in community studies. This in turn has resulted in similar challenges when faced with interpreting the available research base.

As in community studies, the issue of intent in self-injury has been the subject of considerable confusion and discussion. There are a number of clear differences, however, in relation to prison-based studies. For example, most community studies have reported a preponderance of self-poisoning. As noted above, prison studies have, in marked contrast, generally reported low levels of self-poisoning. Therefore studies of intentional self-injury in prisons have tended to be dominated by incidents of self-mutilation (i.e. self-cutting, burning, abrasion and even asphyxiation), since these are by far the most common means of self-injury seen. In contrast to the community at large, self-poisoning appears to be relatively rare in prisons, perhaps as a function of (non-) availability. It remains unclear, therefore, how comparable the results of community-based and prison-based studies are, and how far the results of community studies may be used to inform practice in forensic settings. In addition, it is worth noting that much self-injury in prisons involves methods of high potential lethality (e.g. hanging). This also appears to be markedly different from self-harm in the community.

Research in the context of secure institutions is further complicated by issues of reporting and detection. Community studies have focused primarily on patients who present for treatment to acute or primary-care health services. It is therefore possible that a significant number of incidents of self-injury go unreported in the community, with individuals treating their own injuries, with the possible exception of self-poisoning. In prisons, by contrast, the majority of cases of intentional self-injury are likely to be reported.

One aspect that is not unique to prisons, or other secure environments, is the labelling of those who self-injure themselves. In prison settings, such behaviours are routinely described as 'attention seeking' and 'manipulative', even where such behaviour is of high lethality. There may be some truth in such assertions. Thus an attempted suicide (or actual suicide) may be the only way an individual feels that personal distress or the need to seek help can be expressed; and so in this sense an individual's behaviour is clearly attention seeking. Such terms as the latter are, however, often used in a pejorative sense and may serve to legitimise a hostile response from staff towards the individual (see Dexter and Towl, 1995).

Self-injurious behaviour is also, in prisons and the community alike, associated with the presence of 'personality disorders'. This association can be used as a largely circular explanation, with self-injury being used to define a 'personality disorder', which in turn is seen as explanatory of the self-injury.

Major research into intentional self-injury

There has been relatively little research into ISI in prisons. Two major studies, from the early and late 1990s, are now described.

Liebling and Krarup 1993

The study by Liebling and Krarup (1993) has its roots in earlier work reported in 1991 (Liebling, 1991). It involved 'two years of interviewing, discussion, observation and listening' and the authors state 'no apology is made for its length or content' (Liebling and Krarup, 1993:

2). As might be concluded from this hint, it is a difficult study to summarise and, in fact, any attempt at summary is unlikely to do it full justice.

The study has two main elements, which run concurrently. First, it contains an epidemiological study to collect information prospectively on suicide attempts and self-injury over a 12-month period in 16 prisons. Secondly, it provides a qualitative study covering social, environmental and motivational factors using lengthy semi-structured interviews with staff and prisoners in four establishments.

For the first part of the study, a data-collection form (not illustrated in the report) was devised that was filled out by healthcare staff on actual incidents of self-injury. Of the 343 occurrences recorded, 38 were discarded as they failed to meet the criteria for inclusion. Some of the key findings from this part of the study are thus: there was an overrepresentation of young prisoners and remand prisoners (40 per cent, compared with 20 per cent of the total prison population); 77 per cent of the self-injury incidents involved some form of cutting; and 18 per cent involved hanging. When reasons for self-injury were examined, staff tended to use explanations that were more strategic, ascribing instrumental motives to prisoners; prisoners, in contrast, were more likely to emphasise factors such as depression. Interestingly, both were equally likely to draw upon situational factors.

The second part of the study provides a rich source of personal accounts of staff and prisoners describing their experiences of life in prison from all perspectives, and the factors that are felt to impinge upon the likelihood of risk of self-injury. The accounts are drawn together to underpin a general set of principles about prisoners' adaptation to, or ability to 'cope' with, imprisonment. As suggested above, it would be an injustice to attempt to summarise these findings; instead, the reader is encouraged to read the personal statements and accounts first-hand, for the findings provide a fertile ground for generating exploratory hypotheses that warrant further attention.

Office for National Statistics report (1998)

In 1997 the Social Survey Division of the Office for National Statistics carried out a survey on behalf of the Department of Health (ONS, 1998). Its main aim was to collect baseline data on the psychiatric morbidity of male and female prisoners, both on remand and sentenced. The survey included, *inter alia*, personality disorder, psychosis, alcohol and drug dependency, deliberate self-harm, post-traumatic stress and intellectual functioning.

The survey was based upon lay interviews with a sample of over 3,100 prisoners across all establishments in England and Wales and upon clinical interviews with a subsample consisting of one in five of the main sample. It was thus one of the largest of its kind. The survey highlighted high levels of mental health problems for prisoners generally, compared with rates observed in community studies or household surveys.

Twenty per cent of male prisoners and 40 per cent of female prisoners had received help with mental or emotional problems in the 12 months prior to coming into prison. Prevalence rates for any type of personality disorder were 78 per cent for male remands, 64 per cent for sentenced males and 59 per cent for females. Paranoid personality disorder was the most prevalent personality disorder: 29 per cent of males on remand, 20 per cent of males sentenced, and 16 per cent of females. Borderline personality disorder was more prevalent for females than paranoid personality disorder. Prevalence of functional psychoses in the year prior to interview was: 10 per cent for males on remand; 7 per cent for males sentenced; and 14 per cent for females.

Interviewers asked four questions on self-harm/attempted suicide based on earlier studies (see Paykel and Cooper, 1992):

- *'Have you ever thought that life was not worth living?'*
- *'Have you ever wished that you were dead?'*
- *'Have you ever thought of taking your life, even though you would not actually do it?'*
- *'Have you ever made an attempt to take your life, by taking an overdose of tablets or in some other way?'*

If the interviewee answered 'yes' to any question, they were then asked:

- *'Was this in the last week, last year, or at another time?'*

A separate question was added to touch on parasuicide:

- *'Since you have been in prison, have you deliberately harmed yourself in any way but not with the intention of killing yourself?'*

A number of findings were reported: 46 per cent of male remands indicated thoughts of killing themselves at some time in their life; 35 per cent in the previous year; and 12 per cent in the previous week. Over one-quarter of male remands stated that they had attempted suicide at some point in life and one-sixth reported they had done so within the previous year. For females the figures were higher. And remand prisoners, male and female, showed a higher prevalence of suicidal ideation and attempted suicides than sentenced prisoners. This feature was most striking for the time period covering the previous week: 12 per cent of male remands versus 4 per cent sentenced and 27 per cent of female remands versus 16 per cent of sentenced. Reported rates for suicidal thoughts and attempted suicide were highest among white prisoners; a similar picture was reported for parasuicidal behaviour. Prisoners in custody for less than one month had higher rates of suicidal thoughts, particularly during the previous week.

A secondary analysis of the self-harm data was conducted and reported on in 1999 (ONS, 1999). Although, as the authors of that report acknowledge, any secondary analysis is limited by the absence of key areas that may not have been of prime concern in the initial study, this secondary level of analysis yielded some useful findings. One limitation of the original study is of note: data had not been collected on the precise timings of self-harm/attempted suicide. It was not, therefore, possible to ascertain whether incidents had occurred before or during custody.

The secondary analysis showed overall that prisoners attempting suicide tended to be younger, white, single, born in the United Kingdom, had left school earlier and consequently were more poorly educated. Ethnicity and age were the most significant factors. Female prisoners who had attempted suicide were more likely to have no children.

A number of features distinguished the suicide attempters (in the previous year) from the non-attempters: levels of psychosis (25–50 per cent versus 5 per cent respectively); levels of neurotic disorder and alcohol abuse; co-morbidity for mental health disorders (defined as four or five factors present simultaneously) – suicide attempters were five times more likely to be in this category; psychiatric treatment prior to custody (male suicide attempters were more likely by a factor of four and females by a factor of three, compared with non-attempters). There were a number of other health and social factors that distinguished the two groups.

Some custodial factors were of particular note: one-third of male and female sentenced prisoners and one-quarter of males on remand, who had attempted suicide in the previous year, reported having been held in 'strip cell' conditions. And 41 per cent of the male remands who had attempted suicide reported that they had been threatened with violence compare with 17 per cent of non-suicide attempters. Twelve per cent of the suicide attempters reported no family contact on the outside, compared with 6 per cent of non-suicide attempters.

Although relying heavily on self-report through interview, the scale of this study on a sample comprising 5 per cent of the prison population makes it an important contribution to research in the field. At the very least it provides ammunition to support the view that support for mental health problems is required for many prisoners at heightened risk of self-injury.

Demographic factors in intentional self-injury

The absence of a broad research base makes the identification of correlates of ISI very tenuous. However, a number of aspects of those who self-injure and of the prison environment have been studied.

Age

It is clear that large numbers of young people intentionally injure themselves in prison.

But the question of age and ISI in prisons has been complicated by the age distribution of the prison population, which is anyway skewed towards younger age groups.

There is evidence that within the imprisoned population young offenders (aged 15–21 years) are not at greater risk of ISI when held in young-offender institutions (Thornton, 1990). However, Winkler (1992) suggests that this is not the case for young offenders held in adult prisons, where the risk of ISI appears markedly higher. Beyond this, the picture from the research is somewhat confused. Some researchers have suggested that ISI increases as a function of age (e.g. Winkler, 1992), whilst others have found no clear relationship (Jones, 1986).

What does seem clear from the research is that recorded rates of ISI in prisons are higher than in the community. Winkler (1992) suggests a rate for young offenders five times higher than that seen in adolescents in the community. It remains unclear, though, how far such findings are a reflection of increased detection and how far it is a result of the characteristics of those who come into prison, and the particular environments into which such prisoners come.

Ethnicity

Consistent differences have been reported for the rates of ISI amongst different ethnic groups. Most of the research in this area is North American, and the most robust finding here has been the lower rates of ISI amongst black prisoners, along with higher rates amongst white and Hispanic prisoners.

It has been suggested that rates of ISI are higher for African-Americans in the community (Haycock, 1989). Haycock suggests that the best explanation of this paradox is that predominantly white prison officers selectively attend to ISI; therefore, a large part of the ISI of African-American prisoners will effectively be ignored. This view fails to explain convincingly why Hispanic-American prisoners show higher rates of ISI than African or white American groups.

Other *post hoc* explanations are also possible. For example the rates of imprisonment for black men in the USA are much higher than for white men. As such, it could be suggested that the characteristics of the two groups in terms of risk of ISI will be different.

Gender

As noted above, community studies of DSH in Europe have suggested higher rates of self-harm amongst women than men; a similar picture is found in prisons. This may be greatly influenced by the breadth of definition used in European studies, and by the preponderance of cases of self-poisoning that stem from it.

Studies of women prisoners who have self-injured have been conducted. Cookson (1977) reported that women who self-injured in prison tended to be younger than control groups. They were also more likely to be serving sentences of more than one year, have a history of previous psychiatric treatment and be convicted of violent offences. In a similar study, Cullen (1985) reported that women young offenders who self-injured were more likely to have harmed themselves in the past than other prisoners. They were also more likely to have a history of suicide attempts and of prior custodial sentences or remands.

A pilot study conducted into ISI in women prisoners was reported by Snow (1997). This study involved interviews with a sample of women who had self-injured, as well as interviews with prison staff. Snow reported a wide range of reasons for self-injury, but the role of frustration and anger was evident:

> Ten women reported that they injure themselves as a means of relieving stress, tension, anger and frustration. Seven women said they also injure themselves specifically to draw blood. Reasons for this included feelings of calmness when blood is seen ... Two women reported that they injure themselves specifically to inflict pain on themselves...
>
> (Snow, 1997: 53)

A particularly striking finding from this study relates to staff opinions. All the staff interviewed distinguished between suicide and self-injury. Many also stated that acts of self-injury did not suggest to them an increased risk of suicide. Such opinions were in marked contradiction to Prison Service policy in England and Wales and also run counter to much of the research evidence.

Situational factors affecting intentional self-injury

Prisons and other secure institutions are clearly very different environments from those experienced in the community at large. In particular, secure environments by definition act to impose marked controls on behaviour.

Custodial variables

A number of custodial variables have been studied in relation to ISI. One of the most obvious has been the legal status of those who self-injure, and specifically the remand-versus-sentenced distinction. Studies have reported high rates of ISI amongst remand prisoners (e.g. Wool and Dooley, 1987). However, such a finding is not altogether surprising, given the high turnover of remand prisoners. Therefore a larger number of individuals will be placed at risk of ISI in prison when they are on remand than when under sentence. This directly parallels the research on suicide (see Chapter 2). As noted, early studies of suicide rates consistently overestimated the value of remand status as a marker of suicide risk, simply as a function of calculating rates on the basis of Average Daily Population (ADP)[24] (Bogue and Power, 1995).

Custodial-sentence setting has also been suggested as an important factor in ISI. Those detained in local prisons have been found to be overrepresented in terms of ISI. Again, this may be largely – or wholly – a facet of the means of calculating the rates of ISI. Local prisons have the highest turnover of prisoners and therefore tend to have many more individuals placed at risk than would be suggested by their ADP. In order to make valid comparisons across establishment types, a more sophisticated measure of time at risk is required. Calculations based on ADP or receptions are unlikely to be totally adequate for the purposes of such comparisons.

Time from reception has been another area of research. Livingstone (1997) suggests that the research differs according to whether young offenders or adult prisoners are studied. For adult prisoners, a number of researchers have reported that around one-third of all incidents of ISI are reported within the first week of reception (Albanese, 1983; Kerkhof and Bernasco, 1990). Only one study of young offenders has specifically looked at this. Alessi *et al.* (1984) found ISI to be evenly distributed across the sentence. It is worth noting, however, that the level of analysis in such studies may have been inadequate: Crighton and Towl (1997) in studying prison suicides found that the initial period from reception into an establishment appeared to be a time of very high risk of suicide – something that appeared to be, at least to some extent, independent of the amount of time spent in custody.

The use of isolation

Despite criticism from a range of professional bodies, isolation is still commonly used as a means of managing difficult behaviour such as aggression and ISI (Royal College of Psychiatrists, 1998). Several research studies have shown that there is a clear relationship between the use of isolation and ISI.

Ross *et al.* (1978) report that 70 per cent of all incidents of ISI in their study occurred whilst the self-injuring individuals were in isolation. Liebling (1991) also stated, in her study of young offenders, that many of them did not report their thoughts about self-injuring, or incidents of ISI, because of a fear of being isolated from others.

It was suggested by Lester (1991) that a record of disciplinary offences distinguished those who self-injure from other prisoners. It has therefore been mooted that ISI may be one expression of generally poor impulse management. This notion is supported by Shea (1993), who reports that self-injurers are more likely to display poorly directed hostility to others, especially those in positions of authority. Such individuals are, when in prison, more likely to find themselves isolated as punishment, as well as being isolated as an attempt to prevent ISI. For such prisoners, the end result must appear similar and, indeed, for many staff the distinction may seem at times to be blurred.

Depression and hopelessness

There is a significant body of research that suggests a correlation between ISI and depression for adult men in prison (see Livingstone, 1997). The picture for women is less certain, with research suggesting no clear link (Wilkins and Coid, 1991). Curiously, the link between depression and ISI has been found for both men and women young offenders (Livingstone, 1997). There are a number of possible explanations for the finding relating to adult women: one possibility is that the Wilkins and Coid study used too restrictive a definition of 'depression'; alternatively, it may be that ISI in adult women is markedly different in important respects from ISI in the other groups. Further research is clearly needed to answer this question.

In reviewing the issue of depression and ISI, Ross and McKay (1979) suggest that depression *per se* is not a sufficient cause of ISI but may act along with other influences to increase the risk of ISI occurring. Haycock (1989) also notes that prisoners recovering from depression may be more likely to intentionally self-injure. This clearly parallels the finding that those recovering from depression are at increased risk of suicide, relative to those who are more severely depressed.

A number of researchers have suggested a link between life events and ISI in prisoners (Livingstone, 1997; Ivanoff and Jong, 1991; Coid *et al.*, 1992). In particular, threats to personal relationships and the loss of loved ones have been seen as significant. In the specific case of young offenders, however, it appears that ISI may be more likely to be triggered by factors in the immediate prison environment (Livingstone, 1994).

Aggression and violence

Recent research (e.g. Plutchik, 1997) has suggested that the role of aggression in self-injury and suicide has been neglected. Plutchik defines aggression as a theoretical inner state, whilst violence refers to the overt behaviour resulting from such an inner state.

Various types of life events have been shown to increase aggressive impulses. These would include threats, challenges, changes in hierarchical status, loss of social attachments, physical pain, loss of power or respect, among many others. Whether aggression goes on to be overtly expressed will, in turn, depend on a number of intrinsic and extrinsic factors. Some factors will serve to 'amplify' and some 'attenuate' the aggressive impulse (Plutchik, 1997):

> The balance and vectoral interaction of these factors or forces at any given moment determines whether the aggressive impulse exceeds a threshold and is then expressed in overt behaviour ...
>
> (Plutchik, 1997: 121)[25]

Plutchik refers to 'amplifiers' and 'attenuators' as 'stage I countervailing forces'. [26]

Overt action also requires a goal to be directed towards. The Plutchik model assumes that some variables will result in violence being directed toward the self and some will result in its direction towards others. Plutchik also notes that violence may have a negative feedback function, in that violence towards others may serve to reduce the threat from them. Self-injury may function as a means of managing a crisis or unsatisfactory relationships, by (for example) mobilising help from others:

> The violent behaviour thus functions as a feedback system designed to keep social interactions within certain limits. The process is exactly the same as occurs in emotional reactions ... The study of suicide may thus be thought of as an aspect of the general study of emotion.
>
> (p. 121)

Most recent research on suicide and self-injury has, Plutchik suggests, not adequately addressed the role of aggression in self-injury and suicide. He argues that there are potentially a very large number of variables that will influence violence. Such variables will also act to determine whether violence is directed toward the self, or directed toward others. Future research into self-injury and suicide, he suggests, should not simply limit itself to establishing correlations with traditional sociological, demographic and diagnostic variables.

Summary and conclusions

There is now a significant body of research in the general area of ISI, both community-based and conducted within prisons. However, much of this research has been bedevilled by the use of multiple definitions. Such definitions have in themselves often been confused and confusing, and have had the practical effect of making comparisons across studies difficult. It is probably fair to say that the dominant notion in much of the research so far has been 'deliberate self-harm' (DSH). This term in turn has been interpreted differently by researchers working in North America and Europe. The former have tended to adopt the narrower definition of DSH, focusing on acts of self-injury excluding self-poisoning and overdose. European research, in contrast, has tended to adopt a broader definition, with the result that much of the European research reports a great preponderance of self-poisoning and overdose.

As noted above, whichever interpretation is used, there are a number of marked difficulties with the whole notion of DSH. In particular, the term 'self-harm' is very broad and has been interpreted by some to include behaviours such as nail biting and hair cutting. The term self-harm has also been taken to include overeating, undereating, tattooing, smoking, substance abuse, self-poisoning, self-injury and so on. As such, the concept seems far too broad a basis on which to conduct meaningful research. Indeed, in practice, what appears to have happened is that researchers have narrowed the definition. Thus community studies of DSH tend to involve studies of those referred to medical services for self-poisoning and self-injury.

Another problem with the term DSH is the question of deliberation, implied by the use of the term 'deliberate'. As noted above, the term 'deliberate' implies a judgement in relation to the amount of thought and preplanning involved, suggesting a high level of both. In fact, it would seem more appropriate for this to be seen as a research question in its own right. Although some individuals may deliberate over their self-injuring or self-poisoning, many others do not appear to do so. Thus we would argue that 'intentional' is a far more appropriate (and less value-laden) term to use, since it implies only a conscious awareness of an action at the time it occurred.

For such reasons it has been suggested that the term DSH may have outlived its usefulness in research and practice. Towl (1999b, 2000) advocates the use of the term 'intentional self-injury' (ISI) as being preferable for a number of reasons. First, it focuses on a much more limited range of behaviours, excluding other forms of self-harm such as eating disorders, alcohol abuse, smoking and so on. Whilst all these behaviours are genuinely self-harming, it is unclear how far they share similarities with self-injury and in what ways they differ. Secondly, the notion of ISI places a greater emphasis on the specific behaviours involved. This in turn is likely to allow for the formulation of more precise research questions. Thirdly, ISI does not imply deliberation and planning of behaviour; although it is clear that some individuals intend to injure themselves, it seems premature to decide the extent and nature of this intent beforehand.

By focusing more closely on the specific behaviours involved in ISI, and the meanings these have for individuals, it seems likely that more effective interventions may be developed. In contrast, notions of deliberation and the inappropriate manipulation of others that is sometimes associated with this may help to legitimise punitive responses to self-injury, such as the inappropriate use of isolation.

Overall, there is a good deal of research that is indicative of a number of avenues of further study. Much of the existing research base has been concerned with establishing correlational relationships between intentional self-injury and both demographic and situational variables. It can be argued that this base needs to be built on with the development and testing of theoretical models, concerned with the interactions between individual characteristics, prison environments and ISI (Dexter and Towl, 1995; Towl and Hudson, 1997; Towl, 2000).

4

Risk assessment and management
Graham Towl & David Crighton

Overview

The aim of this chapter is to review the area of risk assessment and management of suicide and self-injury within prisons. In order to do this, it is important to have some understanding of many of the concepts involved in risk assessment and management. Hence, by way of introduction, some of the language used in the literature associated with risk assessment is examined. This involves looking in fairly close detail at the use of three commonly used terms: 'dangerousness', 'prediction' and 'risk assessment'.

This analysis of the three terms is followed by a brief outline of a number of concepts and terms relating to mental disorder. Some understanding of these is important since a substantial proportion of the existing research base has been predicated on concepts of mental disorder such as 'psychoses' and 'personality disorders'.

Following on from this, a framework is outlined for undertaking risk assessments and managing the risk of suicide with prisoners. No framework for risk assessment in the field of forensic practice would be complete without being linked to a clear understanding of ethical issues underpinning such assessments and interventions. It is crucial, therefore, to draw out some of the logical and ethical issues that underpin decisions in relation to risk assessment and management.

Some of the significant contributions of cognitive psychology (e.g. Plous, 1993; Eiser, 1980) and social psychology (e.g. Aronson, 1995) are outlined next, in the context of decision making. Such research allows an examination of the biases and processes associated with perception or what some (e.g. Towl and Crighton 1998) have termed perceptual prejudices, memory and decision making in its social context. The application of such approaches to a better understanding of suicide and self-injury in the prison environment is also analysed.

The chapter concludes with a review of how existing research might best be integrated into a structured framework, and how this might be applied to risk management of suicide and self-injury in prisons. The reader is encouraged to draw upon other chapters in this book to augment the process.

The language of risk assessment

In this section three terms – 'dangerousness', 'prediction' and 'risk assessment' – are defined, and considered in terms of their current and historical use.

Dangerousness

The 1993 *Chambers Dictionary* definition of 'dangerous' is 'full of danger; unsafe; insecure; arrogant, stand-offish'. In the literature, and in forensic practice, the term is used in a number of different – and often incompatible – ways.

It is sometimes used to refer to a particular hazard or to indicate that there is a significant probability of a hazardous event occurring. It has been noted, that such differing uses of the term may result in confusion (Scott, 1977; Monahan, 1981). Some use the term 'dangerous' to refer exclusively to violence to others (e.g. Bowden, 1996), while others use it to mean violence to others or oneself thus the term may be used to include suicide and self-injurious behaviour. Some (e.g. Monahan, 1981; Towl and Crighton, 1996; Towl, 1996) simply prefer the use of specific behavioural descriptions (e.g. 'violent behaviour') to the term 'dangerousness', because of the semantic clarity that such an approach brings. A number of commentators have sought to distinguish between violence and dangerousness. As Sarbin (1967, quoted in Monahan, 1981) states pithily: violence denotes action; danger denotes a relationship. Recently, some researchers have sought to distinguish danger from risk. 'Risk may be said to be the likelihood of an event's occurring, and danger the degree of damage (harm) that may occur should the event happen' (Prins, 1996).

The term 'dangerous' is enshrined in a range of legislative frameworks addressing the management of offenders both in the United Kingdom (e.g. the Mental Health Act 1983 and the Criminal Justice Act 1991) and internationally (e.g. New Zealand, with its Criminal Justice Act 1985). Such legislation has contributed to the resultant erroneous classification of individuals as either 'dangerous' or 'not dangerous'. This process has been referred to as bifurcation (Bottoms, 1977). Research into the utility of such dichotomies has shown them to be both inaccurate and unjust. What is evident from this brief review of the use and abuse of the term 'dangerous' is that it is still used among numerous researchers and practitioners and that it is enshrined in some of the legislation that is highly relevant to the forensic field.

The term needs to be viewed with some caution. It is important to be aware of the usage of the term 'dangerous' in legislation, but this does not mean that it is necessarily helpful routinely to use such ill-defined terms in professional practice. The term is, at best, vague; but also – perhaps most importantly – it is clear that it is used with a range of different unspecified meanings, leading to spurious dichotomies and conceptual confusion (Towl and Crighton, 1997).

Prediction

Once more, the 1993 *Chambers Dictionary* definition comes to the fore, this time of 'prediction': 'the act or art of predicting; something foretold', and 'predict' is defined as 'foretell, especially on the basis of present knowledge'. Thus from X we may predict Y. Criminological studies on prediction are characterised by the identification of a 'predictor variable', such as age (Monahan, 1981) or the offence type (Copas, 1982), which is then tested as to its predictive power for a given criterion variable. Similar methodology can be used to study suicide and self-injury.

Clearly defined predictor and criterion variables are key elements to the methodology of prediction studies in criminology (Farrington and Tarling, 1985). Such studies aim for the accurate prediction of specified events, i.e. criterion variables, and for our purpose in this context the variables are suicide or self-injury.

In terms of the complexities of any human social behaviour, it is logically implausible to maintain that such predictors will ever be 100 per cent accurate in terms of predictor variable X *always* predicting criterion variable Y. To judge the utility of prediction studies on the basis of whether or not the predictor variable always predicts the criterion variable would be illogical. A useful test of prediction studies is to check the degree of accuracy of the estimated probability of the relationship between the predictor and criterion variables. Thus, for example, if a specified predictor variable was shown to predict a specified criterion variable in 70 per cent of the time, data could be examined to test and retest this estimate of the statistical relationship.

One logical consequence of such a conceptualisation of prediction studies is that if the presence of the predictor variable does not result, in an individual case, in the manifestation of the criterion variable, then this does not 'disprove' the prediction. A direct parallel of this can be seen in forensic decision making. McHugh and Towl (1997) provide a further and fuller discussion of the point with suicides in prison. The thorny issue of decision rules, in terms of the acceptability or otherwise of what is a reasonable level of risk to take, will be discussed in greater detail below (Monahan, 1981; Towl and Crighton, 1996; Towl and Hudson, 1997).

Risk assessment

Three basic concepts lie at the root of good practice in risk assessment:

- **Clearly defined predictor variables (PV) and criterion variables (CV).** The term 'prediction' has just been discussed. Central to the language of prediction are the terms 'predictor variable' and 'criterion variable' (Monahan, 1981). Predictor variables are those variables that may be used to predict an event at a specified level of probability – in this context, for example, the risk of suicide within a particular timeframe (a criterion variable).
- **Base rates.** The 'base rate' is the relative frequency with which a specified event occurs (Plous, 1993). The base rate for suicide is low, and such low base rates result in particular problems of prediction, with infrequently occurring events being notoriously difficult to predict (Towl, 1996).
- **The notion of the acceptability of a specified level of risk of a criterion variable occurring.** This is an important and conceptually distinct issue. Attempts to set guidelines for such areas of practice are sometimes referred to as 'decision rules'. Thus the problem is in how we make judgements about the cut-off point where levels of risk are deemed acceptable. This is, understandably, a very contentious area with regard to both suicide and self-injury.

Having looked at the research base for risk assessment in suicide and self-injury, it is clear that much of the research is drawn from the psychiatric literature. It is therefore important to have a basic understanding of a number of the conceptual bases of such research. A brief overview is given below of some of the relevant aspects of mental disorder.

Mental disorder

A significant proportion of the research into suicide has focused on the role of mental disorder. The definition of mental disorder is far from clear-cut, however. Different terminology and explanatory models are used by different disciplines. Definitions of mental disorder also depend upon the application of social and cultural standards. These in turn are not fixed, but clearly vary between cultures and over time within cultures.

Psychiatric models of mental disorder have traditionally emphasised the detailed description and classification of disorders based on apparently common features. Such approaches have been increasingly codified in recent years into diagnostic frameworks, the most widely used of these being DSM IV (American Psychiatric Association, 1994), which tends to be used in North America, and ICD 10 (World Health Organisation, 1993), which tends to be used elsewhere in the world. A substantial proportion of research into the area of risk assessment and mental disorder has drawn upon these classification systems.

It is worth noting that there are a number of profound criticisms of both these approaches, not least of these being the question of how valid the categories described are and how accurately they can be identified. Brockington *et al.* (1978) studied ten widely accepted operational definitions of schizophrenia and applied these to a group of 119 mentally disordered individuals. The number defined as schizophrenic ranged from three to 45 depending on the definition used.

Further difficulties arise in the context of forensic practice, where a number of other considerations may influence the categorisation of mentally disordered offenders. In particular, it is possible for some chronically 'psychotic' individuals to be relabelled as 'psychopathic' and 'untreatable'. As Taylor (1994) points out, in forensic contexts it is not uncommon for the emphasis to shift from psychotic aspects of mental disorder to personality aspects.

An increasing number of models of mental disorder are being drawn from psychology. Such models tend to focus on the specific aspects of cognitive and/or behavioural functioning as the basis for identification and analysis – for example, focusing on hallucinations *per se* (e.g. see Towl, 1990) rather than treating such phenomena as indicative of a hypothesised syndrome. These approaches have the advantage of being more specific than broad groupings of mental disorders, and also being less open to reinterpretations dependent on context. However, such approaches have not yet been widely applied in mental-health settings.

Psychotic disorders

Psychotic disorders are one group of mental disorders and would generally be taken to include schizophrenia, manic-depressive psychoses, and psychotic disorders due to organic causes (e.g. Korsakoff's syndrome). Psychotic disorders occurring in the absence of any known organic cause are often termed 'functional psychoses'.

The main characteristics of psychotic disorders are the presence of delusions and hallucinations (often called positive symptoms). A number of so-called 'negative' symptoms may also be observed, and these would include such behaviours as social withdrawal (Gelder *et al.*, 1996).

Delusions

Although delusions are a major characteristic of a number of mental disorders and are often defined as pathological beliefs, this description perhaps raises more questions than it answers. In particular, the term 'pathological' implies a value judgement on the part of the assessor. This is the case because what constitutes a delusion cannot be simply defined. So, for example, it is not the case that delusions are simply false beliefs. A large number of people hold beliefs that are demonstrably false; many more hold beliefs where truth or falsity may be demonstrated (e.g. religious beliefs). Equally, an individual may hold a belief that is true but is nevertheless delusional. An example of this might be an individual who believes – correctly – that other people are talking about that person but bases this belief on irrational evidence.

Distress is evident as a characteristic of some delusions; but, again, is not definitive since it is not *always* evident. In a number of individuals the affective response to delusional beliefs that would distress most people is incongruous or flattened.

Given some of the failings associated with psychiatric models of mental disorder, a number of alternative frameworks have been suggested. For example, Oltmanns and Maher (1988) suggest that delusions are perhaps best viewed as complex and multifaceted cognitive phenomena, characterised by a marked conviction in the belief, a preoccupation with it, and a sense of personal reference – a view that is largely in keeping with earlier research in cognitive psychology (e.g. Watts *et al.*, 1973).

Hallucinations

Hallucinations can be defined as 'sensory experiences in the absence of external stimuli to the relevant sensory organ'. Definitions of hallucinations have traditionally excluded such experiences during sleep (dreaming), whilst falling asleep and whilst waking (McNeil, 1994). This appears to relate to the fact that such 'hallucinatory' experiences in these contexts are very common, tend to be very transient and will generally have no effect on an individual's social functioning.

Hallucinations have been reported for all sensory modalities and can be attributable to a number of causes. Thus they are known to occur frequently following prolonged isolation, during sensory, food, sleep or water deprivation, and in the face of extreme stress. Hallucinations have also been reported to occur commonly in a significant proportion of the general population in the absence of any reported mental disorders (Haddock and Slade, 1996). Hallucinations are also frequently reported as sequelae of drug use, particularly LSD, phencyclidine (PCP), cocaine and amphetamines.

Those experiencing psychotic symptoms have been shown to be at an increased risk of suicide relative to the general population (Hawton, 1994). Rossau and Mortensen (1997) also report that, for those diagnosed as 'schizophrenic', the risk of suicide is highest during the first six months after their first admission. A number of possible explanations might be suggested for this finding – for example, the experience of hallucinations and delusional beliefs may be more distressing when the experience is novel. Similarly, it has been suggested that the effects of such symptoms on an individual's social functioning may be critical. Further research is needed to clarify this area, but recent diagnosis of a major psychotic disorder such as schizophrenia appears to signify increased risk both in the community and in hospitals.

Depression

Depression is the most common form of mental disorder and the one most closely associated with suicide and attempted suicide. Depressed mood states have high reported prevalence with rates of depressed mood found to be higher amongst those of lower socio-economic status, the unemployed, women and the divorced or separated (see Boyd and Weissman, 1982).

Epidemiological studies in North America report rates of major depressive disorder to be 1.6 per 100 men and 2.9 per 100 women (Reiger *et al.*, 1988). Depression was also found to be much more common in the unemployed, in urban areas and in the 18–44 years age range (Klerman and Weissman, 1989). Kendell (1994) looked at the prevalence of depression in the community over a six-month period. Based on an analysis of 3,000 people living in five sites in the United States, the rates of prevalence were in the range 6.0–8.3 per cent for women and 2.7–4.6 per cent for men. Surtees and Sashidharan (1986), after allowing for differences in the criteria used, report similar rates in the United Kingdom. Multicentre studies conducted by the World Health Organisation have also reported the occurrence of depression in a wide range of cultures, although this has often been misreported in earlier studies because of cross-cultural differences in the presentation of a depressed mood (Jablensky, 1981).

The gender differences in rates of depression appear to be a very robust finding, but the explanation remains unclear. They may be due in part to differential reporting rates of depressed mood, with women being more willing to express such feelings. It seems unlikely, however, that this fully explains the differences seen, and other factors are very likely to have an effect. For example, poverty and low income may have a greater negative impact on women.

Table 4.1 Classification of depressive disorders

ICD 10 system	DSM IV system
Depressive Episode	*Major Depressive Episode*
Mild	Mild
Moderate	Moderate
Severe	Severe
Severe with psychosis	Severe with psychosis
Other Depressive Episodes	
Atypical depression	
Recurrent Depressive Disorders	*Major Depressive Disorder (recurrent)*
Currently mild	
Currently moderate	
Currently severe	
Currently severe with psychosis	
In remission	
Persistent Mood Disorders	*Dysthymic Disorder*
Cyclothymia	
Dysthymia	
Other Mood Disorders	*Depressive Disorders not otherwise specified*
Recurrent brief depression	Recurrent brief depression

Source: Gelder *et al.* (1996: 209). Reproduced by permission of Oxford University Press

The distinctions between mild, moderate and severe depression, as outlined in Table 4.1, tend to be somewhat arbitrary. However, some aspects of an individual's thinking and behaviour do appear to be indicative of more severe depression. These can be tapped by psychological tests such as the Beck Depression Inventory (BDI), which can be used in research and practice to provide a more reliable estimate of the severity of depression than clinical impression alone (Beck, 1967). Probably more useful in the context of suicide is the Beck Hopelessness

Scale (Beck *et al.*, 1979), since this appears to tap some of the aspects of depression most closely associated with suicide (Dexter and Towl, 1995).

In some cases of depression, an individual's beliefs may appear to become delusional, with themes relating to guilt, persecution and punishment being common. Interestingly, such delusional beliefs may be in keeping with the depression in mood, or they may be entirely out of keeping, as for example in the case of someone expressing grandiose beliefs whilst depressed (Gelder *et al.*, 1996). Perceptual disturbances may also occur in depressed clients – for example, auditory hallucinations. The behaviour of depressed clients can vary dramatically, and it has long been known that moderately and severely depressed individuals can present as being agitated, retarded or stuporous (Gelder *et al.*, 1996).

Personality disorders

A considerable portion of mental disorders is composed of 'personality disorders'. The definition of these is even more controversial than for psychotic disorders.

Table 4.2 Classification of personality disorders

ICD 10 system	DSM IV system
Paranoid	Paranoid
Schizoid (Schizotypal[27]	Schizoid
Dissocial	Antisocial
Emotionally unstable	
– Impulsive type	
– Borderline type	Borderline
Histrionic	Histrionic
	Narcissistic
Anankastic (Obsessive–Compulsive)	Obsessive–Compulsive
Anxious (avoidant)	Avoidant
Dependent	Dependent
Other	Passive–Aggressive

Source: Reproduced from Gelder *et al.* (1996) with permission from Oxford University Press.

As can be seen from Table 4.2, both DSM IV and ICD 10 divide personality disorder into similar typologies. Despite the fact that a large amount of research has been based on these systematic frameworks, there is considerable disagreement over the approach on a number of grounds. Not least of these is the way that such systems divide personality characteristics into apparent dichotomies. The reliability and validity of these classifications is consistently poor, and the value of this type of approach to personality disorders is both questionable and out of keeping with psychological research (Needs, 1989). What certainly seems clear is that these systems manage, in very broad terms, to describe a number of aspects of interpersonal functioning that cause difficulties, both for individuals and those around them.

As with depression, alternative psychological approaches emphasise the continuity between normal personality variations and more extreme presentations of particular personality characteristics. One example of this is antisocial personality disorder (APD). Here, psychological measures of the detailed characteristics of APD have been developed – for example, the Psychopathy Checklist (Hare, 1986) – so as to provide an estimate of the degree of APD characteristics shown, rather than use of a simple dichotomy. Such approaches appear much more promising in terms of future research and practice.

Thus far, the focus has been on outlining a number of the fundamental concepts involved in risk assessment, such as dangerousness and prediction. The logical difficulties inherent in such terms have been discussed. In addition, much of the research into suicide and self-injury is drawn from a psychiatric base. Therefore a number of the key concepts in relation to mental disorder have been outlined.

Below, a structured framework for the assessment of risk in suicide and self-injury is elaborated. As will be seen later, the process of risk management follows logically from the structured assessment of risk.

The Cambridge model of risk assessment

Figure 4.1 outlines the Cambridge model of risk assessment. It is derived directly from the earlier influential work of Towl and Crighton (1996; 1997).

Stage 1 refers to the specification of the relevant criterion variables (CVs) as the first step in the risk assessment. There may be more than one criterion variable for each client; for example, in forensic settings, CVs may include violence towards others, as well as suicide. Thus criterion variables need to be precisely defined and, where appropriate, separately assessed. This more readily enables practitioners to structure risk assessments so that distinctions may straightforwardly be made between the likelihood of the occurrence of distinct criteria. This

is important partly because of the unfortunate tendency of some practitioners simply to assess risk as if it were a global and homogenous
term.

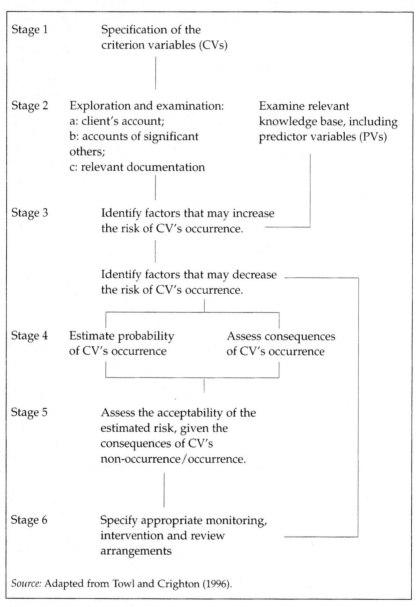

Figure 4.1 The Cambridge model of risk assessment in flowchart form

Stage 2 essentially consists of an information-gathering process. It is
important that practitioners have a well-developed and developing

knowledge base in areas where they are conducting risk assessments (Towl and Crighton, 1996). It is only with such a knowledge base that practitioners may best be enabled to fully explore and examine individual cases. The client's[28] account of events will be of paramount importance in the assessment process. The views of significant others will also be important – for example, the views of friends and the individual's family. Where the assessment is taking place in an institution (e.g. prisons, special hospitals, medium/ low secure health-service units, or police custody), it would be particularly prudent to solicit the views of a range of members of staff (e.g. forensic psychiatric nurses, probation officers, social workers, occupational therapists, teachers, prison officers and police officers). Good and effective communication between professionals is absolutely imperative to help inform accurate risk assessments. Prins (1996) helpfully highlights three major aspects of adequate communication within forensic practice: first, the need to have good inter-professional communication; secondly, the need to have adequate communication between the practitioner and the offender, with an understanding of some of the inherent tensions in such a relationship (for example, Prins (1996: 49) perceptively observes that 'denial is by no means the sole prerogative of offenders'); and, thirdly, the need to listen. Prins is chiefly concerned here to draw attention to the expertise of those responsible for the day-to-day care of an individual.

Stage 3 of the framework involves the identification of those factors that may serve to increase the risk of an individual completing suicide. It is also important at this stage to make an evaluation of those factors that may act to reduce the level of risk. In making such an analysis, practitioners need to draw on the available knowledge base in relation to the specific assessment being made.

Stage 4 involves estimating the probability of the criterion variable(s) occurring and the consequences of such an occurrence. This leads very directly into Stage 5, which relates to the decision process involved with the acceptability or tolerability of the level of risk.

The final stage, Stage 6, of the Cambridge model involves the specification of monitoring, intervention and review arrangements for each client assessed. Thus this stage involves outlining and implementing a programme of risk management.

Criterion variables

A major and fundamental criticism of many studies concerned with 'risk' and 'mental disorder' has been the failure to define terms adequately. In particular, many studies have failed to define adequately the criterion variables being used (Monahan and Steadman, 1994).

Past research into suicides in prisons has also been bedevilled by definitional problems, and this in turn has made the task of practitioners in conducting accurate risk assessments more difficult. In recent years, however, this problem has been resolved in the context of prisons by deeming all cases of self-inflicted death as suicide (McHugh and Towl, 1997).

The Office of Population Censuses and Surveys (OPCS) publishes details of trends in suicide rates and methods for England and Wales (Charlton *et al.*, 1992). In their report on trends in suicide, Charlton and colleagues give two definitions of suicide, based on the World Health Organisation's ICD codes for cause of death:

a) recorded suicides (World Health Organisation, 1948; 1955; 1965; 1977): 6th ICD E970–E979; 7th ICD E970–E979; 8th ICD E950–E959; 9th ICD E950–959 (as used in population trends 35); and
b) suicides and undetermined (from 1968 onwards only): as (a) above plus E980–E989, excluding E988.8 after 1978.

Charlton *et al.* (1992) point out that an understanding of how suicide deaths are certified is important in informing the choice of definition used:

> The Coroner investigates every case where violent or unnatural death is suspected, and sudden deaths of unknown cause. The verdicts that may be recorded are homicide, accidental death, suicide, and open verdict. A verdict of suicide should only be recorded if there is clear evidence that the injury was self-inflicted and that the deceased intended to kill him/herself. If there is any doubt about the intentions of the deceased either an accidental or an open verdict should be recorded.
>
> (Charlton *et al.*, 1992)

Those authors point out in the same work that a reliance on officially certified suicides inevitably leads to some under-recording of suicide deaths, and that it seems likely that most open verdicts returned on adults are in fact cases of suicide that were not proven. This is supported by them, too, by the fact that the trends for recorded suicide and suicide and undetermined deaths have followed a similar pattern. Platt *et al.* (1988) have shown that the main difference between open verdicts and recorded suicides, in the community at large, is the method of killing, with passive methods (e.g. drowning) being less likely to receive a suicide verdict.

Only in recent years have researchers into suicides in prisons adopted the broader definition (b) described by Charlton *et al.* (1992). This definition is also in line with the definition adopted by the Suicide

Awareness Support Unit for the Prison Service in England and Wales. Previous studies into prison suicides, and the majority of older studies into suicides in the community, have adopted a range of definitions (Topp, 1979; Dooley, 1990; Bogue and Power, 1995). This has had the effect of introducing a number of systematic and unsystematic biases into the research. For example, Diekstra and Hawton (1987) suggest that coroner's courts are more likely to return a verdict of suicide where there is a history of mental disorder amongst those who kill themselves. Another example of such biasing in research is illustrated by an analysis of coroners court verdicts. For the years 1988–1995, the proportion of self-inflicted deaths that attracted verdicts of suicide ranged from 58 per cent to 84 per cent for men (McHugh and Towl, 1997). For women, from 1988–1996 an overall rate of 27 per cent was reported (Towl and Fleming, 1997). It appears that self-inflicted deaths among women prisoners are less likely to attract a verdict of suicide.

In the context of risk assessment and management, it makes little sense to make the type of legalistic distinction outlined above. Yet in practice this often seems to occur, with inferences made about intent often being conflated with the process of assessing and managing risk. Similarly, although it makes little sense to distinguish between the risk of a 'genuine' suicide and some other hypothesised form of self-inflicted death, it is important to note than some older research is predicated on exactly this type of distinction.

Practitioners need to be clear, therefore, about the criterion variables being used. They also need to be clear about the criterion variables used in previous research. So, for example, where they are assessing the risk of a self-inflicted death occurring in prison, they will need to draw on research using similar criteria. A number of early studies into suicide in prisons have drawn exclusively on cases where coroner's courts have returned suicide verdicts (e.g. Dooley, 1990). Such work is perhaps best interpreted with some caution.

Developing a knowledge base

A number of researchers have identified background factors that may increase the risk of suicide. For example, a disrupted family background, a family history of suicide, drug and alcohol addiction, failure at school, unemployment and depression all feature in the research results (Diekstra and Hawton, 1987; Van Egmond and Diekstra, 1989). One of the most striking aspects of such factors is how closely they reflect many of the social factors identified in prospective studies of criminal careers (e.g. Farrington, 1993) as being associated with prisoner populations (Towl and Crighton, 1996). In this sense, prisoners may include a disproportionately large number of individuals who may be at a higher risk of suicide than average. Unemployment may be a particularly strong factor in increasing the risk of suicide (Platt and Kreitman, 1984; Moser *et al.*, 1984, 1990). Interestingly, two recent studies indicate that the unemployment rates for the suicidal immediately prior to imprisonment are very high (Dexter and Towl, 1995; Jones, 1996), reporting rates of 77 per cent and 76 per cent respectively. This perhaps highlights the potential importance of constructive supervised employment for prisoners, either in a job or in education whilst in custody (Towl and Hudson, 1997).

As was indicated in Chapter 2, a close read of the research on suicide strikingly indicates two limitations to a number of the studies. First, the studies are often based upon small sample sizes (e.g. Dexter and Towl, 1995). Secondly, studies are sometimes based simply on one population subgroup, such as young offenders (e.g. Liebling, 1992). Both of these potential limitations may result in an overgeneralisation of results.

In two recent studies Crighton and Towl (1997); Towl and Crighton (1998) included all cases of self-inflicted death recorded by the Prison Service Suicide Awareness Support Unit from 5 February 1988 to 5 November 1995. This provided an analysis of all 377 self-inflicted deaths (SIDs) occurring within this timeframe. Of the sample, 369 were men and eight were women. Of the men, 181 were sentenced and 188 were on remand: of the women, five were sentenced and three were on remand. The average age of the whole sample was 29 years 6 months. Table 4.3 sets out the data on rates of SIDs for sentenced prisoners, subdivided by sentence length. Data is also presented for prisoners remanded into prison custody. Broadly, the results described in Table 4.3 suggest that the greater the sentence length, the greater the risk of suicide. Life-sentenced prisoners appear to have an appreciably higher risk of suicide than determinate-sentenced prisoners.

Table 4.3 Rates of self-inflicted deaths by sentence length, for sentenced male prisoners, 1988–95

Sentence length	Number	ADP 1988–93[34]	Rate per 100, 000 ADP p.a.
Up to and including 6 months	11	3,761	38
6–12 mths (inclusive)	9	3,759	31
12–18 mths (inclusive)	11	3,436	41
18–36 mths (inclusive)	39	8,262	61
36–48 mths (inclusive)	16	3,468	60
48–60 mths (inclusive)	13	2,642	63
> 60 mths, excluding life sentences	40	6,917	75
Life sentences	39	2,834	178

Table 4.4 Rates of self-inflicted deaths for male remand prisoners, 1988–95

Remand Prisoners	Number	ADP 1988–95	Rate per 100,000 ADP p.a.
Number of deaths by ADP	191	10,372	238
Number of deaths by reception	191	63,562[29]	39

Table 4.5 Self-inflicted deaths by age, 1988–95, amongst male sentenced and remand prisoners

Age	Number 1988-95	ADP 1988-95[30]	Rate per 100,000 p.a.
15–17 Years	15	810	239
18–20 Years	43	4,215	132
21–24 Years	66	7,546	113
25–29 Years	95	7,772	158
30–39 Years	93	8,477	142
40–49 Years	39	3,843	131
50–59 Years	15	1,458	133
60+ Years	3	428	90

The data in Table 4.4 illustrates powerfully the effects of the method of measurement used when calculating suicide rates among remand prisoners. Thus, when rates are calculated for this group using the average daily populations (ADP), the rate per 100,000 prisoners appears very high. This is in keeping with the traditional wisdom, based on earlier research, that remand prisoners are at particularly high risk of suicide. However, when the rates are calculated using the number of deaths by remand reception numbers into the Prison Service, the rates are markedly lower (i.e. 39 per 100,000). This compares with rates for determinate-sentenced prisoners of between 31 and 75 per 100,000 ADP and a rate of 31 per 100,000 sentenced receptions per annum. The data suggests that remand prisoners are at a similar risk of suicide to those given short determinate sentences (under 18 months) and are at a lower level of risk than those given longer or indeterminate sentences.

Taken together, Tables 4.3 and 4.4 provide some evidence to support the view that remand status as an individual marker for an increased risk of suicide has perhaps been overemphasised (Towl and Hudson, 1997).

Table 4.5 gives the suicide rate per 100,000 ADP by age group. This data allows exploration of the popular hypothesis that younger age groups (e.g. 15–24 years) will be overrepresented in the figures for prison suicides. Whereas there appears to be some evidence to support the hypothesis that the juvenile group (i.e. those aged 15–17 years) are at increased risk of suicide, younger age groups in general do not appear to be overrepresented in the figures. This finding was also evident in earlier findings examining suicide data in prisons for the periods 1988–90 and 1994–95 (Crighton and Towl, 1997), where a similar picture was described.

Mental disorder

Mental disorder has often been posited as a factor in suicide. Barraclough *et al.* (1974) claimed that around 90 per cent of suicides in the community had experienced psychiatric disorder; with depressive disorders being the most common group at 70 per cent. Later studies have questioned this assertion, and Hawton (1994) points out that, by drawing exclusively on cases with a suicide verdict, the proportion of those with a history of depression and psychiatric involvement is likely to have been increased. Even allowing for this factor, it seems clear that those with a history of mental health problems are at increased risk of suicide in the community. Hawton (1994) suggests that around 15 per cent of those diagnosed as having severe depressive disorders go on to kill themselves. This represents a thirtyfold increase in the lifetime risk relative to the general population. Drug and alcohol abusers similarly appear to be at a far greater lifetime risk of killing themselves, with around 15 per cent of those with a recorded history of alcohol abuse going on to take their own lives.

A number of studies have suggested high rates of mental disorder in the prison population. Gunn *et al.* (1991) reported that 37 per cent of a sample of the prison population showed clear evidence of such disorders. Included in their definition of 'mental disorder' were: substance abuse (experienced by 23 per cent of the prison population), neuroses (5.9 per cent) and sexual deviations (1.9 per cent). The rates of psychotic disorders within the prison population were also reported as 1.9 per cent.

A more recent study found even greater prevalence of psychiatric disorders (ONS, 1998). The prevalence rates for personality disorder, for example, were 78 per cent for male remand prisoners, 64 per cent for male sentenced prisoners and 50 per cent for female prisoners. Prevalence rates for functional psychosis were 7 per cent for male sentenced, 10 per cent for male remand and 14 per cent for female prisoners. The prevalence of neurotic disorders was 40 per cent for male sentenced, 59 per cent for male remand prisoners, 63 per cent for female sentenced, and 76 per cent for females on remand.

It should be noted that such studies have adopted an unusually broad definition of what constitutes mental disorder – certainly one broader than that within the meaning of the United Kingdom's Mental Health Act 1983. However, what seems clear is that those with a history of mental health problems have an increased lifetime risk of suicide. This in turn is complicated by, and appears to interact with, social factors such as unemployment and poverty. Crighton and Towl (1997) examined the prevalence of psychiatric histories and records of drug abuse using the 377 records of self-inflicted deaths covering over seven years.

Table 4.6 Self-inflicted deaths by psychiatric history

	Number	Percentage
Psychiatric history	142	38
No psychiatric history	235	62

Table 4.6 shows the proportion of those who killed themselves who had a prior history of psychiatric assessment or treatment. In all, 37 per cent of those who killed themselves had such a history. This figure is clearly very much higher than would be found in the general community but is similar to the rate of mental disorder reported by Gunn *et al.* (1991). Although further research, based on a more rigorous definition of mental disorder, is needed in order to determine whether or not those with particular mental disorders have an increased risk of suicide and self-injury, the existing research suggests that broadly defined mental disorder is not an indicator of increased risk of suicide in the prison population. The significance of particular types of mental disorder in relation to increased risk is illustrated in Table 4.7.

Table 4.7 Self-inflicted deaths by history of drug abuse

	Number	Percentage
History of drug abuse	108	29
No history of drug abuse	269	71

Table 4.7 shows that 29 per cent of those who killed themselves were recorded as having a history of drug abuse. This compares with estimated rates for the prison population of around 11.5 per cent (Gunn *et al.*, 1991). Whilst there are again a number of definitional problems inherent in determining what constitutes a 'history' of drug abuse, it does seem that individuals deemed within the definition may have an increased risk of suicide. Indeed, Hawton (1994) has suggested that mental disorder and drug abuse may interact to further increase the

risk of suicide, although further research is necessary to test this notion in the context of prison.

Table 4.8 Suicide and self-harm monitoring in relation to psychiatric history

	Psychiatric history	No psychiatric history
Suicide/self-harm monitoring in prison	49 per cent	29 per cent
No monitoring	51 per cent	86 per cent

Table 4.8 illustrates the proportion of those who killed themselves who had ever been subject to Prison Service self-harm monitoring. Data is presented for those with and without a history of psychiatric assessment. As can be seen from the table, those with a history of psychiatric involvement were much more likely to be subject to monitoring and support procedures. Those with a past history of psychiatric involvement were more likely to be currently subject to monitoring and support procedures in prison.

Just under one-third of suicides had a recorded history of drug abuse. This is markedly higher than existing estimates for prevalence in the prison service as a whole. Thus a history of drug abuse would appear to be indicative of increased risk of suicide. It is also clear that over two-thirds of those who kill themselves have no recorded history of drug abuse.

It is worth considering the robust finding from other studies (e.g. Bogue and Power, 1995; Crighton and Towl, 1997), namely that, during the first few weeks of custody, prisoners in general are at a far higher risk of suicide than during subsequent weeks. One possible contributing factor may be that some prisoners are experiencing withdrawal effects from drugs. This may or may not come to the attention of the appropriate authorities.

Table 4.8 shows the application of monitoring and support procedures with those who subsequently killed themselves. It is clear from the data that those with a history of psychiatric treatment and/or assessment were much more likely to be identified as being at inflated risk of suicide and subject to monitoring and support. There is a variety of possible explanations for this. It may, for example, be that the psychiatric assessment itself makes the identification more likely of an individual as at an unacceptably high risk of suicide. Another possible contributing factor is that prisoners with a known history of psychiatric assessment are more likely to come to the notice of Prison Service staff as being at increased risk of suicide. The historical and often unhelpful emphasis on medical assessment of the risk of suicide seems likely to increase any such tendency. Alternatively, it may be a product of the emphasis placed on past history of mental health problems during prison service reception procedures.

What seems clear is that Prison Service staff appear to have been much more successful at identifying those at risk of suicide where a prior history of psychiatric treatment and/or assessment previously existed.

The prison environment

The different functions of the various categories of prison establishment are reflected in their regimes. For example, in local or remand prisons there is a high 'throughput rate' amongst prisoners from, and to, the courts, and to other prisons. Such throughput rates tend to be lower in other types of Prison Service establishment. This is likely to be an important factor to consider when attempting to understand suicide in prisons. The majority of deaths (65 per cent) occur in local/remand prisons, with much lower rates being seen in Category C training prisons (10 per cent), youth custody centres (9 per cent), and dispersal and Category B training prisons (both 8 per cent). Furthermore, in 71 per cent of cases, death occurs while the individual is located in a single cell, compared with 23 per cent of cases involving shared cells. (In 7 per cent of cases this information was not recorded.) There were no recorded cases where death occurred while an individual was located in a ward setting in prison (Towl and Crighton, 1998).

Bogue and Power (1995) conducted a study of suicides in the Scottish Prison Service and concluded that remand prisoners were as a group at a higher risk of suicide as a proportion of ADP. They suggested that this might be a facet of the much higher turnover of remand prisoners, resulting in a larger number of individuals being placed at increased risk of suicide. Indeed, it is important when attempting to understand suicide to be aware of the significance of the social context (Wilkinson, 1996). Such contexts, or environments, are of potentially great significance in informing our understanding of suicide in prisons. Various features of particular prison regimes may effectively serve to increase or decrease the risk of suicide for individual prisoners (Dexter and Towl, 1995).

Environmental factors, such as aspects of the organisation of regimes, are liable to have a significant impact on suicide rates in prisons. Support for this is evident in the finding that (as quoted above) two-thirds of suicides for the period of study occurred in local/remand prisons. There is a lack of research into the specific effects of high throughput rates. However it seems likely that a number of factors might be implicated, including the transience of the population being held. High throughput within an establishment is also likely to lead to a greater need to relocate individuals. This is liable to disrupt social contacts and increase uncertainty amongst both staff and prisoners. Perhaps most importantly, we would suggest that as the transience of a population increases, so the full development of positive staff–prisoner relationships will become progressively more difficult to develop and maintain.

Other studies have identified factors that may have an impact on suicide rates within regimes (Dexter and Towl, 1995; Jones, 1996). In both studies, positive and constructive staff attitudes towards prisoners at a high risk of suicide seemed to be particularly significant. The importance of staff attitudes in having an effect towards the efficacy of suicide prevention has been highlighted and reflected in studies of staff training programmes (Lang *et al.*, 1989; Cutler *et al.*, 1997).

Establishing the probability of criterion variable occurrence

This approach derives from analysis of the characteristics of each individual case and needs to be based on as many relevant variables as can be reasonably gathered. However, many of the variables discussed above will be available.

Equally, there are significant gaps in the research upon which individuals working in the area can draw. Therefore there is limited information on the interaction between specific aspects of, for example, the prison environment and suicide. It is to be hoped that such gaps will increasingly be addressed by future research (McHugh and Towl, 1997).

Acceptability or tolerability of levels of risks

So far the focus of this chapter – as for the vast majority of the research – has been on the frequency with which particular outcomes might occur. In many respects this is simply a facet of adopting an empirically based approach. However, a useful risk assessment needs to go beyond simply stating how likely a broad category of behaviour is; some consideration of the acceptability or tolerability of the level of risk of suicide is necessary. There has to date been remarkably little direct research into this area. A recent and notable exception is a study by Cudby (1997), which looked at both the assessment of risk by staff, and the acceptability of particular levels of risk in relation to outcome criteria (including the risk of suicide).

The question of the acceptability of risks tends, in general, to be addressed by multidisciplinary teams. In a number of cases, judicial or quasi-judicial bodies undertake consideration of risk. Ultimately, such decisions are trans-scientific (Towl and Crighton, 1996); however, there exists a body of evidence from social and cognitive psychology that can be used to inform decisions. In particular, research in cognitive and social psychology has gone a long way toward illuminating the processes, and biases, involved in making decisions.

Eiser (1980) argues that cognitive psychology makes certain basic assumptions concerning the way people deal with the world around them:

- The individual is an active processor of information.
- The interpretation of a stimulus depends both on the attributes of the stimulus and on the perceiver's prior expectations and standards of comparison.
- The individual tries to organise his experience: such organisation typically involves selection and simplification.
- The function of such organisation is to provide a guide for action and a basis for prediction.

These basic assumptions have been well supported by research in cognitive and social psychology (Eiser, 1980). Indeed, it would be impossible for individuals to function, in a world with effectively unlimited amounts of information, without being able to process such information actively and selectively.

What seems equally clear is that a number of the processes used to achieve such functioning can lead to specific errors. When dealing with complex information, people have been demonstrated as using a number of characteristic intellectual short-cuts, or 'heuristics' (Tversky and Kahneman, 1974). In comparison with logical or mathematical analyses, these heuristics often produce inaccurate results. A number of them are of particular relevance when looking at the area of risk assessment with the suicidal.

Representativeness

The term 'representativeness' refers to a group of heuristics used by people making a wide range of assessments. It refers, in essence, to the tendency for people to make such assessments on the basis of how 'representative' an event is, even when other information might be more significant. An example in the context of suicide might be the tendency to underestimate the risk of suicide in those without a history of mental disorder. As noted above, particular forms of mental disorder are clearly associated with suicide; however, the majority of those who kill themselves show no evidence of mental disorder. This is especially so in prisons (Towl and Crighton, 1996; Crighton and Towl, 1997).

Adjustment and anchoring

This term refers to the trend for people to alter their assessments (adjustment) only with reference to their initial starting point (anchoring). It seems clear that people are resistant to making radical changes in their evaluations, and to a large extent this is resistant to contradictory information. In the case of suicide, this suggests that an initial assessment of low risk will be adhered to, and similarly an initial assessment of high risk will not easily be revised downwards. In fact, such a rigid approach to assessments is untenable, because it is evident that a client's level of risk may vary dramatically with changes in circumstances; indeed, this variation should be even more marked in the face of a good risk-management strategy.

Availability

The heuristic of 'availability' refers to the information that is actually attended to in a cognitive task. A very basic example is the tendency for the majority of people, when asked, to say that more words begin with the letter K than have K as the third letter. In fact this is incorrect, but it is much easier for people to retrieve from memory on the basis of the first letter, rather than the third letter (Evans, 1989). This may at one level serve to illustrate the importance of suicide awareness *per se*, whether through training or proactive management.

Such availability biases can also be triggered by expectancies and prior beliefs, an example being 'illusory correlations'. Chapman and Chapman (1967; 1969) found in a study that clinicians reported patterns of relationships between clinical tests and diagnoses that confirmed their prior beliefs but that were not, in fact, present in the information presented. Indeed, there is now considerable evidence to support the notion that information is selectively encoded and retrieved in ways that confirm prior beliefs (Evans, 1989). Thus, with the risk of suicide in prisons, a prisoner's distress may be dismissed as 'not genuine', 'manipulative' or 'attention seeking' (and see Dexter and Towl, 1995 and Towl, 2000 for a useful critique of such pejorative terms).

Vividness

Nisbett and Ross (1980) proposed the notion of 'vividness' to explain some of the weightings given by people to social information. The authors argued that people have a clear tendency to overweight vivid, concrete information and a tendency to underweight dull, pallid and abstract information. The vividness of information appears to be determined by:

- its emotional interest;
- its 'concreteness' and 'imaginability';
- its temporal and spatial proximity.

In the context of suicides in prison, it is perhaps not difficult to see some possible implications. For example, information suggesting an increase in suicide risk is likely to have more emotional interest where staff–prisoner relations are positive; and is likely to be of even greater interest for staff with more direct contact. Similarly, the temporal and spatial proximity may be quite distant for staff involved in assessing the risk of suicide.

Confirmation bias

'Confirmation bias' is an inferential error that suggests people have a fundamental tendency to seek information that is consistent with their current beliefs, theories or hypotheses, and to avoid the collection of potentially falsifying evidence (Evans, 1989). Thus, if a prisoner is believed to be 'manipulative', that prisoner's behaviour is interpreted in relation to such a label.

Risk management

Managing the risk of suicide follows logically from the process of risk assessment described above. In particular, stage 3 of the Cambridge model (see Figure 4.1) should have served to highlight the factors that are acting to increase or decrease the risk of suicide. Management of risk will, therefore, to a very large extent involve attempts to decrease the former and increase the latter.

The Prison Service for England and Wales uses Form F2052SH as a tool for assessing and managing the risk of both suicide and self-injury. The document is designed to facilitate effective monitoring, good com-munications, and a focus on helping each prisoner with his or her prob-lems (Towl and Hudson, 1997). The form dovetails well with the systematic framework for risk assessment outlined above, providing a system for implementing, and documenting, effective risk-manage-ment strategies.

Towl and Hudson (1997) stress the importance of focusing on the thoughts and behaviour of individual prisoners, rather than basing risk-management strategies exclusively on groupings of those who have been shown to be at an increased risk of suicide. They draw on the example of health education strategies such as those employed in the area of HIV and AIDS, where the focus in the United Kingdom has increasingly been on high-risk behaviours rather than on high-risk individuals. One robust finding from recent research is that prisoners are at greater risk of suicide in the early stages of their stay at a new establishment. Individuals, given time, are better able to develop a network of social contacts and support, both with staff and other prisoners. This is supported by a recent study (Jones, 1996) that found that 75 per cent of those recorded as being at 'high risk' of suicide in a local prison were not in an established relationship. This compared with 47 per cent of those not assessed as being at 'high risk'.

It has been suggested that particular thoughts, feelings and beliefs will be evident in those at high risk of suicide (see Crighton, 1997). Dexter and Towl (1995) helpfully suggest a typology of thoughts relating to suicide:

- Thoughts indirectly related to suicide, but no evidence of suicide having been considered as a possible option.
- Thoughts suggesting suicide has been considered, but no intention of carrying it out.
- Thoughts suggesting a desire to complete suicide, but no evidence of making plans to carry it out.
- Thoughts indicating a desire to complete suicide and planning how to do it.

Dexter and Towl also provided an analysis of the correlations between each type and scores on the Beck Hopelessness Scale (BHS), uniquely and powerfully using a 'repeated measures' experimental design. They went on to suggest in their 1995 study that the BHS may serve as a useful tool for assessing the risk of suicide amongst prisoners.

The Prison Service clearly contains – and manages – a large number of prisoners with psychological problems. Thus a more detailed analysis of the nature of such difficulties prior to, and during, imprisonment may be used to inform more effective risk management of suicide in prisons. Community studies have consistently shown markedly increased lifetime risk of suicide among those with particular mental disorders. There appears to be, however, a marked absence of empirical data on whether these groups are at higher or lower risk of suicide whilst in prison custody. Similarly, a more detailed analysis of those with histories of drug or alcohol abuse may be valuable in evaluating the relevance of these factors in assessing the risk of suicide relative to the prison population (see Towl and Hudson, 1997).

In line with previous research (Towl and Crighton, 1997), one area where further research is crucial is the interaction between the prison environment and individuals' characteristics. This will inevitably require a shift of emphasis away from quantitative approaches and towards more qualitative analyses. Crighton (1997), in line with the views of Shneidman (1987), suggests that suicide is often best seen as an attempt to resolve problems that are causing intense psychological suffering. In so far as prison regimes can be developed to provide alternative means of resolving such problems, they are likely to be successful in reducing the risk of suicides.

Risk assessment and risk management is concerned with uncertainty. As such, it is logically impossible for any risk assessment, however good, to predict an outcome with 100 per cent accuracy. A parallel example might come from the field of civil aviation, where risk assessment has been developed to a very high degree. Even so, aircraft still – very occasionally – crash. This does not mean that the engineers made incorrect risk assessments (Towl and Crighton, 1996) but that the riskiness of flying is sometimes demonstrated in such a dramatic manner. What is very clear, though, is that the quality of risk assessment in the behavioural sciences has perhaps fallen short of the rigour of some other disciplines.

The knowledge base in relation to suicide in prisons, on which individuals must draw in making assessments, remains limited. In particular, little is known about the effects of particular prison regimes on levels of suicide risk. Even less is known about the interactions between psychological disturbances, such as depression, and prison regimes. A number of hypotheses can be suggested from community studies but research is needed to test them.

A number of risk indicators are nevertheless already clear from the existing research (Crighton and Towl, 1997). One robust finding is that men are at higher risk of suicide in prison than women. This reflects the findings of community studies that have shown a wide, and increasing, gender difference in suicides and undetermined deaths (Charlton *et al.*, 1992; The Samaritans, 2000). Perhaps the most robust finding is that individuals appear to have an increased risk in the early stages of their reception into a particular establishment (Bogue and Power, 1995). This effect is evident in those received from the community and also in those transferred from other institutions. Towl and Crighton (1998) report from their findings that over 10 per cent of suicides occurred within one day of reception into a new establishment, and over 45 per cent killed themselves within one month.

The popular notion that remand prisoners have a higher risk of suicide than sentenced prisoners is not borne out by recent research (Crighton and Towl, 1997) and appear to be an artefact of the way in which suicide rates in prison have been calculated. Hence, when rates are calculated on the basis of average daily population, the suicide rate for remand prisoners appears very high. When calculated in terms of the number of individuals remanded into custody (a more accurate estimate of the number of at-risk individuals held in prison custody), the rate is broadly similar to that for sentenced prisoners. Among sentenced prisoners, the level of risk appears to increase as sentence length increases, with a particularly marked increase for those serving life sentences.

Caution is needed in interpreting the existing research in relation to mental disorder and suicide in prison. This is because of a number of methodological problems inherent in some of the research. However, it seems possible that mental disorder and a history of mental health problems may have been overstated as an indicator of risk of suicide in prisons. Equally, the significance of substance abuse as an indicator of risk may have been underestimated.

Summary and conclusions

This chapter has reviewed the area of risk assessment and risk management of suicide in prisons. The chapter began with a review of a number of important concepts, both current and historical, in relation to risk assessment and management. The review was followed by an outline of a number of constructs concerned with 'mental disorder'. These are significant in understanding suicide, since much of the research to date has been based on such concepts.

Following on from this, a systematic structure for assessing risk was outlined with reference to suicide in prisons. A review of the existing research base followed, together with an outline of how such information might inform risk assessment and management. A number of robust indicators of increased risk are evident. Most strikingly, prisoners appear to have a greater risk of suicide during the early stages of their stay at an establishment. Some demographic factors appear to suggest increased risk – for example, males and those who were unemployed prior to imprisonment both appear to be overrepresented amongst prison suicides.

It is clear that further research is needed into suicides and self-injury in prisons, so as to inform future risk assessment and management. Even given the limitations of the existing research base, it seems clear that there is considerable scope to improve existing practice by the rigorous application of existing research evidence.

5

Working with suicidal prisoners

Graham Towl and Danielle Forbes

Overview

In this chapter, we detail a range of considerations that we hope will be of practical use to staff working with prisoners who are suicidal. Our discussion is structured under two main headings: 'organisational and management matters', and 'one-to-one help'.

Throughout the chapter, the term 'staff' is used to refer to all types and grades of staff in prisons, whether or not directly employed by the Prison Service. There will, of course, be differences in terms of appropriate types of work that staff of various grades and disciplines should engage in with suicidal prisoners; however, we wish to stress that it is by working together in partnership across disciplines and agencies that we may most effectively help the suicidal (Longfield, 1999).

Working with the suicidal in forensic environments is one of the most challenging roles for staff. Forensic environments in general, and prisons in particular, are fundamentally coercive and this can, in itself, contribute to an increased risk of suicide. Thus working with the suicidal in prisons brings into sharp focus for staff their sometimes competing roles in both the care and control of prisoners (Towl, 1994). Considerations of security are of key importance to all staff working in prisons. These considerations serve to limit the possibilities in terms of what precisely may be provided to help the suicidal prisoner. However, there is still a great deal that staff can offer.

Suicide involves loss of life and is therefore both irreversible and extremely serious in terms of its consequences for all those involved. Hence, there is a significant emotional dimension to the work of staff with suicidal prisoners. Thus a good starting point for such work can be for staff to consider their own attitudes towards suicide and the suicidal. The primacy of the human relationship between the suicidal prisoner and the staff exercising supervision is at the core of providing the best quality help and underpins the effectiveness of a prison's suicide awareness policy and practice.

Organisational and management matters

Individual staff clearly need to be aware of the Prison Service policy with regard to working with the suicidal. Such knowledge will serve more helpfully to structure staff responses to working with suicidal prisoners. The details of the Prison Service policy are described in Chapter 1 of this book and also elsewhere (e.g. McHugh and Towl, 1997; Towl and McHugh, 1999). Ensuring that staff are appropriately aware of policy is largely a matter for managers in prisons, e.g. senior (prison) officers, principal (prison) officers, senior probation officers, governors and healthcare managers. The training of managers, who potentially play a key role in supporting staff in their work with the suicidal, is an important – but perhaps sometimes overlooked – cornerstone of training requirements in establishments.

A number of practical steps can be taken to improve the management of the suicidal. One key issue is to ensure that there is a continuity of care and communication between all staff working with a prisoner. A number of steps can be taken to improve prisoners' care and the communication between staff. For example, once an F2052SH has been opened, it is useful to attach a photograph to the form so that staff unfamiliar with the prisoner will quickly be able to recognise her or him. At some establishments, in order to enhance communications, the F2052SH documentation is kept in the wing office in a racking system that is regularly checked by prison governors and wing managers.

The quality of completion of the 'Daily Supervision and Support Record' in the F2052SH varies within and between establishments. It is important that written comments or 'observations' of staff are appropriately detailed in their nature, timely and relevant. It is probably axiomatic to state that 'observations' should involve meaningful details of the prisoner's thoughts, feelings and behaviours. Active intervention is often required to elicit good-quality information. A written account of a conversation between a prisoner and a member of staff is, in general, of far more use than a comment such as 'appeared down' or 'appeared brighter', based simply upon distant observation.

A formal (recorded) handing-over procedure on wings of 'open' F2052SHs across shifts is good practice. This helps facilitate a continuity of care and also helps ensure that there is a clear line of accountability. Good working relationships between healthcare staff and wing-based staff in prisons are essential if the best care is to be given to prisoners. There can be a great deal of expertise across both these settings, and it is important to work together in achieving the best possible service for the suicidal prisoner.

Each prison is different in terms of its environment and culture. The differences exist on a number of dimensions. Some environmental factors have been identified that are associated with an inflated risk of suicide in prisons, and these are outlined in some of the most recent research on completed suicides in prisons (Towl, 1999b). The subject of risk assessment and management is dealt with elsewhere in this book (see Chapter 4). Clearly, such information is of potential use in informing both good policy and practice in prisons.

Perhaps the single most important environmental factor is the enormously inflated risk of suicide associated with the 'high throughput' of prisoners in some establishments, as discussed in Chapter 3. Thus, in local prisons, there are disproportionately large numbers of completed suicides. It is difficult for staff to establish good-quality relationships with prisoners when they only see each other for very short periods of time. The 'induction process' in prisons generally, and in local prisons in particular, is critical to the effective implementation of a good-practice-based approach to working with the suicidal. This is because a prisoner's risk of suicide is especially high in the days and weeks following induction. Hence, the quality of the relationships between newly arrived prisoners and induction unit staff may very well contribute to whether or not those individual prisoners will or will not report suicidal feelings to staff in their first few days after arrival and also at later stages of imprisonment. Therefore the importance of treating prisoners with respect cannot be overemphasised.

Having examined a number of elements of the organisation and management of the suicidal within prisons, we now move on to address some of the practice-based issues and techniques associated with helping suicidal prisoners as part of the F2052SH policy and procedures.

One-to-one help

It is of key importance, for the success of the Prison Service strategy to manage the suicidal, that individual prisoners share any suicidal thoughts and ideas with staff, in order that staff can develop effective management and support plans. Clearly, prisoners are more likely to share such thoughts in the context of a private, one-to-one discussion with a supportive and trusted Listener (prisoner or staff) than they are in a public or group setting. However, as mentioned previously, the coercive nature of the prison environment does not, in general, encourage the development of fully open relationships between staff and prisoners. In addition, suicidal individuals – whether or not they are prisoners – are likely to experience feelings of ambiguity about the usefulness of sharing their concerns and plans with others. Following initial interviews in which suicidal intent is established, staff go on to be involved in the management and support of individual prisoners, which often involves ongoing one-to-one contact or one-to-one help.

When seeking to make some analysis of what constitutes good one-to-one help, it can be useful to look on two levels: first, at the level of process and content; and, secondly, at the level of skills and values. That is to say, the way in which discussions are conducted can be equally as important as the nature of what is discussed. Although clear distinctions are made here between the two areas, in reality significant overlap and convergence exists.

Ground rules

When initiating work with a suicidal prisoner, ground rules should be established to enable the development of an effective and ethical helping relationship by structuring prisoners' expectations. The nature of the ground rules that need to be set will, in large part, be dictated by the designation of the members of staff involved, but are likely to include issues of confidentiality and issues surrounding the nature of future contact.

Someone employed directly by the Prison Service would need to make explicit to a prisoner the limits to confidentiality that this implies. The member of staff would be required to report matters that could impact upon the security of the prison environment or any of the individuals held within it. This would mean reporting any stated intention to self-injury. On the other hand, an individual conducting this sort of work in a prison who was not employed directly by the Prison Service (for example, a member of The Samaritans or a prisoner 'Listener') would not be confined in that way and could offer complete confidentiality. What is important to establishing a good relationship is that, wherever possible, prisoners are made aware of the limits of confidentiality before they start to work with a member of staff.

The nature of the follow-up help or contact between a particular member of staff and a suicidal prisoner will vary enormously depending upon the situation. It can range from no more than a brief acknowledgement of the other party, to a series of extended, private interviews. The nature and regularity of contact or help will be influenced to some extent by the grade of the staff involved and the nature of the difficulties experienced by the prisoner. For instance, an instructor in a prison workshop may work with a prisoner during weekdays but not at weekends; similarly, individual prison officers have relatively short working hours. Inevitably, this serves to limit the level of contact. What is vital is that the nature of the contact is discussed, agreed and implemented between the staff member and the prisoner.

Content

Chapter 4 outlined how important it is for a staff member assessing a prisoner's risk of suicide to have a good knowledge and understanding of those factors generally associated with an increased or decreased risk of suicide. However, in addition staff must build up a good knowledge of each individual prisoner's situation. Prisoners' own expertise on their situation is central in this process. Unfortunately, such expertise is often insufficiently recognised (Medlicott, 1999). One obvious method of tapping into such expertise is simply to ask prisoners to give their accounts of what has led to their current feelings. As well as establishing facts from a prisoner's point of view, this opportunity to discuss thoughts and feelings with a supportive listener may also serve a highly therapeutic purpose. Furthermore, openly acknowledging the difficulties associated with imprisonment can often be helpful. One function this may serve is to help 'normalise' the individual's behaviour, thoughts and feelings.

Nevertheless, depression, or at least lowered mood, is a common feature of those who are contemplating suicide. However, it is important to be aware of the possibility that sometimes a prisoner may have an *elevated* mood, which may serve to mask the fact that they have decided to kill themselves. The mood elevation from depression may, in such cases, reflect contentment at the decision having been arrived at about taking one's life. Such observations are not uncommon in psychiatric settings. Generally, it is useful to help inculcate some sense of structure to the day when working with those who are depressed. Structured activity is important, although opportunities for providing such structure within prison settings may be limited. This is perhaps partly why it is particularly helpful for staff working with prisoners to have the support and confidence of managers. Healthcare staff are in a position to advise, if appropriate, on drug treatment for depression, which can be an important element of helping individuals be better placed to work through their depression. It is always worth checking whether a prisoner has a history of any mental health difficulties. This will not be the case for the majority of prisoners, but if there is such a history it is worth knowing. It is also very important to find out whether the prisoner has self-injured or attempted suicide in the past, because research has shown that a high proportion of those who go on to complete suicide have self-injured or attempted suicide previously.

Staff working with the suicidal must be cautious when attempting to alleviate a prisoner's feelings of hopelessness and helplessness by introducing certain, apparently more positive topics. For example, it may be helpful to discuss with the prisoner some of the past brighter and more positive times in the prisoner's life. The act of such discussions implicitly acknowledges the prisoner's capacity for further positive experiences. However, it may simply contrast somewhat depressingly for them with their current experiences. Similarly, managing uncertainty can be the source of considerable anxiety and distress. The prison environment is in some respects an uncertain one and adapting to this uncertainty can be problematic. It may well be helpful to distinguish with prisoners those areas of their life that they remain able to influence and change. This can help focus thoughts on how to take areas forward. However, such conversations could also serve to highlight the possibility that prisoners may not be able to change or influence those things that are most important to them. Therefore, staff need to maintain a balance between a focus on the positive and the reality of the individual's current situation.

Skills and values

In order to maximise the effectiveness of one-to-one work with a suicidal prisoner, staff should aim to demonstrate a high level of respect for, and a non-judgemental attitude toward, an individual prisoner's thoughts, ideas and concerns. There are certain key communication skills (basic counselling skills) that can help staff to demonstrate these values. We would stress that we are not advocating that all prison staff are trained as counsellors, but rather that all staff are able potentially to use some basic counselling skills to positive effect when working with the suicidal. Some relevant counselling skills may be summarised under four general headings: attending, active listening, empathy, and active exploration.

'Attending' is quite simply demonstrating to someone that you are giving them your full attention. Ways of achieving this include maintaining an appropriate level of eye contact during conversations, and using relaxed and open body language. The antithesis of a relaxed open presentation would be to sit upright with one's arms folded.

When attending, you are in an excellent position to conduct 'active listening', which means demonstrating that you are listening carefully to everything that someone is saying as well as picking up on their non-verbal cues. Remembering and referring back to points that they had made earlier would be an example of demonstrating active listening.

A member of staff demonstrating 'empathy', would be making every effort to understand the prisoner's world from the prisoner's perspective. Checking things out with the prisoner and never making assumptions about thoughts and feelings would be examples of empathic communication. Even so, it is probably best to avoid saying: 'I understand how you feel' because this can often be interpreted as the contrary.

Finally, 'active exploration' involves exploring issues by asking questions in a supportive manner, in order to build up a clear, detailed and accurate picture of a prisoner's thoughts, feelings and ideas. Skills of active exploration are perhaps the most challenging for staff to become skilled at. However, such skills are important in helping the suicidal.

Labelling

Some of the research on suicide in prisons has drawn from 'coping theory', suggesting that some individuals who become suicidal differ from those who do not largely as a function of their 'coping ability' (e.g. Liebling, 1991). To follow this theory to its logical conclusion, individual prisoners might be labelled as 'poor' or 'good' copers. However, we would suggest that it is unwise and unhelpful to label individuals in this way. We all experience difficulties in adapting to our environments at different points. Problems with labelling people (particularly potentially pejoratively) at difficult times in their lives are well documented elsewhere (e.g. Goffman, 1961). Labelling prisoners at times of personal crisis as 'poor copers' could serve to reinforce institutional stereotypes about suicidal prisoners, namely that they are, in the less liberal parlance of prisons, 'inadequate'.

When working with the suicidal, such stereotypes may be harmful on a number of levels. First, such terms may set limits to individual potential to change in the minds of both the prisoner and the member of staff who is in the helping relationship. Secondly, a great deal may be missed by the act of focusing upon such stereotypes rather than the behaviour, thoughts and feelings of the individual prisoner. Particularly important is the fact that the areas missed may well be the very aspects of the person and their situation that could be crucial in helping them through their difficulties.

Self-awareness

Working with the suicidal can be emotionally demanding for staff. Discussions with individuals who are suicidal may trigger responses in staff members that are a struggle for them to deal with. Honest self-reflection is therefore an essential part of professional practice. We must be aware of our own emotional reactions, first in order to protect ourselves emotionally and, secondly, in order that we can monitor our own behaviour to ensure that we maintain high standards of professionalism.

One common reaction to this work is a feeling of self-doubt. Because we are dealing with an uncertain, but potentially very serious, outcome, we can doubt our ability to manage the situation effectively. Staff of all grades and disciplines often feel that they are 'unqualified', 'untrained' or 'unskilled' when conducting this type of work. Staff need to manage their feelings in this regard in order to ensure that they do not allow themselves simply to avoid further work or contact with a suicidal individual. Anyway, avoiding contact could serve to increase the risk of suicide by a particular prisoner through increasing feelings of isolation and decreasing the level of information that is available to staff to inform risk-management decisions.

Another common reaction when working with suicidal prisoners, particularly someone who is repeatedly self-injuring, is a feeling of frustration, anger, desperation or futility. These feelings are likely to underlie what has become a common and well-documented response by prison and hospital staff to the work, namely describing prisoners (or patients) as 'attention seeking', 'manipulative' or 'not genuine'. While these terms are sometimes used out of a frustration with what can be difficult work, such language may serve to increase the risk of an individual completing suicide (Dexter and Towl, 1995; Towl, 2000).

In one sense, it does not matter whether or not prisoners are 'genuine' in intending to take their own life. First, if prisoners are not 'genuinely suicidal' but report to staff that they are, they must feel very desperate to go to such extremes to bring matters to the attention of staff. Secondly, people can – and do – kill themselves without the intention of going through with it and, sometimes, reporting such feelings can be a last attempt to get help. Thus such prisoners need help. We cannot accurately distinguish prisoners' motivations, particularly since, as the following quotation illustrates, a simple dichotomy ('genuine' or 'not genuine') does not reflect the complexity of suicidal experiences: 'Sometimes acknowledged suicidal ideas have other meanings; in some they can be a way of influencing a life situation rather than an actual wish to destroy the self, though quite often both mechanisms may be present in the same patient' (Morgan et al., 1998).

Summary and conclusions

We have identified that working with the suicidal in a prison environment is a challenging area for good practice but an important one. The term 'working with' the suicidal is intended to convey the importance of the relationship and rapport that can develop between staff members and suicidal prisoners. It is this relationship that underpins good policy and practice.

We have seen how the language used in relation to the suicidal can have a significant impact upon the effectiveness of our interventions. Further, we hope that we have sufficiently emphasised the need for good basic counselling skills and values in this work. Other chapters should be of assistance in providing a sound knowledge base on suicide in prisons and on the process of risk assessment. We hope that the contents of this chapter are of some use to those engaging in work with the suicidal within the challenging constraints of a coercive environment.

6

The role of formalised peer-group
support in prisons

Louisa Snow

Overview

This chapter focuses initially on the impact and effects of imprisonment
(from sociological and psychological perspectives) and on prisoner
adaptation and adjustment. This is followed by a discussion on the
introduction and development of formalised peer-group support for
prisoners and the difficulties in quantifying the impact of support networks for the suicidal (both within and outside prison custody). A
review of previous evaluations of formalised support schemes is then
provided and a recent study on prisoners' preferred sources of support
is described. Finally, a number of conclusions are drawn and their
implications for the development of such support schemes are discussed.

Introduction

It is suggested by Gresham (1971) that deprivation of an individual's
liberty is a fitting punishment for crime. Thus, prison itself should not
induce distress amongst those held (Biggam and Power, 1997). However, there is evidence that prison is indeed stressful to the extent that
it precipitates psychological problems in some (Toch, 1992; Zamble and
Porporino, 1988; Cooper and Livingston, 1991), although the evidence
is far from conclusive as to the precise nature or extent of the stress (or
distress) experienced, by whom, when or why. The issue of prison-
induced stress or distress has become more focal with recent concern
over the rate of suicide in prisons within the United Kingdom (Biggam
and Power, 1997) and the increasing rate among prisoners in England
and Wales (as discussed in Chapter 1). The Prison Service is taking a
number of steps to reduce the number of completed/attempted suicides and self-injury amongst prisoners. An important aspect of work
is this area is the improvement in prisoners' access to (community-

based) organisations such as The Samaritans and their prison-based equivalents, 'Listeners'. Listeners (like Samaritans) are carefully selected and trained to actively listen in a reflective and sympathetic way to the distressed, the suicidal or the despairing.

This chapter examines the role of such formalised peer-support schemes for prisoners, particularly among those experiencing what they perceive to be problems. The provision of support to such individuals is crucial because of the relationship between recent negative life experiences and problems and suicidal behaviours (see, for example, Wicks, 1972; Wool and Dooley, 1987; Ivanoff and Jong, 1991; Coid *et al.*, 1992; Dexter and Towl, 1995). It is suggested that listener schemes are a source of support, acting as an important protection against suicide, particularly amongst those with limited access to alternative sources. It is well understood that perceived absence or lack of support can foster feelings of loneliness[31] (Weiss, 1975), sometimes leading to desperation (Shaver and Rubenstein, 1980) and depression (Shaver and Rubenstein, 1980; Russell *et al.*, 1984) – factors that are correlated with increased likelihood of suicidal ideation or behaviour (Morgan *et al.*, 1998). Thus intervention at an early stage can be crucial.

The effects of imprisonment

Although well documented, research on the effects of imprisonment is inconclusive. Some studies suggest that imprisonment is damaging to the extent that it induces extremely negative effects, while others contentiously suggest the reverse – that prison may in fact be conducive to *good* health (Bonta and Gendreau, 1990: 357). Arguably, inconsistent findings are further encumbered by methodological problems. As Zamble and Porporino (1988) argue, studies have employed contrasting indices and definitions, have varied in the types of populations/establishments included in the samples and have typically been based on simple correlational or cross-sectional designs. Further, there is a paucity of longitudinal research, which limits our understanding of the longer-term effects of imprisonment. These difficulties should be borne in mind when reading the following overview of key research in the area.

Early (predominately sociological) studies focused on the unique characteristics of the prison environment that reportedly influenced prisoners' general well-being and behaviour, both during and after imprisonment. Some authors suggested that inadequate living conditions (characterised by, for example, poor sanitation and overcrowding) were a source of stress (Mathieson, 1965; Nagel, 1976). Others argued that particular aspects of institutional life exerted negative influences on prisoners' attitudes, values, modes of interaction and self-concepts.

For example, Sykes (1958) characterised the prison experience and its environment as detrimental in preventing prisoners from fulfilling certain basic needs and causing extreme material deprivation, loss of personal security and autonomy. Such factors constitute what Sykes termed the 'pains of imprisonment'. Goffman (1961) suggested that the very structure and organisation of the 'total institution' exacerbates the already-present difficulties in adjustment to institutional life. Total institutions, argued Goffman, foster dependency by infantilising, undermining the self-esteem and limiting the autonomy of the incarcerated. Similarly, Foucault suggested that these and other effects are intrinsic to the very notion of punishment in what are described as 'complete and austere institutions' (1979: 235–236).

By comparison, analyses of the ostensible harmful[32] effects (from psychological, clinical and psychiatrically oriented perspectives) have sought to quantify the range of cognitive, emotional, attitudinal and personality changes apparently induced by imprisonment, at least for some. Variants of what Zamble and Porporino term the 'psycho-syndrome' include defects in cognitive functioning, emotional problems, difficulties in relating to others, and the appearance of various psychotic characteristics. Some (for example, Gunn *et al.*, 1978) have reported immediate negative effects (in the form of high levels of distress, disturbance and psychological discomfort), which, although remaining high, appear to dissipate following adjustment to imprisonment. Similarly, Zamble and Porporino (who conducted one of the few longitudinal studies on the effects of imprisonment) found that almost half their sample had experienced difficulties with depression, anxiety and sleep one month into their sentence, whilst more than one-third had clinically significant levels of hopelessness. After three months, depression and anxiety levels had decreased significantly, although one-quarter of the participants had increased levels of depression. After 15 months, mean depression and hopelessness levels were not significantly different from those at three months, although anxiety levels and problems with sleeping had decreased further.

As intimated, although it is probable that some prisoners develop psychological problems during imprisonment, other studies have failed to demonstrate any long-term or overall aversive effects on cognitive, perceptual-motor and personality functioning (see, for example, Banister *et al.*, 1973; Heskin *et al.*, 1973; Sapsford, 1978). It is important to emphasise that inconsistent and inconclusive findings are likely to be related to the application of inconsistent methodological, conceptual and definitional approaches (Zamble and Porporino, 1988; Coid, 1984; McKay *et al.*, 1979). Notwithstanding these difficulties, a relatively robust finding is that any psychological difficulties, disturbance, stress and/or consequent distress are likely to be maximal during the initial phase (Toch and Adams, 1989) and subsequently to diminish following a period of adjustment (Gunn *et al.*, 1978.). This finding is supported by Backett (1987), who suggests that imprisonment induces a continuum of distress, which may induce feelings of despair if a critical threshold is exceeded. As Backett argues, such a threshold is individually specific and dependent on a balance between the factors that cause distress and individuals' resources to manage distressing situations (both generally and within the prison context). Findings such as these are especially pertinent to the issue of suicide in prisons, given that research has consistently shown that the majority of deaths occur in the earlier period following arrival at a prison, at a time when prisoners are likely to face the greatest amount of uncertainty (as suggested by Towl and Crighton, 1998; Bogue and Power, 1995; Towl, 1999a; Towl, 2000).

Having briefly considered the possible consequences of imprisonment, attention now turns to the issue of prisoners' adaptation.

Adaptation to imprisonment

The importance of successful adaptation to imprisonment has long been recognised (see, for example, Clemmer, 1940; Sykes, 1958; Sykes and Messinger, 1960; Goffman, 1961; Cohen and Taylor, 1972; Coid, 1984). Early (predominately sociological) theorists suggested that prisoners manage the deprivations imposed upon them through the development of normative systems, by adherence to subcultural norms and attitudes, and through the adoption of institutional dialect (Zamble and Porporino, 1988). Affiliation to the prison counterculture or so-called 'inmate code' may facilitate a prisoner's adjustment in the sense that opposing the authority of staff and promoting acceptance amongst prisoners' peers may reduce feelings of isolation and allow prisoners to regain some sense of control over their lives. Such factors may improve an individual's self-esteem, promote a sense of autonomy and, argue Goodstein and Wright (1989: 231), improve their self-respect.

Rather than seeking to demonstrate either the presence or absence of psychological, emotional and/or psychiatric consequences of imprisonment, some researchers (for example, Zamble and Porporino, 1988; Power *et al.*, 1997; Backett, 1987) recognise that any negative consequences – if, indeed, they occur – are not inevitable and, moreover, are individually specific, rather than generalised or uniform. Further, as Biggam and Power (1997) acknowledge, researchers in the area have recently become aware of the 'process' or multidimensional nature of stress (Lazarus, 1966), which incorporates an individual's physical environment as well as the psychological and social realms. Stress and subsequent distress stems from a person's appraisals of the interaction of such factors (Cox, 1978). Thus, how one interprets current situations (and any problems being encountered) may be equally as important as the frequency or severity of the problems themselves (Zamble and Porporino, 1988: 11).

Recognising the multidimensional nature of stress (in the context of imprisonment), Power *et al.* (1997) examined prisoners' perceptions of adaptation. The results of the study suggested that, generally, one's coping/adaptive abilities are multifaceted and determined by a complex interaction of background, individual, situational and environmental factors. Adapting to imprisonment, however, requires the additional skill of successfully socialising with one's peers, as Biggam and Power remark:

> Coping in a closed, crowded and potentially aggressive environment is determined largely by one's ability to interact successfully, form alliances, establish allegiances, develop social networks and, most importantly, acquire acceptance.

(p. 390)

Thus, successful adaptation depends on a combination of factors, including previous life experiences, acquired techniques of managing stress and distress (the utilisation of which may be curtailed by incarceration), current psychological and psychiatric states, relationships with significant others outside prison, the development and continuation of such relationships, and the cultivation of relationships and networks with peers. Arguably, if integration into a supportive (prison-based) social network is not achieved, the problems or difficulties experienced by prisoners are likely to become intensified.

Biggam and Power (1997), examined the structure and function of social support (considering self-perceived actual and ideal levels of support and the discrepancies between them) in a group of young offenders. The authors concluded that those who report higher levels of psychological distress (anxiety, depression and hopelessness) desire higher ideal levels of support (emotional and practical) and reported a higher discrepancy between overall actual and ideal levels of support. Thus, those experiencing higher levels of psychological distress regarded themselves as more deficient in social support. Similarly, Liebling (1992) argued that, in the case of young offenders, 'poor coping skills', manifested as difficulties in adjusting to imprisonment and successfully associating with others, are among the main factors distinguishing suicidal from non-suicidal prisoners. Others have questioned the accuracy and utility of the use of the term 'poor coping' (e.g. Dexter and Towl, 1995; Towl, 2000).

Having introduced the concept of social support and its ostensible importance to individuals' general well-being and in the successful adaptation to imprisonment, attention now turns to the contribution of formalised (as distinct from informal) support, particularly that provided by other prisoners.

Formal support for the suicidal: the role of prisoners

Biggam and Power (1997), in consideration of the availability and utilisation of support to prisoners and in their experience of anxiety, depression and hopelessness, distinguish between external and prison-based relationships (including, for example, a well-known or personal officer or, less formally, a close friend). Their results suggest that those with higher levels of anxiety report less than optimum practical support from other prisoners and less than optimum practical/emotional support from best-known/personal officers. Those with higher levels of depression reported less than optimum emotional/practical support from prisoners/officers; and those with higher levels of hopelessness reported less than optimum emotional/practical support from officers. The authors conclude that an overall discrepancy in emotional support was the greatest predictor of anxiety, depression and hopelessness. As observed, this finding reflects other research (e.g. Brown *et al.*, 1986) that suggests that the unexpected absence of social support in times of crisis (which could, feasibly, include imprisonment) can precipitate depression.

The benefit of social integration has long been recognised. For example, Durkheim's study of suicide (1888) proclaimed the importance of environmental, situational and demographic factors, such as marital status, socio-economic class and, importantly, degree of social integration (Baron *et al.*, 1990). Other research highlights the importance of supportive relationships in the maintenance of one's health and general (physical and psychological) well-being (see, for example, Cohen and MacKay, 1984; Cohen and Wills, 1985; Turner, 1983; Brown *et al.*, 1986.; Wills, 1991) and in reducing the likelihood of psychological distress in response to stressful situations. Generally speaking, social support appears to partially protect individuals in the experience of stressful life events (Cohen and Wills, 1985). Within the prison context, the relevance of the so-called 'buffer effect' of social support – whereby people who feel supported are less affected by stressful life events and conditions than those who feel unsupported (Cohen and Hoberman, 1983) – is clear. Since imprisonment is likely to be perceived to be stressful by at least some prisoners, it may be argued that the existence and utilisation of positive supportive relationships are crucial for the psychological well-being of prisoners – an observation supported by Biggar, 1996; Carolissen, 1996; Biggam and Power, 1997; Power *et al.*, 1997.

Recognising the importance of prison-based (and external) relationships and the positive influence that prisoners can exert over one another, the Prison Service's multidisciplinary strategy on suicide awareness and prevention emphasises the role of prisoners in the care of the suicidal (for a more detailed account of current Prison Service policy, see Chapter 1). The strategy utilises and formalises the informal help and support that invariably takes place between prisoners in times of stress and distress (Biggar, 1996; Carolissen, 1996) through what are commonly termed 'listener' schemes, the majority of which are developed under the supervision of The Samaritans (a nationwide charitable organisation that provides confidential, emotional support to anyone who is suicidal or despairing). Some prisons offer befriending/'buddy' schemes, which operate under a different philosophy. That the generic term 'listener' is applied to a number of quite different schemes has resulted in some confusion; nevertheless, for the current purpose the terms 'listener' and 'listener scheme' are used to refer both to Samaritan-supported and other schemes.

Prison listener schemes

The first listener scheme, similar to the scheme established in Charles Street Jail, Boston, in the United States in 1979, was introduced into Swansea Prison in 1991. Samaritan-supported schemes have since been expanded to operate in more than 100 prisons of all types in England and Wales (over two-thirds of the prison estate). This development has been actively encouraged by the Prison Service because it is recognised that prisoners experiencing difficulties may prefer to confide in their peers rather than staff or someone from 'outside' the establishment. Furthermore, prisoners are an underused source of support although, as emphasised in Prison Service guidance, support from them must be regarded as an *addition* to (rather than an alternative to) the support provided by staff and other external agencies. In addition, individual prisoners (unlike residential staff, Personal Officers, Prison Visitors or Samaritans) can be available 24 hours a day. Further, staff–prisoner (listener) relationships may improve as a result of both groups working towards a common objective (i.e. the amelioration of distress). Finally, prisoners acting as listeners may gain personal benefits, in terms of improvements to their own self-esteem, their sense of self-worth, and an enhanced sense of responsibility.

Samaritan-supported listener schemes are founded upon similar principles to community-based Samaritans. Individual prisoners who possess the necessary skills to help and support others (such as empathy, understanding and acceptance) are carefully selected by staff and Samaritans. They are then trained to listen actively in a reflective and sympathetic way to those in crisis or despair; as with Samaritans in the community they are not trained as counsellors but as *listeners*. Like Samaritans, listeners encourage the suicidal to accept help from others, which is more likely if trust between listener and prisoner is established. Clearly, if prisoners think that listeners may divulge the issues they raise to others, they may be discouraged from disclosing their distress – which may, in turn, enhance their feelings of despair. For this reason, listeners (like Samaritans) are bound by a strict code of confidentiality.[33] Although not included in the surveys reported in this chapter, some prisons run listener-type schemes without Samaritan involvement, where a principle of privacy applies (for an account, see *Suicide Awareness Bulletin*, No. 2, HM Prison Service, November 1999). The privacy rule affords a degree of confidentiality but at the same time offers reassurance to staff that where extreme risk of 'self-harm' has been identified they will be informed.

It is important to acknowledge the contextual differences between community-based Samaritans and prison-based listeners, which means that adequate support from The Samaritans and sympathetic understanding from staff is vital. Recognising this need, The Samaritans provide regular and crisis support to listeners through visits and telephone contact. One difference between Samaritans and listeners is their relative proximity: prisoners live with those they befriend, which means that they may be unable to disengage in quite the same way, or that they may be on-call more frequently. Further, whereas only a small proportion of Samaritan community work is face-to-face, all listener work operates in this way without the degree of anonymity afforded by telephone contact. Also, the reactions of fellow prisoners may be challenging: listeners may face criticism from others for supporting those they may regard as unworthy of such support – due to the nature of their offence, for example. In addition to the contextual differences between community and prison-based support schemes, it should be acknowledged that the introduction of listener schemes presented a considerable challenge to prison culture. The principle of confidentiality, for example, is the subject of controversy, in the sense that for a listener to keep confidential a client's expressed wish to die places considerable demands upon them. This issue will be discussed more fully later in the chapter.

It is important to note that listener schemes may not be suitable for all types of establishment. There may, for example, be problems running such schemes with young offenders, where there may be a shortage of prisoners with the right qualities or the required degree of maturity. It is accepted that, in common with Samaritan work in the community, Samaritan-supported listener schemes are inappropriate with juveniles (aged under 18 years), where individual befriending by external Samaritans is regarded as more appropriate.

Assessing the impact of listener schemes

Having described the introduction of listener schemes, an overview of previous evaluations of support schemes for the suicidal and prison-based (listener) schemes is now provided. Although it is important that evaluations of suicide prevention services (such as The Samaritans and listener schemes) are made, particularly with a view to improving service provision, assessments of the efficacy of such services, in terms of their impact on incidence of completed and/or attempted suicide are, in short, inconclusive. While some have suggested that The Samaritans are 'successful' in preventing suicides (Bagley, 1968) others (such as Barraclough *et al.*, 1977; Cutter, 1979; Lester, 1994) suggest otherwise. The disparity in research findings is clearly related to the complex nature of the behaviours. The causes of suicide are usually multifactorial, and to prove that any one factor (e.g. Samaritan/listener support) either contributed to or prevented death is unlikely to be possible. The number of potentially intervening variables precludes straightforward evaluation. Because of the inherent difficulty in accounting for other factors (which may have a bearing on whether someone chooses life or suicide) any statistical studies are likely to be spurious (Bagley, 1968). Quantification is problematic also because the most visible measure is failure – i.e. completed suicide – which is fortunately a comparatively rare event, and to expect the demonstration of a simple effect upon such a very rare event is unrealistic. Furthermore, analysis of Samaritan contact by those who do die by suicide is difficult because of the confidential nature of their work (Gunnell, 1994).

Nevertheless, it is important that suicide prevention and support schemes are monitored, in order that best practice and potential problems may be highlighted and addressed, so as to ensure that improvements and developments are made. To this end, three (unpublished) reviews of listener schemes have been conducted, which are now summarised. See also Appendix 5A (I) of the Thematic Review, *Suicide is Everyone's Concern* (HMCIP, 1999).

Review by Suicide Awareness Support Unit, 1995

Firstly, an unpublished national review was conducted in 1995 by the Suicide Awareness Support Unit (Prison Service Headquarters) using a postal questionnaire. The sample consisted of 120 staff and 270 listeners. The majority of staff (89 per cent) felt that the listener scheme had had a positive impact on the establishment, of whom 41 per cent reported a resultant reduction in suicidal behaviours. Other positive effects reported included a reduction in absconds (from open prisons) and improvements in awareness of those at increased risk of suicide (on the part of staff and prisoners). The vast majority of staff (87 per cent) reported no problems with the principle of confidentiality (in the sense that they thought it should be adhered to). Reported concerns related to security, staff feeling uneasy about not knowing whether or not a prisoner was planning to kill him/herself, and the possibility of collusion between listeners and other prisoners. Negative effects reported included opposition to the scheme and suspicion – on the part of staff

Listeners reported similar opinions: 65 per cent stated that the schemes had a positive impact, of whom 49 per cent felt that there had been a ensuing reduction in suicidal behaviours. Most (73 per cent) reported having had no problems with confidentiality (or its preservation). Problems reported included concerns over keeping confidential prisoners' expressed wishes to die and application of pressure by other prisoners (for example, to carry messages). Almost half (48 per cent) felt that being a listener improved their attitude towards staff; 59 per cent felt that it improved their relationships with other prisoners, and 54 per cent felt that being a listener helped them better manage difficulties faced during imprisonment. The majority (83 per cent) said their training (from The Samaritans) helped them considerably and 74 per cent were satisfied with the support they received.

Review at a Category C establishment, 1995

Secondly, a review was conducted at a Category C training prison in 1995. The sample included staff (44), Samaritans (8), listeners (12) and prisoners (124) of whom 11 per cent had used the Scheme. The majority of staff (84 per cent) reported a workable understanding of the scheme and 68 per cent said that they found it helpful in their day-to-day work. Almost half (40 per cent) reported that introduction of the scheme had resulted in an improvement in staff–prisoner relationships; half reported no effect; and 7 per cent reported a negative effect. Just over half (55 per cent) reported that listeners 'always' or 'nearly always' adhered to confidentiality. On a less positive note, 66 per cent felt that listeners tended to 'misuse' their status in some way. Turning to the views of listeners themselves, all but one felt that their training enabled them to cope either 'well' or 'very well' with their work. All felt that The Samaritans provided at least adequate support, although half felt that they received inadequate support from staff. Most (75 per cent) reported that they were able to help prisoners 'always' or 'often', and all but one reported that adherence to the principle of confidentiality was unproblematic.

With regard to the views of prisoners, almost half (42 per cent) reported recently experiencing a problem they wanted to discuss with someone; and, of these, 14 per cent spoke to their friends or family and 17 per cent spoke to staff. Reported reasons for *not* seeking support from a listener included their unapproachability (17 per cent), beliefs that the prisoners' problems were too trivial (11 per cent), concerns about confidentiality (7 per cent) and a lack of awareness of the existence of such a scheme (5 per cent). The majority (72 per cent) thought that the listener scheme was a good idea in principle; 5 per cent did not; and the remainder (23 per cent) were unsure. Slightly more than one-third (36 per cent) said that they would consider using the scheme in the future, 33 per cent would not, and 19 per cent were unsure. The majority of those who had used the scheme reported no difficulties in obtaining access to a listener. Further, most felt sure that confidentiality was always adhered to and most felt that listeners do not misuse their status.

Review at a high security prison, 1998

Thirdly, a review was conducted at a high security prison in 1998. The sample was restricted to 74 prisoners, of whom 26 had used the listener scheme. Two-thirds of the sample had never spoken with a listener about their problems, for a number of reasons: they had no confidence or trust in listeners (43 per cent); they felt it unnecessary (14 per cent); they generally discussed their problems with others (20 per cent); and some (7 per cent) would not divulge problems to other prisoners. Although almost half regarded the scheme as a good idea in principle, respondents suggested that improvements could be made in the areas of training, information and selection (and more than half felt that the then current listeners were unsuitable).

The majority of prisoners who had used the scheme (77 per cent) reported no problems in contacting a listener, although 6 per cent reported experiencing 'a great deal of difficulty'. More than half (59 per cent) described the scheme as either 'useful' or 'quite useful'. Almost half (44 per cent) reported feeling better about their problems after speaking with a listener, whilst 20 per cent reported feeling worse. With regard to the issue of confidentiality, more than half (54 per cent) reported being 'unsure' or 'not confident' that the principle was adhered to. Regarding future use, around a third stated that they would (either 'definitely' or 'probably') use the scheme.

Inferences drawn

A number of inferences may be drawn from these surveys:

- From the staff perspective, the majority response implies that listener schemes reflect an improvement in the care of suicidal prisoners in terms of enhancing staff–prisoner relationships. On a negative note are the findings (from the second review mentioned above) that two-thirds of staff feel listeners 'misuse' their status and that a significant proportion do not adhere to confidentiality.

- Responses from listeners indicate satisfaction with the level of training and support provided and feeling capable of assisting with the majority of problems with which they are approached. Of significance is the apparent ease with which confidentiality is adhered to, contrary to the views of staff and prisoners.
- Views of prisoners (who had not used the scheme) indicate a preference for alternative sources of support in times of distress, largely because of concerns regarding the preservation of confidentiality – a view in fact shared by users of the scheme. With regard to the quality of service they received, those who had used a scheme appeared satisfied; however, in the case of the third review mentioned, 20 per cent reported feeling worse about their problems after having confided in a listener.

A review of listener schemes by the author, 1998

Building upon, and developing further, the reviews outlined above, the author of this chapter conducted a survey of prisoners, listeners and staff at five prisons (Snow, 1998). The main aims of the review were threefold:

1. to explore the frequency and range of problems experienced by prisoners;
2. to ascertain the availability and utilisation of support networks for those who reported problems;
3. to explore perceptions of the value of listener schemes and how to improve them.

The study sample consisted of four groups, comprising 28 prisoners who had used the listener scheme ('users'); 44 prisoners who had not used the scheme ('non-users'); 40 prisoner listeners, currently active; and 31 members of staff from operational grades. The five prisons included in the sample were chosen in consultation with the Suicide Awareness Support Unit at Prison Service Headquarters, on the basis of suitability (i.e. having a Samaritan-supported Listener Scheme) and type – all prisons were local-type establishments and chosen because of the comparatively high rate of suicide in these establishments (Liebling, 1992; Towl and Crighton, 1998; Towl, 1999b).

A semi-structured questionnaire was distributed to the participants in each of the four groups at each of the five prisons. In order to test the independence of the participants' responses (i.e. to test whether statistically significant differences existed between the groups), Pearson chi-squared tests were conducted. This test examines whether or not the number of positive or negative responses to particular questions differs across the groups or, in other words, whether certain categories within the variables co-occur (or not) with a higher frequency than would be expected by chance.

Results obtained

The following results illustrate a number of significant differences between the groups (particularly with regards to users and non-users of listener schemes) – which, notwithstanding the relatively small sample size, have implications for how such schemes can be improved and developed nationally.

The majority of prisoners in the sample (68 per cent) reported recently experiencing what they perceived to be problems. Not unexpectedly, more of those who had used the listener scheme reported problems (89 per cent, compared with 55 per cent of non-users). The difference between the groups on this issue is statistically significant: x^2 = 9.499, df = 1, p =< 0.01.[34] As illustrated in Table 6.1, there were also significant differences in the range of problems reported: users were more likely to report relationship problems (outside of prison), bullying, difficulties in coming to terms with imprisonment, and concerns over forthcoming court appearances. Further, as predicted, more users reported experiencing feelings of suicide and/or self-injury: 21 per cent compared with 5 per cent of non-users There were no significant differences between the groups with regard to their concerns about release, debt, drug-related problems or problems with other prisoners.

Table 6.1 Range of problems reported for listener scheme help

Problem-type	Non-Users		Users		Level of significance
	No.	per cent	No.	per cent	
Relationships (outside)	10	23 %	15	54 %	p <0.01
Bullying	2	5 %	7	25 %	p < 0.05[35]
Coming to terms with imprisonment/sentence	2	5 %	6	21 %	p <0.05
Court appearance	3	7 %	7	25 %	p <0.05
Drug-related	2	5 %	2	7 %	ns[36]
Debt	2	5 %	1	4 %	ns
Release	3	7 %	1	4 %	ns
Problems with other prisoners	1	2 %	2	7 %	ns

To determine the availability and utilisation of social support networks, participants were asked who, if anyone, they had talked to about their problems. Only a minority of non-users (39 per cent) had talked about their problems, whilst the majority (82 per cent) of users had; this difference is statistically significant (x^2 = 13.117, df = 1, p < 0.001[37]). Although, as a group, non-users were less likely to have discussed their problems, the same proportion of both groups confided in their friends or family outside the prison (non-users, 25 per cent; users, 25 per cent). Proportionally fewer non-users had discussed their problems with friends in prison (21 per cent, compared with 39 per cent of users) or with staff (18 per cent, compared with 32 per cent of users).

It is important to note that over two-thirds of users (68 per cent) sought the support of a listener about their most recent problem(s). Given that more users than non-users speak to friends inside prison about their problems, it could be predicted that they would perceive their peers to be more understanding (than staff) of their problems. Indeed, 92 per cent of users said that they regarded other prisoners to be more understanding (compared with 72 per cent of non-users) – a statistically significant difference (x^2 = 4.094, df = 1, p < 0.05).

Analysis of the views of those who had not used the scheme produced very positive findings. First, the mere frequency with which prisoners sought support from listeners indicates that at least some have found the scheme beneficial. Most had spoken to a listener more than once: 36 per cent had done so once or twice, whilst 62 per cent had spoken to a listener more than three times. Furthermore, a substantial proportion (44 per cent) reported that they always felt better after confiding in a listener, while 52 per cent felt better at least 'sometimes'. Only one respondent (4 per cent) reported that they felt better 'rarely'. Moreover, the vast majority (84 per cent) said that they had always found experience helpful. Few (8 per cent) found it helpful 'sometimes' and a further 8 per cent 'rarely'.

Similarly positive views were expressed regarding the approachability of listeners. The majority (61 per cent) said that could talk to a listener about anything that was worrying them. Equally positive responses were reported regarding listener availability; most (74 per cent) said that they had experienced no problems in contacting a listener when they had requested help, and thus listeners appear to be relatively accessible. Finally, users were asked whether they thought they would seek the help of a listener if they faced a similar problem in the future. That the majority (57 per cent) responded that they were likely to do so suggests that they were satisfied with the support they had received; 21 per cent said that they would possibly seek help from a listener, and 21 per cent reported that it was unlikely.

Overall, these findings suggest that the majority of users of listener schemes were satisfied with the support they received, indicating that listener schemes are beneficial, at least to some. Of equal importance, however, is the issue of why the majority of prisoners do not utilise such support networks. Reported reasons for not using the scheme are as follows: 70 per cent said that they simply prefer to deal with their own problems; 42 per cent said they had confided in someone else; 7 per cent found listeners unapproachable; 5 per cent were unaware of the scheme; and 37 per cent were concerned about the preservation of confidentiality.

Despite confidentiality being fundamental to Samaritan-supported listener schemes, there are very clear concerns about its preservation in practice, to the extent that a significant minority are reluctant to discuss their problems with listeners for this reason. The vast majority of both groups regarded the preservation of confidentiality as being very important. Interestingly, slightly fewer of those who had used the scheme felt it was very important (86 per cent, compared with 95 per cent of non-users). Likewise, 11 per cent of users regarded it as important (compared with 5 per cent of non-users), whilst 4 per cent of users (and no non-users) felt that it is unimportant. Furthermore, there were statistically significant differences between all the groups of participants (including staff and listeners) on their views regarding its preservation in practice ($x^2 = 32.296$, df = 3, p < 0.001). As predicted, the least confident were non-users, 81 per cent of whom did not think listeners kept confidential everything they were told: 46 per cent of users, 52 per cent of staff and 18 per cent of listeners were unsure that, in practice, confidentiality was always preserved. The majority of both groups of prisoners reported that their lack of certainty in the preservation of confidentiality would prevent them from confiding in a listener in the future (74 per cent of non-users, compared with 85 per cent of users). Interestingly, proportionally more users said this would prevent them from using the scheme – although, in practice, most had done so on more than one occasion.

Finally, all participants were asked how they thought the listener scheme could be improved. As illustrated in Table 6.2, a number of differences between the groups exist in their interpretations of problems associated with the scheme and how, therefore, it might be improved. The majority prisoner response was that selection of different individuals to train as listeners would improve the scheme, whilst listeners and staff felt that more information about the scheme was necessary.

Table 6.2 Ways suggested for listener schemes to be improved

Improvement	Non Users		Users		Listeners		Staff		Level of significance
	No.	per cent	No.	per cent	No.	per cent	No.	per cent	
Access	7	16 %	6	21 %	21	53 %	6	19 %	p < 0.01
Listener support	6	14 %	9	32 %	10	25 %	6	19 %	ns
Selection	17	40 %	18	64 %	10	25 %	14	45 %	p < 0.05
Information	6	14 %	9	32 %	25	63 %	16	52 %	p < 0.001

Inferences drawn

The review described above has generated some important findings regarding the availability and utilisation of formalised support networks for prisoners, which have implications for how such schemes can be improved and developed nationally. Unlike previous surveys, this had the advantage of including staff, listeners and prisoners (as both clients and non-clients) across a range of establishments. Notwithstanding any limitations, a number of significant findings emerged concerning differences between those who had used listener schemes and those who had not.

First, there are differences in the frequency and range of problems reported. Those who sought formalised (listener) support were likely to experience what they regarded as problems more frequently than those who do not; more than half of non-users, but almost all users, reported experiencing problems ranging from personal, offence/sentence-related and situational difficulties. Users of the scheme were more likely to report experiencing difficulties with relationships, bullying, coming to terms with their sentence and concerns over forthcoming court appearances. Perhaps unsurprisingly, they were more likely to report having experienced thoughts of suicide, although of concern is that two non-users reported feeling suicidal, neither of whom had discussed their feelings with anyone.

There were also differences between the groups in their respective utilisation of support when faced with problems. Users were more likely (than non-users) to discuss their problems with friends or staff in prison; both groups were equally likely to discuss their problems with family/friends outside prison. That users of the scheme tend to talk to more and to different groups of people implies that they simply prefer discussing their problems with others. Indeed, non-users' reasons for not using the scheme included a preference for managing problems personally and/or confiding in others, although a sizeable proportion reported concerns over the preservation of confidentiality.

Although the majority of non-users and a significant proportion of users reported that their concerns over the preservation of confidentiality would prevent them from confiding in a listener this did not in practice appear to preclude users from utilising the scheme, the majority of whom had done so on more than one occasion. The frequency with which users sought the help of listeners suggests that they were satisfied with the support they received. They felt better after discussing their problems and thought that they would probably utilise the scheme if facing problems in the future. These reactions suggest that they found listeners approachable, accessible, understanding and helpful.

Of further importance was the view of some staff that the scheme encourages prisoners to help and support one another without their intervention. Awarding prisoners the opportunity of resolving problems between themselves may also have an empowering effect. Opinions expressed by staff suggested that listeners provide an extra avenue of support for distressed prisoners, thereby complementing the support already provided for those experiencing difficulties. Staff acknowledged that they might not always have the time or the skills necessary to support those in crisis. As one officer remarked:

> [We] are not routinely trained in counselling skills. It is often difficult, therefore, to counsel prisoners with severe emotional difficulties. Listeners have the time, ability and training to listen to someone's problems – more so, in many cases, than staff. Listeners are therefore a source of reassurance for staff, especially [those] who arouse particular concern.

Although Prison Service policy clearly states that listener schemes should be complementary to, and not a substitute for, the work of staff, this is clearly an area that needs to be kept under supervision when resources are stretched.

Finally, a range of views were received regarding potential areas for improvement to listener schemes and the responses of prisoners (users and non-users) differed from those of staff and listeners. For example, both groups of prisoners said that a fully representative range of listeners was necessary, highlighting the need for careful selection of listeners. Tied in with this was a view expressed by both listeners and staff that increased information about, and access to, listener schemes was vital. For an individual perspective on this latter point, see also 'A Listener's Concerns' (in *Suicide Awareness Bulletin*, No. 2, HM Prison Service, 1999).

The results of my 1998 study indicate that those who seek formalised (listener) support are likely to experience what they regard as problems more frequently than those who do not. A broad range of problems (including personal, offence/sentence-related and situational) were described. That prisoners sought the formalised support offered by listeners is important because of the correlation between recent negative life events/problems and suicidal behaviour/s, both generally and within the prison context, as discussed earlier. Conversely, however, the majority of prisoners do not utilise the support offered by such schemes.

Summary and conclusions

Positive association with one's peers is advantageous to successful adaptation to imprisonment, particularly in the early stages of confinement when other support networks may be unavailable (a suggestion supported by Coid, 1984; Goodstein and Wright, 1989; Biggar, 1996; and Carolissen, 1996). However, as Coid (1984) suggests, social acceptance within the prison context is neither immediate nor equally available to all. Some may be excluded because of the nature of their offence or particular aspects of their personality. Exclusion may enhance a prisoner's vulnerability, which is likely already to be elevated during the early stages of imprisonment (Gunn *et al.*, 1978). It is in such circumstances that alternative support networks (such as listener schemes) may be particularly worthwhile.

As discussed, the relative impact of suicide support and prevention services (such as The Samaritans and listener schemes) is difficult to quantify. Whilst there exists no unequivocal evidence that such help is effective in preventing suicides, the above review suggests that they are effective in reducing distress amongst some. However, the results of the current survey suggest that the vast majority of prisoners (including those who report experiencing problems) do not utilise such support, partly because of concerns over the preservation of confidentiality. The general response was that, although a sound and necessary principle, confidentiality is simply not adhered to by all listeners in all circumstances – a factor that precluded many from sharing their distress. Users, too, expressed concern about the issue, although they continued to use listeners as a source of support (perhaps in the absence of alternative sources). Similarly, a significant proportion of staff expressed scepticism about the preservation of confidentiality. Comments suggested that it was generally felt that, for listeners, preservation of confidentiality can be too great a responsibility (especially following expression of suicidal thoughts, for example); some questioned the support that listeners receive in this regard.

Although a key issue, as demonstrated by the reported surveys, confidentiality (and its preservation) has been the source of much debate. It is fundamental to the successful operation of Samaritan-supported schemes, since it is a central tenet of The Samaritans' philosophy. There is no discretion for an establishment running a Samaritan-supported scheme – which, for the Prison Service, is a rare example of a straightforward, clear-cut issue. However, the concept does not sit easily within such an organisation where confidentiality and privacy are, by definition, normally subservient to security. A core task of the Prison Service is to keep prisoners safely in custody.

The tensions that arise between two organisations with substantially different cultures are brought into sharp relief on this issue. The degree of empowerment to individual listeners, which accrues from confidentiality in Samaritan-supported schemes, is foreign to the expectations of many staff and prisoners. For some it appears out of step with the multidisciplinary approach to suicide prevention with *shared* responsibility.

It is interesting to note that opinions are divided, as has been demonstrated in this chapter. Difficulties associated with total confidentiality can sometimes be blown out of proportion with case scenarios centred on the worst possible case. In reality, such scenarios are likely to be rare; listeners are trained to encourage the client to give their permission to seek help in extreme circumstances. Nonetheless, the concept of confidentiality on this scale is alien to the working of many staff and for some requires a powerful stretch of the imagination to understand its importance. It is worthy of note that many establishments have embraced comfortably the concept of confidentiality and are able to accept it.

It is debatable whether there exists any organisation other than The Samaritans with the skills, experience and capacity to provide the level of support required for listener schemes on this scale. Although the issue of confidentiality is likely to continue to be a source of considerable debate, it is of note that in the last of the surveys reported here, distressed prisoners using the listener scheme continued to do so even where they expressed a lack of confidence that confidentiality would be guaranteed.

A quite different approach to the use of peer-group support can be seen in New York City Department of Corrections, whose overall suicide-prevention strategy is mentioned in Chapter 1 (see also Snow, 2000). There, prisoners are selected, trained and paid as 'Observation Aides' who provide a 24-hour observation-and-support service to prisoners. If they feel a prisoner may be at risk of suicide, they report their concerns to staff. The programme operates within a wholly different approach from strategies in England and Wales and to that extent care needs to be taken in cross-cultural comparisons. The scheme is, however, impressive and is one that features in the recommendation from HMCIP's thematic review (1999).

In conclusion, although formalised peer-group support schemes clearly have an important role to play in providing support for those in crisis, their impact – in terms of actual levels of self-injury or suicide attempts – has not been examined with rigour. Notwithstanding the difficulties in demonstrating any such impact, there is much scope for further research in the area. It would also be of interest to understand more about the actual experience of being a listener, and the influence that this experience has (on, for example, the likelihood of prisoners re-offending). The rapid growth of listener schemes is in itself a degree of testimony to their success – it is very unlikely that they would have been adopted with such enthusiasm were they not responding to an unfulfilled need. The surveys reported here describe a number of positive outcomes.

7

Training staff in suicide awareness

Jo Bailey, Martin McHugh, Lisa Chisnall, and
Danielle Forbes

Overview

In this chapter we outline the stages involved in identifying training needs and developing a staff training programme. The processes are illustrated with reference to the particular issues that arise in suicide awareness training. The chapter concludes with a brief description of some of the current developments and plans for the future.

Defining training

Training is sometimes viewed by organisations as a kind of universal panacea. Where problems of performance arise – whether manifested by knowledge or skill deficits, or by inappropriate behaviour or attitudes – the problem is frequently defined as indicative of a training need. Eagerness both to address and be seen to address the problem can result in premature adoption of a training initiative of dubious benefit to the organisation and maybe even to the individual. Apart from the obvious costs associated with training in terms of time and resources, there is the potentially adverse impact of poor-quality training, which may, at best, have little effect and, at worst, be counterproductive. Some would argue that training that is not evaluated is not training at all, because in the absence of a method of assessing its effectiveness, it is not possible to state whether trainees have in fact been trained.

Above all, training is no substitute for good management. What is often perceived as a 'training need' may in fact be a symptom of ineffective management rather than a training deficiency. These principles apply equally in the area of suicide awareness. It is axiomatic that staff training is an essential requirement in effective delivery of a suicide prevention programme, but it is equally essential that the training is of good quality.

There have been a number of definitions of training. A useful definition is found in Goldstein (1993):

'The systematic acquisition of skills rules concepts or attitudes that result in improved performance is another environment.

(p.3)

The term 'systematic' is important within this definition. Identification of training needs, the most appropriate methods for training delivery, and evaluation of its effectiveness, should be based on a systematic approach.

The above definition views the goal of training as making an impact upon the behaviour exhibited by a trainee in the performance of a job or task. The components of that behaviour have traditionally been classified as Knowledge, Skill and Abilities or KSAs (Prien *et al.*, 1987). *Knowledge* is the foundation upon which abilities and skills are built. (Note that this is a necessary but insufficient ingredient in training; its possession is no guarantee of its use.) *Skill* refers to the ability to do the job with ease and precision. *Ability* usually refers to the level of cognitive capabilities required to perform the job, most often involving the application of a knowledge base. An additional dimension, whose importance should not be overlooked, is the extent to which a trainee is emotionally prepared to perform an assigned task, i.e. who displays appropriate attitudes. This latter point can, of course, have a significant impact on how receptive the trainee is to any training. These distinctions serve to illustrate the range of facets which must be addressed in the training environment.

A framework for training in suicide awareness

Systematic approaches to training usually adopt a framework with the following common elements:

- assessment of training needs;
- training design and delivery;
- transfer and evaluation of training.

For a full and detailed consideration of the issues involved in these stages, the reader is referred to texts such as Goldstein (1993). In this chapter the stages will be illustrated with specific reference to training in suicide awareness.

Assessment of training needs

Identifying the training needs of staff in suicide awareness presents particular challenges. The starting point of a needs analysis is the task and job analysis, i.e. what is it that staff do? Note that this may not be the same as the job description. Relating that question to what staff have to do in suicide awareness and suicide reduction in the prison setting, it quickly becomes apparent that the specific tasks, dictating training needs, will vary according to the particular roles played by differing grades and specialties of staff. Front-line staff have a wide-ranging job to perform in the direct day-to-day supervision of prisoners; specialist staff have specific roles to play in a more limited context; and managers have specific roles to play in monitoring, supervising and supporting staff.

Although roles differ, there is a need for common agreement and understanding on the principles underlying the nature of suicide and self-injury in prisons, and how it can be handled most effectively. The more straightforward element is familiarisation with the process, i.e. the procedures that have been devised to identify prisoners at risk and to provide adequate management. The more difficult part is raising the level of understanding about the nature of suicide and self-injury, and deciding what is achievable. This difficulty arises in part from the differing range of experiences that individual staff and prisoners bring to the topic. Morgan *et al.* (1998) stress the importance of professionals' views on suicide and clients' levels of responsibility. Personal experience from friends and relatives, previous experience of suicides and self-injury in prisons, religious beliefs, and many other factors can affect powerfully how staff approach suicide prevention. One outcome of this may be erroneously held beliefs which find fruition in widely held myths. Challenging myths must be a primary aim of staff training.

To the authors' knowledge, the Prison Service has never conducted a full-scale and formal training needs analysis in suicide awareness – or at least certainly not in recent years. What has been accumulated, however, is a large body of experience through formal and informal consultation with staff and prisoners, dialogue with other agencies, and evidence from independent reviews and inspections, which has provided an informed understanding of the issues that concern staff in carrying out work in this sensitive area. Informal assessment highlights the following core issues as training needs:

- a clear understanding of the procedures for the management of suicide and/or self-injury;
- an understanding of risk indicators;
- a sense of ownership of the problem;

- an understanding of what options are available to support prisoners in crisis;
- staff confidence in their ability to make a positive impact;
- staff confidence that they will be supported through line management.

This list covers a range of KSAs and attitudes. It reflects the understandable anxieties that are associated with work in an area that carries much risk and responsibility. The first point on the above list is worthy of expansion. It is vital that staff are trained in the appropriate use of standard procedures. To an external observer, the emphasis on process may appear excessive. However, used appropriately, procedures are an effective tool that will assist in building up staff confidence by allowing an audit trail indicating the quality of care delivered.

A further issue to be addressed in the needs analysis is the definition of 'staff'. In the prison setting a distinction can be made between staff who have regular day-to-day contact with prisoners and those in administrative roles with less, or minimal, contact. There is a strong argument for provision of common training to all staff, irrespective of their role, as a means of emphasising the importance attached to the task, and also because this approach highlights the contribution that all may play and of which some staff may be unaware. To take but one example, a switchboard operator handling calls from concerned relatives may benefit from an understanding of how information coming in will be acted upon.

Training design and delivery

Identification of the training needs informs the next stage of the staff-training process: definition of the aims and objectives of the programme. It is recommended good practice for the objectives to be as specific (and measurable) as possible.

In designing a training programme, key issues are efficacy and practicality. There is usually a tension between the ideal and the achievable. There is a danger in being too focused on the practicalities at the outset, and this can result in restrictive and unambitious thinking. On the other hand, ignoring the realities of what is deliverable will result in a programme that may fail at the implementation stage.

The shape of the training programme needs to reflect the KSAs identified in the needs analysis. Each element lends itself to a different type of training approach. Knowledge can be developed by attendance at lectures and reading. Skills may be developed by a range of methods – trial and error, or imitation, for example – but one key feature of good-quality skills training is the opportunity to practise with constructive feedback on student performance. The level of skill possessed will depend upon experience and practice in performing that skill, whether the skill be mental, physical or social. Attitudes affect the successful performance of tasks – an individual may, for instance, possess the necessary knowledge and skill, but not perform the task adequately because of an inappropriate attitude.

This is one of the most potentially challenging aspects for training, but there are broadly two paths open to the trainer. First, to provide information or *knowledge* as to why the desired attitudes are important for acceptable performance. Secondly, to develop *skills* to encourage a particular way of reacting to a situation. Hence, modifying attitudes is closely associated with the development of knowledge and skills.

An important factor to be considered is level of prescription within the curriculum. Suicide awareness as a topic well illustrates the dilemma. A common baseline set of knowledge can be prescribed as an achievable target, for instance covering information about suicide and self-injury and current procedures for management. However, in training on the skills involved in providing adequate care for those identified at risk, there may be a range of options tailored specifically according to the type of establishment. Good practice in management develops with experience; furthermore, some issues will be of greater concern in one type of prison – for example, repeated self-injury may be a more salient management problem in one prison than risk of fatality. An overprescriptive curriculum will be too restricted and stifling; clearly, a balance is required which permits flexibility whilst ensuring that core issues are covered.

Design and delivery of training go hand in hand. In deciding the most appropriate format for delivery there are a number of considerations. Style of presentation should be influenced by the range of KSAs to be covered in the programme. One important distinction is the use of a Socratic versus didactic approach, the former emphasising a less formal and participative approach drawing from within the audience, and the latter focusing more on a 'chalk and talk' approach where knowledge is imparted to the audience. Both approaches have advantages and disadvantages.

The benefits of the formal didactic approach lie mainly in the ability to put over a large amount of information in a relatively short time, to a large number of people. Formal sessions appear the most cost-effective method of training staff in terms of time and numbers. A disadvantage is that this approach encourages passivity and reduces the opportunity for participants to develop rapport and support networks, both of which may be an important aid to learning.

The participative approach aims to draw the material from the participants and is therefore a more active form of learning. There are various advantages in using this style. It encourages active participation, allowing the tutor more flexibility in pitching the level to suit the audience, and it enables teaching points to be generated from within the group that may aid credibility and acceptability. A further advantage is the opportunity this approach allows for the tutor to tune into the levels of understanding of individuals within the group and thus to adjust the training plan accordingly.

In many training settings tutors will use a combination of both approaches within a session, depending upon the nature of the material and the objectives. However, it is worth reflecting on the most appropriate methods of delivery for suicide awareness issues given the nature of the subject. We have already referred to the anxieties which surround this area of work and the need for staff confidence to be built up. From that perspective, an interactive approach with an emphasis on discussion and the sharing of information and ideas would appear sensible.

A variety of different methods and techniques can be employed to deliver the training – for example, main group discussions, subgroup discussions, brainstorming sessions, chart lists, role-plays and demonstrations. Small-group training is the basic unit for participative training. There are a number of advantages to employing small-group working in training. For example, it is relatively easy to involve everyone and participation may be less threatening than in a large group; participants are afforded the opportunity to learn from each other; small groups are flexible and allow the trainer to restructure to enhance learning; and individual needs can be more readily recognised. Small groups lend themselves to skills-based training.

Many individuals may experience some anxiety at working with those who self-harm or who contemplate suicide. Skills-based training aims to develop skills and confidence to combat such concern, in addition to working on attitudes. Ideally, staff would all receive training in basic counselling skills, with a particular emphasis on various areas of concern, such as suicide and self-harm. However, training time is limited and suicide training can aim to address skills deficits. The most common method of imparting skills is through demonstration. It is generally acknowledged that demonstrations of good practice have most value; bad practice models may serve to illustrate points dramatically but there is a danger that they may overshadow the good model. Course members ideally need to practise the appropriate skill until they reach the standard identified by the teaching points. Various organisational constraints may limit the amount of practice available; however, limited practice is better than nothing as it serves to reinforce the teaching points and help clear up issues for both the person practising the skill and those observing.

Other commonly used methods include discussion. The reason for using a discussion will depend upon whether the aim is to develop knowledge or modify attitude. Where knowledge is the aim, discussion can be used before or after an input with different effect. Used beforehand, discussion can motivate participants by encouraging active participation rather than passive listening, prepare participants for new information by relating it to current knowledge, and to test existing knowledge to aid the trainer in pitching the level of the input. Discussion following the input can serve to clarify points and reinforce learning by encouraging active processing of the information.

Where the aim is to modify attitudes, discussion can be used by the trainer to test the attitudes and feelings on a subject, encourage reflection and questioning of such attitudes, and hence attempt to modify attitudes. A skilled trainer is required to manage sessions sensitively where the content may be emotive, such as suicide awareness. But modifying attitudes via discussion depends upon a range of issues – for example, how entrenched the attitudes are, how much the attitudes affect the participants' behaviour, whether attitudes are based on fact or prejudice, and the credibility of the trainer.

Hence, the advantages of informal sessions are the increased group participation, the opportunity to identify and assess individuals' performance, a better chance of 'pitching' the training at the correct level and the possibility of matching the pace and mood of the group. However, there are a number of disadvantages to informal sessions. Tutors require experience and skills, for example to maintain control over the material and the timing, and in steering group contributions to the desired outcome. A good range of groupwork skills, in addition to basic presentational skills, is necessary for effective informal sessions. Informal sessions require smaller-sized groups, or additional tutors if subgroups are used for skills-based sessions. They are therefore not as 'cost-effective' in training large numbers of people, although the long-term benefit in quality may compensate.

A final, but crucial point on training delivery concerns the quality of the trainers. It is manifest from the preceding discussion that, in our specific context, the subject matter of suicide awareness requires particular sensitivity. The core tutoring skills are common to those required to train in any subject, but it is unlikely that an individual forced into the training role against his or her will would have either the credibility or the motivation needed to inspire confidence in an audience. It is a subject that is much more than nuts and bolts; it needs trainers who are committed to the subject, who are confident, and who can inject some feeling and passion into the training sessions. It is not unusual for individuals who have had personal experience of the subject matter to volunteer to be trainers.

Transfer and evaluation of training

A common problem in training is ensuring that the results of the training are transferable into the working environment (Cutler *et al.*, 1997). If they are not, then the value of the training is severely limited, although there may still be benefits accruing from the training, such as a political or organisational imperative to demonstrate that training has been delivered, or the networking and time-out opportunities it has afforded the participants.

There may be a number of impediments to the transfer of learning. Common factors are:

- **Peer-group influence.** Highly trained and motivated staff may find themselves under heavy peer-group pressure that is resistant to change. This experience is often encountered by new staff. It is part of the paternalistic approach that adopts a rather patronising approach to training and the outside world, considering all such approaches as inferior, and largely irrelevant, to local ways of working.

- **Cultural factors.** The peer-group pressure may be part of a whole culture that is resistant to change and that will view any new ways of thinking with suspicion. Thus the trained member of staff may find large obstacles placed in the way of implementation of training modules.

- **Inadequate line-management support.** Circumstances may arise that hinder the opportunity for practice and development of skills learned.

These points demonstrate the importance of training being placed within a developmental role rather than in the kind of ad-hoc style that sometimes results from the need for training quotas to be achieved. It also demonstrates the crucial contribution that line managers have to make in ensuring that opportunities are made for investments in training to be put into practice.

The transfer of training can be assisted if the training programme has been developed around practical objectives that have both strong face validity and content validity for the trainees. Choice of materials has a part to play – for example, ensuring that where case studies are used in exercises, they are credible and realistic.

Evaluation of training is essential as well and, as mentioned earlier, it can be argued that training without any evaluation is wholly redundant since it cannot be ruled out that the training is having a negative effect over the desired outcome. It is slightly puzzling that rigorous evaluation of training is rarely conducted by organisations. Part of the problem is that rigorous evaluation of training is complex and expensive; but also it is probably true that many organisations can ill afford to handle the consequences of discovery that their training programmes do not work.

According to Goldstein:

> Evaluation is the systematic collection of descriptive and judgemental information necessary to make effective training decisions related to the selection, adoption, value, and modification of various instructional activities. (1993: 147)

One of the difficulties in measuring the effectiveness of training is in identifying reliable outcome measures. This can be illustrated in suicide awareness training. Although the ultimate goal of an effective suicide-prevention strategy is to prevent suicides, it would be surprising if a *direct* link could be established between staff training and reduced numbers of suicides as an outcome. This is partly because suicide is such a rare event, but also because there will be many other factors between the start and end of training that could have impacted on the likelihood of suicides occurring. Levels of self-injury offer more potential as an outcome measure. Outcome measures can be examined at a number of different levels: reactions and opinions about the training programme; evidence of learning, for instance increased knowledge; evidence of behavioural change, such as an improved quality of work within the suicide awareness strategy; and, finally, results – the ultimate impact of change on numbers of incidents of self-injury.

'Validity' is a central concept in the evaluation of training. There are two aspects: internal validity and external validity. Internal validity concerns the extent to which the training programme has changed behaviour in the desired direction. External validity concerns the extent to which the training outcomes have generalised to the work setting.

Evaluation of training programmes therefore poses significant challenges. Often, it is overlooked and included as an afterthought; in contrast, good practice would be to identify and build in the evaluation strategy at the training design-and-delivery stage. This significantly increases the likelihood that evaluation can and will be carried out in as systematic a manner as possible. A full-scale evaluation of the impact of an suicide-awareness staff-training programme has yet to be undertaken within the Prison Service. From an ethical perspective there would be some difficulties in conducting a carefully controlled experiment requiring various treatments where staff were randomly allocated to training versus no training conditions. It is clear, however, that a better understanding of the impact of staff training in this area is needed.

HM Prison Service training programmes

When the suicide awareness strategy was revised in the early 1990s a comprehensive training programme was devised on a modular basis with six modules consisting of: (a) foundation on basic issues; (b) identifying stress and despair in custody; (c) listening and supporting; (d) management of prisoners at inflated risk of suicide; (e) appearing at an inquest; and (f) suicide awareness for prisoners. Most of the modules required around two-and-a-quarter hours for delivery. It was not intended that all staff would require training in all of the modules; they are geared towards the particular roles that staff have to play.

In practice, it has proved difficult for the training programme to be fully implemented. During 1994 and 1995 a number of major training initiatives had to be completed and each was competing for limited and stretched training time. The reality was that most trainers found themselves forced to adapt the suicide awareness module into a manageable chunk that could be delivered within the constraints of a single session but that retained the core concepts and philosophy. A good example of an evaluation of a modified version of the modules is outlined by Cutler *et al.* (1997). While modifying the national pack to meet local needs, Cutler and colleagues described their primary aim as to cover the key teaching points identified in the manual, while acknowledging the need to convince staff of the validity of the research that formed the rationale of the new policy. A number of different training methods were used to put across the learning points, including brainstorms, discussion and formal input. The training was evaluated using a 'before' and 'after' questionnaire which aimed to assess knowledge and knowledge/attitude through weighted questions. The results of the evaluation indicated a statistically significant improvement between the before and after scores on both the knowledge and knowledge/attitude weighted questions. Cutler *et al.* concluded that the training was effective in terms of improving the reported attitudes and knowledge of the staff trained.

Since 1994 there have been a number of developments in staff training, including: revision of suicide awareness training for new-entrant prison officers and new reception officers; inclusion of suicide awareness training in managerial training on accelerated promotion schemes; and a re-examination of the basic modular programme to produce a common core module that is deliverable. The years 2000 and 2001 will see the implementation of this revised core module, which is based around an interactive style of presentation, consisting of group discussions aided by a quiz, and focusing on a case-study approach aimed at illustrating examples of good-quality care and management practice. Another new development during the period will be the introduction of special training for managers in prisons who have lead responsibility for delivery of suicide awareness programmes locally.

A major goal within this context must be to ensure that training does not become too heavily focused upon process and procedure. This was a criticism that was raised by HM Chief Inspector of Prisons in the thematic review *Suicide is Everyone's Concern* (1999). It was recommended that staff be given more training on skills to increase their confidence to approach prisoners they believed to be at heightened risk of suicide. The new core module has been developed to address this point.

The differing needs of establishments

A particular problem faced by the Prison Service is the range of differing needs presented by what are, arguably, quite different populations across the age ranges and gender. This was an issue that HMCIP raised (1999) in the context of implications for staff training. The following recommendations and observations were made:

- **Local prisons (paragraph 6.16):**
  There should be much better training for all local prison staff in recognizing and responding to vulnerable prisoners.
- **Women's prisons (paragraph 5.18):**
  An increased understanding of the impact of abuse, a knowledge of how to help and the limits of work in a prison setting, active support for and the maintenance of self-help groups and information sources of specialist help are all essential for staff.
  Distressed women will often mutilate themselves. Staff need to know this and understand both the self-loathing which often stems from the experience of abuse and the powerlessness which can lead to the use of self-mutilation as a way of coping with and experiencing distress. Deliberate self-mutilation and eating disorders are specific examples. Staff need to be prepared for this and encouraged to help women find more acceptable ways to seek help and express distress.
- **Young Offenders' Institutions (paragraph 5.17):**
  Understand suicidal behaviour in the context of adolescent risk taking, the early onset of mental health problems, the experience of loss and poor coping.
  Understand and manage the impact of work with disturbed and disturbing young people.
  Be someone to talk to and someone who can seek specialist help when needed.

This point in the discussion is perhaps an appropriate place to raise the notion that although there will always be a role for specific training in suicide awareness, there is a considerable overlap into other areas of custodial care, e.g. mental-health issues, and strategies for reducing bullying. In fact there are some dangers in treating the topic of suicide awareness in isolation. Some very productive co-operative work has been conducted between the Prison Service and the Trust for The Study of Adolescence in the developments and production of staff-training manuals focusing on working with adolescent offenders and women prisoners.

An example of tailoring training to the needs of an establishment

The following example describes the development of a training package for staff working with women prisoners. This was felt to be a priority issue in view of the high prevalence of self-injury within women's prisons, and the attention rightly paid to this area by HM Chief Inspector of Prisons (1999).

Despite the training given to new entrant officers, many staff lack the relevant knowledge and adequate skills to work effectively with prisoners who self-injure or contemplate suicide. Lack of relevant training can be damaging to both the staff and the prisoners concerned. Lack of knowledge may also contribute to staff feeling disempowered and under pressure. Such feelings may then impact negatively upon the prisons in their care, and also upon the staff in terms of attendance at work. Letters published by 'SHOUT' (undated) indicate that the reaction and attitudes of others when faced with self-harm have an extreme impact upon the individual engaging in self-injurious behaviour. Arnold (1995) found that 'women who self-injure found a high level of dissatisfaction in services, apart from counselling/psychotherapy' and that 'most women's distress and dissatisfaction with the services was caused by negative or dismissive attitudes whether this was expressed in terms of condemnation, disinterest or failure to provide any real help'.

A training package developed by Arnold (1997) aims 'to increase understanding of self-injury amongst the public and professionals'. The pack was developed as a result of extensive work with women who self-injure and is aimed at trainers working in a variety of settings. This pack has been adapted for implementation within a women's prison (Chisnall, 1999).

The aims of the training pack are listed below. They are presented as flexible in their importance, depending upon the working context.

- to develop participants' knowledge and understanding of self-injury, its nature and reasons for it;
- to identify some of the important issues arising in working with people who self-injure and to consider ways of dealing with these issues;
- to explore the needs of clients who self-injure;
- to assess the value of various professional approaches to self-injury;
- to provide the opportunity for course members to reflect on their own practice (and that of agencies) in working with clients who self-injure;
- to develop participants' skills, resources and confidence in responding helpfully to those who self-injure;
- to explore the impact on workers of supporting people who self-injure, identifying workers' own needs for supervision, support etc. and looking at ways of ensuring these needs are met;
- to provide an opportunity for sharing of experience, knowledge and views.

The package is flexible, with helpful module plans and training notes. The predominant learning method is through informal sessions. Hence techniques such as activities, brainstorming, card games, subgroup working and role plays are used to encourage participation and active learning. The package makes no assumptions about trainers' knowledge of group members. The detail provided serves to empower trainers and ensure consistency in delivery. This would appear essential when dealing with an emotive subject area such as that under consideration in this chapter, where many individuals will already have their own opinions regarding self-injury and suicidal behaviour.

One aspect of the package that may be seen as a strength in some settings, but that does not sit easily within the Prison Service philosophy, is the concept of an individual's *right* to self-injure. Although not formally stated within any instruction or guidance, there is an implicit assumption within the prison culture that all self-injury is negative, which leads to an attitude of zero tolerance. The validity of this approach is the subject of debate. The concept of 'right to self-injure' is reinforced in the package by the emphasis on self-injury as a coping mechanism or as a means of survival from the difficult experiences of individuals.

Through the establishment of a working group within a women's prison, the Arnold package was adapted so as to produce the following outline. Each module contains a range of learning methods to put the material across, based upon the aims of each session and the teaching points identified.

- **Module One**: What is self-injury? Why do people self-injure?
- **Module Two**: What issues does self-injury raise for prison staff? What are the staff's own needs?
- **Module Three:** What are the needs of prisoners who self-injure?
- **Module Four**: Approaches to self-injury.
- **Module Five**: Exploring the alternative to self-injury within the prison setting.
- **Module Six**: Skills development.

Evaluation of this training package is based on before-and-after questionnaires, the procedure being supported by monitoring of the quality of care inputs as indicated in case records (F2052SH documents) following a suggestion made by Cutler *et al.* (1997). The aim is to assess whether any changes in attitude and knowledge are being translated into behaviour and reflected in working practices.

Summary and conclusions

This chapter has reviewed the main considerations in developing and implementing an effective suicide-awareness training programme for staff. A general consensus supports the view that adequate staff training is a vital underpinning for a suicide prevention strategy. There is less consensus over the scope of the curriculum, but some common core issues have been identified – notably the need to build staff confidence in working in such a sensitive area.

Training has been defined in this chapter from a formal perspective. The less formal methods of reinforcing messages through information provided at the working level and good-quality supervision and management must not be overlooked. Nor should the need for refresher training be ignored. The key challenge for the Prison Service in this area is to undertake more systematic delivery and evaluation of training in order to maximise its effectiveness.

8

The aftermath of a death in prison custody

Louisa Snow and Martin McHugh

Overview

In this chapter we examine the largely unexplored area of the impact of a death in prison custody on the different groups who are likely to be affected, namely family and friends, other prisoners, and staff. Also, although every establishment consists of a collection of staff and prisoners, each of whom may be affected in her or his own way, there is a sense in which the prison as a whole, as a community, is affected.

There are a number of reasons for devoting a chapter to this topic. First, it is necessary to acknowledge that even the most effective suicide prevention and healthcare programmes cannot guarantee the elimination of all deaths. Sadly, it is probable that some deaths are not preventable (McHugh and Towl, 1997); some people will be determined to end their lives, some may die by accident, and some may die by natural causes. Secondly, it can be argued that the experience of death generally, and suicide in particular, deeply affects how individuals – both staff and prisoners – approach the task of suicide prevention. Thirdly, it is a fundamental requirement of the Prison Service duty of care to handle the aftermath of a death with professionalism and sensitivity, as reflected in the Prison Service Vision and Objective: 'to protect the public by holding those committed by the courts in a safe, decent and healthy environment'.

There are four main elements to the chapter. Initial attention is on the wider context of bereavement and on the differences that may be experienced following a death by suicide. A brief overview of the purposes of the inquest procedure follows, before considering the impact of a death in custody from differing perspectives. Next the key responsibilities of the Prison Service in the aftermath of a death in custody are outlined. Finally, a brief exploration of future developments in the area is provided. The chapter is largely reflective, drawing upon the authors' experiences of work within the Suicide Awareness Support Unit at Prison Service Headquarters since April 1994, during which time there have been over 400 self-inflicted deaths and around 300 deaths from natural causes.

Although the discussion is largely restricted to the impact of self-inflicted deaths, we acknowledge that this is a somewhat arbitrary distinction. Any sudden, violent or unexpected death (in prison custody or elsewhere) may have similar consequences for those immediately affected, whether it be from natural or non-natural causes, such as suicide or homicide. Whilst the latter is a rare event in prisons in England and Wales, its impact is profound. The focus on self-inflicted deaths is not to deny or attempt to minimise the impact that other types of deaths have on relatives and friends; it simply reflects the main focus of this book. Much of what is discussed here will have resonance with deaths in prison custody under *any* circumstances. A powerful and personal account of the impact of a homicide on a family has been written by Paul and Audrey Edwards (in Liebling, 1998).

Death and bereavement in context

Before examining the impact of a self-inflicted death, it is worth considering the wider context of death and bereavement – issues that have, in recent years, been the subject of a great deal of inquiry, and while much has been of a largely descriptive nature, many common threads have emerged. A brief overview of commonly experienced feelings and reactions to death is presented; the main terms to be discussed are clarified; and an introduction to the social and historical context of death and bereavement is provided.

Hauser (1987) describes bereavement as encompassing complex psychological, behavioural, social and physiological patterns that are displayed by an individual following significant loss (usually through death) and as having two main components: grief and mourning. Grief refers to the feelings and emotional responses following death, whilst mourning refers to the social customs, rituals and ceremonies that assist the bereaved in their grieving by enabling the expression of thoughts, feelings and memories related to loss (Hauser, 1987: 58).

Although highly individual in character, responses to dying, i.e. grief and bereavement, appear to some extent to be historically and socially specific, in the sense that there are distinct differences in reactions in different cultures and in different periods. Seale (1998), in his analysis of varying responses to death, charts some of these changes, suggesting that a universal fear of death led to the modern tendency to deny the existence of death or, at the very least, to keep it hidden by, for example, hospitalisation and institutionalisation. Further, an associated reluctance to talk about death and dying and a decline in the extent of ritual and ceremony following death has occurred. These factors, suggests Seale, contributed to the exclusion and abandonment of the dying and bereaved and a consequent heightening of their loneliness, which did not exist in previous historical periods. Similarly, Walter (1994) suggests that with the advent of the 'modern' death, communal rituals were replaced by the introduction of privacy for the dying and bereaved and that the previous influence of the church was replaced by the medicalisation of death and dying. The reduced death rate, the hospitalisation of death and the fact that the dying and bereaved continually kept their pain to themselves resulted in the banishment of death as an explicit feature of everyday life (p. 185).

Since the 1960s, there appears to have been a shift in attitudes towards death and the dying, taking Western culture towards what may be termed a more 'humanist' approach that is defined by Walter as 'neo-modern'. This is most strongly evident in the recent upsurge of academic interest and literature on the subject, which has coincided with the growth of the hospice movement and the development of counselling and communicational expertise in relation to dying and bereavement; emphasis is upon the emotional, psychological, private and personal meaning of death. Walter regards the development of the hospice movement as being highly important in this regard – as is the work of Kubler-Ross (1970), who actively promoted the rights of the dying and their need to talk openly about their feelings. Thus, it may be suggested that bereavement has recently gained legitimacy as an experience and grief has become a more socially acceptable response following the death of a loved-one.

Although bereavement itself may be more socially acceptable than formerly, it does not necessarily follow that this is the case in all circumstances – bereavement following death by suicide being a case in point. Responses and reactions to suicide are rather more complex since suicide disrupts what is socially acceptable. Thus, it is important to point out that different responses to death and others' treatment of the bereaved are likely following death in different circumstances. For example, responses to foreseen death (perhaps after a long illness or of an elderly person) are likely to differ from reactions to an untimely or sudden death of a young person (by suicide, for example); similarly, reactions to and treatment of the bereaved are likely to depend, to some extent, on the circumstances of the death. These issues will be discussed in greater detail, following an overview of what are understood to be typical reactions to death.

The bereavement process

Although, as acknowledged above, bereavement is profoundly personal, the emotional, psychological, physical and behavioural responses that follow the death of a loved-one share similarities from one person to another, to the extent that there exist common patterns whose features are distinguishable and that may be broadly termed 'normal' bereavement.

Hauser (1987) describes bereavement as a homeostatic process, namely one that allows us to overcome the loss experienced following the death of a loved-one, widely acknowledged as one of life's greatest stresses (Holmes and Rahe, 1967), enabling us to 'recoil, react, adjust to the loss, and then continue on with life' (p. 57). Similarly, Bowlby and Parkes (1970) and Parkes (1972) understand bereavement as a staged process (comprising various psychological and physiological aspects), beginning with initial responses to the trauma (usually numbness or shock) and ending with reorganisation and recovery. Parkes (1970) suggests that although each stage of the process has its own characteristics and duration (which vary from person to person), bereavement generally takes between 18 and 30 months to traverse.

While the concept of stages provides a useful framework for our understanding of the complicated and often chaotic processes of bereavement, it should be acknowledged that, in reality, one's experiences may be more complex than is implied by such models (Wertheimer, 1991). For example, the phases of grieving may be indistinct – individuals may not pass neatly from one stage to the next. Indeed, such a criticism is recognised by Parkes (1972), who states that instead of understanding bereavement as a 'set of symptoms which start after a loss then gradually fade away', it should be regarded as 'a succession of ... pictures which blend into and replace one another' (p. 27). The advantage of such models is that they enable us to focus on key aspects of bereavement reactions. For this reason, the models mentioned above are briefly outlined.

The first stage of bereavement in Parkes's model is distinguished by various physical, behavioural and psychological aspects, most characteristically feelings of numbness, disbelief or shock. These are aspects that, suggest Parkes, protect the individual against overwhelming feelings. During this stage, extreme distress may break through the numbness or the bereaved may feel physically ill. Even in cases where the individual's death is accompanied by feelings of relief, numbness and difficulty in accepting its occurrence are common.

That first stage is superseded by a period of 'separation anxiety' or pining, defined by Parkes as a 'persistent and obtrusive wish for the person who is gone, a preoccupation with thoughts that can only give pain ... the subjective and emotional component of the urge to search for a lost object' (p. 61). Behavioural reactions include alarm, tension, restlessness and a preoccupation with thoughts of the deceased person.

According to Parkes, feelings of 'disorganisation and despair' succeed the 'pining' phase. In contrast to the feelings of anger and guilt experienced during earlier phases, feelings of apathy and despair are likely once the intense pangs of grief are past their peak. Finally, once these stages have been surpassed, healing and recovery begins. As with other stages, recovery occurs at different times for different people: there is no finite period after which an individual will automatically pick up the threads of normal living (Wertheimer, 1991).

Bowlby and Parkes (1970) provided a very similar explanation of the bereavement process, describing it as a series of four phases ranging from shock to 'reorganisation' or, in other words, acceptance and recovery (a useful summary is provided by Hauser, 1987). Like Parkes (1972), Bowlby and Parkes suggest that the initial reaction – shock – is characterised by feelings of numbness and disbelief, feelings that may protect a person from the full impact of death. Typically, this phase lasts for about seven days and is superseded by a phase of 'yearning' or 'protest', during which the full impact of the loss may become manifest; intense yearning, anxiety, tearfulness and sobbing are common during this phase, which, typically, peaks between two and four weeks after death but can continue for several months. The third stage, 'disorganisation', is characterised by feelings of apathy, emptiness, aimlessness and preoccupation with the deceased. The final stage, 'reorganisation', which typically occurs around a year after death, is characterised by a relinquishing of the past and the rebuilding of life with an altered self-image and different social networks. The final step in the process of recovery is acceptance of the finality of death and recognition of the fact that the deceased person will not be seen again; inevitably when the bereaved person has lost their spouse or partner, this may involve significant life-style adjustment and reorganisation.

As Hauser (1987) suggests, what has been termed the 'normal' bereavement process is affected by a number of different factors including the biological, psychological and social characteristics of those involved, the nature of the relationship between the deceased and bereaved and the sources of support available to them. As mentioned above, of particular importance are the circumstances of an individual's death – sudden, unexpected, violent or traumatic deaths, for example, may be more difficult to overcome. In addition, absence of the ritual and ceremony of mourning can affect a bereaved person's recovery. And if an individual feels in any way responsible for another's death, bereavement itself may be hindered. Moreover, the age of the deceased may be an important factor, for it is widely understood that the death of a child is more stressful than the death of an older person (Hauser, 1987).

Even though any of the preceding factors can affect subsequent adjustment and reorganisation, death by suicide is especially significant (Hauser, 1987). The distinctive characteristics of bereavement following suicide (when compared with bereavement following other types of death) are the focus of the following section.

Bereavement following suicide

It is widely acknowledged that bereavement following suicide differs from that following other types of death, both qualitatively and quantitatively, in the sense that those who experience the loss of a loved-one by self-inflicted means face additional stresses and what is commonly termed the 'normal' bereavement process is hindered (Wertheimer, 1991). As Stillion and McDowell (1996) suggest, there are numerous studies that support this premise (see, for example, Wertheimer, 1991; Dunn and Morrish-Vinders, 1987; and Hauser, 1987), to the extent that the term 'survivors of suicide' has been coined to highlight the specific experiences of those bereaved by suicide (McIntosh, 1987).

Suicide brings a number of extra dimensions to the 'normal' bereavement process – dimensions that affect the experience itself and that may prolong and protract the process. Although there will be some commonality with bereavement following death under other circumstances, certain aspects are unique, although they may be similar to other types of violent or unexpected deaths (for example, homicide). The key difference for those who have experienced a loss through suicide is that, in addition to the feelings of sorrow and loneliness common to all types of grief, intensified feelings of guilt, shame, abandonment and anger may be experienced. Moreover, in common with other types of unexpected deaths, there are rarely opportunities to say goodbye or resolve any outstanding issues; thus, the unexpected nature of suicide can affect one's reactions to it. That death by suicide often involves violent means adds a further dimension (Hauser, 1987). Most importantly, however, survivors of suicide must face the fact that the death may have been the result of a deliberate and conscious act (Wertheimer, 1991: 17). This in itself places death by suicide in a quite distinct category.

As indicated above, shock, incredulity, denial and disbelief are common responses in the early stages of the grieving process. However, when a person has consciously chosen to end their life, the 'normal' feelings of the bereaved are likely to be intensified and prolonged. Because suicide is invariably sudden, usually unexpected or untimely, and often violent, relatives or loved-ones are unlikely to have had time to prepare (either psychologically or practically) for the death, for there has been no warning and no prior anticipation. All such factors are likely to influence initial and subsequent responses to the death and may prolong the bereaved's eventual recovery from it. Such feelings are likely to be further magnified when an individual has died away from home (for example, if abroad or in custody) and when the news of the death is delivered by strangers (for example, by police officers or prison staff). These particular factors are discussed in more detail in the following section.

Another common response is blame – whether directed toward the self or others. In the search for an explanation for the death (which may not be immediately apparent), family and friends may search for a scapegoat as a focus of blame. Illich (1976) suggests that, rather than regarding death as the natural and inevitable end to life, some seek to attach blame and responsibility to something or someone, out of a widespread belief that death is somehow avoidable; this response may be intensified when the death is self-inflicted. Culpability following death is a very complex area and is clearly open to contextual differences and social expectations. A critical issue is the extent to which individuals are viewed as having control over their destiny and/or are influenced by others. For example, if a young person in the wider community has taken their life and there is a suggestion that they may have been a victim of bullying, there is understandable concern. In custody – by definition an environment in which individuals have restricted influence over their lives – feelings of anger and a need to seek culpability are likely to be intensified.

The search for blame may be accompanied by feelings of anger: toward the person who took their life because of the implied rejection; towards a God, a higher being or the world generally for allowing it to happen; toward any professionals involved; toward friends for not being as supportive as perhaps they could; and toward the self for not having been able to prevent the act. Similarly, Dunn and Morrish-Vinders (1987) suggest that, in addition to the feelings of shock and disbelief that are common following most types of death, survivors of suicide experience feelings of fear and anger and a need to discuss the death with others – a need often impeded by a general reluctance of those involved to do so. Again, these feelings may be heightened if the death occurs in custody.

Guilt is an emotional response that features in all types of bereavement, although it may be magnified (in intensity and duration) following death by suicide (Hauser, 1987; Sheskin and Wallace, 1976). Relatives and friends may question whether they personally could have acted differently to prevent the death, or they may scrutinise the extent to which they have in some way been responsible. Cain and Fast (1972) suggest that because suicide is such a deliberate, intentional act the degree of guilt experienced by survivors is heightened. As

Wertheimer suggests (1991), guilt can take on many forms and depends very much upon the circumstances of the individual's death. If the death was sudden and unexpected, for example, survivors may berate themselves for not noticing something was wrong. Even if the suicide was a foreseen possibility, survivors may blame themselves for not being available to provide crisis support. Thus, deep self-scrutiny is a natural response; a search of the extent to which one's own behaviour may have been a contributory factor in the reasons for the death is not uncommon.

It has been suggested that relief is a response that sometimes follows suicide. This reaction may occur in cases where individuals were known to have been suffering for some time, similar to the way in which one may experience relief after the death of someone with a prolonged illness. After a suicide, there may be a reluctance to admit to such feelings because of the feelings of guilt that survivors may be experiencing.

Wertheimer (1991) suggests that survivors of suicide may become stuck in an endless and fruitless search for the definitive answer as to why the suicide occurred; or they may decide that they were responsible for the death. As discussed above, it is widely acknowledged (by, for example, Werthemier, 1991; Parkes, 1972) that the final stages of the normal bereavement process involve acceptance (acknowledging the finality of death and the reality of loss) and recovery. For the reasons discussed, acceptance may be more difficult when the death has been self-inflicted. A crucial issue here is the need for information and support, which is generally limited at best (Wertheimer, 1991), particularly when the death has occurred in prison or in any other 'closed' institution.

Another important issue is that death by suicide can compromise usual mourning rituals (Hauser, 1987: 65). In order to avoid dealing publicly with the nature of a loved-one's death, perhaps because of feelings of isolation, distinctiveness or (in some cases) shame, families may avoid the usual mourning ceremonies or rituals – rituals that ordinarily facilitate the mourning process by providing, at least potentially, an arena for comfort and support.

Finally, it should be noted that, in England and Wales, unnatural deaths (including suicide) are subject to legal investigation by a coroner, who is required to hold an inquest that is conducted in public and sometimes before a jury. As will be discussed in greater detail later, the purposes of the inquest are to establish the identity of the deceased, and how, when and why that person died. The inquest is usually formally opened within a few days of the death, at which time identification of the deceased will take place and the body released for burial/cremation. The inquest is then adjourned while the coroner calls witnesses and gathers evidence to be heard at a later date. As

Wertheimer (1991) discusses, it is not unusual for the full inquest to be held several months after death has occurred. Such delays can obviously be very distressing for those concerned, particularly if they regard the inquest as an opportunity to learn more about the circumstances of their loved-one's death. In this sense, delays can prolong the bereavement process, thus hindering acceptance of loss and delaying subsequent recovery.

To summarise, there appear to be a number of distinct differences between the process of bereavement following suicide and that following death under other circumstances. As has been discussed, in addition to a general protraction of the process of bereavement (Staudacher, 1988), death by suicide appears to induce additional dimensions, or feelings such as anger, guilt and culpability. In the next section we discuss the relevance of each of these issues in the context of deaths in prison custody.

Bereavement following an apparent suicide in prison custody

There can be a tendency to treat the custodial setting in isolation from wider society, thus ignoring some of the commonalities between prison and the community. Whilst there may also be an inclination to differentiate between a suicide in prison and a suicide in the community, it would be incorrect to assume that the impact of such a death in these contexts is wholly different. In the vast majority of instances, any sudden and unexpected death has a major impact upon those involved, irrespective of where it occurs. However, when a sudden death occurs in prison custody, there are a number of additional dimensions that may heighten the strain upon those involved; later in this section we examine the impact of a death upon those involved. Although the primary focus for bereavement is family and friends of the deceased, it is important not to overlook the relevance of the stages of bereavement to others involved, both staff and fellow prisoners. In particular, in cases where family support has been largely absent, the prisoner's family equivalent may be the prison community.

By definition, prisons are physically isolated from the community. This means that deaths in custody occur while an individual is separated from those significant others who would normally – but by no means exclusively – be close at hand. Information about the death is likely to be more difficult to ascertain than in the community although, even in the latter, some may be denied full access and may feel that the 'incident' has been taken out of their control (Wertheimer, 1991).

Following a death in prison, family and close friends are caught in a double bind. They start from a relatively powerless position, unaware of the details surrounding the death, which are unlikely to be established fully with immediacy, but also aware that the facts will enter the public domain through channels outside their control – the death may be reported in the media, and the circumstances surrounding it will be aired at an inquest that is conducted by strangers in an unfamiliar and public arena. Thus, despite the personal and private nature of the event, any death in custody in England and Wales will be investigated by a coroner, in public and normally before a jury as a requirement under English law (see next section for details). The bureaucracy is formal, may be foreign and is outside the control of the bereaved individual. For some, this will be their first detailed encounter with the criminal justice system. However professional, helpful and sensitive the conduct of prison staff, the police, and coroners and their staff, the common experience for the bereaved is one of bemusement and bewilderment.

We saw earlier that bereavement following a suicide may be more prolonged than that following other types of death. When the death has occurred in custody, there are a number of factors that may prolong the process; there are several hurdles that have to be overcome on the road to acceptance and recovery. The underlying key issue may simply be the need to establish the truth about what happened. The importance of establishing the narrative of events as a crucial feature in acceptance of a tragedy is well documented from work on critical-incident debriefing (Dyregrov, 1997). To arrive at a coherent account of what has happened involves progress through a number of official procedures, each of which may impact upon the process of bereavement. Of primary importance is the coroner's inquest, the purposes of which are now briefly outlined.

The coroner's inquest

A coroner is an independent judicial officer, acting on behalf of the Crown, whose role is to investigate the causes and circumstances of violent, unnatural or sudden deaths of an unknown cause (Dorries, 1999: xxix). The laws to which coroners, the jury, legal representatives and witnesses must abide are contained in the Coroners Act 1988 and the Coroners Rules 1984. Section 8.1 of the Coroner's Act 1988 (cited in Dorries, 1999: 22) states that an inquest must take place if a person:

(a) has died a violent or unnatural death;
(b) has died a sudden death of which the cause is unknown; or

(c) has died in prison or in such a place or in such circumstances as to require an inquest under any other Act.

Thus, in certain circumstances – and in all cases of deaths in prison custody (or shortly after detention in prison custody, or if the illness which led to the death arose during or shortly after such detention) – a coroner must hold an inquest.[38] The actual cause of death in such circumstances is not technically germane. Such is the concern about deaths in prison generally that the coroner (within whose geographical jurisdiction the prison falls in which the death occurred) has an obligation to inquire into the death (Dorries, 1999: 33). All inquests for such deaths are held before a jury and, as stipulated in Rule 17 of the Coroners Rules 1984, the inquest must be held in public except in cases where evidence is likely to reveal matters of national security.

In contrast to criminal and civil courts, which are essentially adversarial, a coroner's inquiry is strictly inquisitorial. Whilst criminal and civil courts involve a trial between two parties, the purposes of which are to establish proof of liability or guilt, the purposes of an inquest are solely to inquire into the circumstances of an individual's death, ascertaining the identity of the deceased and how, when and why the person died. Coroners are prohibited from expressing an opinion on any other matter outside these requirements. Rules 36 and 42 of the Coroners Rules clarify the purposes of the inquest as follows:

36.   (1) The proceedings and evidence at an inquest shall be directed solely to ascertaining the following matters, namely–
    (a) who the deceased was;
    (b) how, when and where the deceased came by his death;
    (c) the particulars for the time being required by the Registration Acts to be registered concerning the death.
    (2) Neither the coroner nor the jury shall express any opinion on any other matters.

...

42.   No verdict shall be framed in such a way as to appear to determine any question of–
    (a)   criminal liability on the part of a named person, or
    (b)   civil liability

(Excerpt from the Coroners Act 1988 (cited in Dorries, 1999: 138)).

It is therefore not within the coroner's remit (indeed, a coroner is prohibited from doing so by Rule 36) to apportion guilt or attribute blame for an individual's death or to determine questions of civil or criminal liability, but simply to establish the facts as outlined above. Thus, there are no 'parties', nor formal allegations or pleadings and no cross-examination of witnesses. Rather, it is the coroner's responsibility to ensure that the circumstances are fully investigated, that a balanced and fair account of the death is presented, and that relevant witnesses are called to give evidence – witnesses who may be questioned by 'properly interested persons'[39] for the purposes of determining how, when and why an individual died (Dorries, 1999: 118). However, the coroner is entitled to make written observations to a person or authority who has the power to prevent similar fatalities from recurring (under Rule 43 of the Coroners Rules 1984).

As Dorries suggests, considerable significance is placed on a verdict recorded by a coroner and, although there exists no definitive list of verdicts, it is customary for coroners to stay within a suggested list (including suicide, unlawful killing, accidental death,[40] misadventure,[41] an open verdict, and natural causes). Before returning a verdict, the coroner or jury must be satisfied on the necessary facts to the required standard of proof. In order to return a verdict of suicide or unlawful killing, the standard of proof set is the same as in a criminal court: that is, 'beyond reasonable doubt'. For all other verdicts, the lesser (civil) standard applies: that is, 'on the balance of probabilities' (Dorries, 1999: 199–205).

Although strictly inquisitorial, it is perhaps inevitable that inquests into deaths in custody have become increasingly adversarial in tone. This is understandable, given the closed nature of the prison environment and the natural level of concern aroused when deaths occur amongst those in the care of the state. It has become standard practice for the authorities and professional witnesses to secure legal representation for themselves and their parent organisations. Similarly, it is increasingly common for families to be legally represented. However, there is currently no provision for legal aid in respect of representation in coroner's courts. The absence of legal aid (criticised in HMSO, 1971) and families' consequent difficulties in securing legal representation have tended to fuel bereaved families' suspicions of cover-up and generally to increase their feelings of frustration and helplessness.

An issue of further concern is the often lengthy time delay between the opening and adjournment and the reopening of an inquest. This can be a great source of frustration to relatives and others affected, who will wish to see this phase brought to a conclusion. For many of those directly and indirectly involved, the inquest represents a crucial phase, the completion of which plays a vital role in the bereavement process.

For deaths in custody, it is not unusual for family/relatives to leave the inquest dissatisfied. This may result from a misunderstanding and unrealistic expectations of the function and role of the inquest, sometimes fuelled by a misperception that the inquest is able apportion blame, as suggested in the following statement:

It is of critical importance to recognise the true purpose of an inquest. Sadly, the public's perception of such purpose does not always match the reality, and those caught up in the process expect more ... than it can, or is permitted to, deliver, thereby adding to their distress.

(*R. v. Birmingham Coroner ex parte Benton* [1997] 8 Med LR
362 (cited in Dorries, 1999: 144))

Having outlined the nature and purposes of the coroner's inquiry, in the following section we explore the impact of a death in custody from the varying perspectives of those who may be affected.

Differing perspectives on the impact of a death in custody

Various groups of people may be directly affected by a death in custody. For the purposes of clarity, they are grouped thus:

- family and friends;
- prisoners;
- staff;
- the prison establishment.

Family and friends

Of the impact of a death in custody on the four groups outlined above, the most well documented is that of family and friends, and rightly so. The death of any prisoner is the death of a son/daughter or mother/father, husband/wife, sister/brother; it is entirely appropriate that the immediate family should be the focus of greatest concern. In recent years, case studies and examples have featured in a range of media: newspaper and journal articles; radio; and television. First-hand accounts are powerful and moving and vividly illustrate the deep emotions aroused and the difficulties experienced (see, for example, HM Chief Inspector of Prisons, 1999). Unsurprisingly, it is mostly negative accounts that have featured in the media; the extent to which this may, or may not, reflect the overall picture is simply not known. An unusual account, in the sense of a perspective rarely reported, is to be found in the *Prison Service Journal* (1999).

For family and friends, the process of bereavement is impeded from the very outset by the fact that the relative has died in a place by definition with limited access, and all that that entails. Hearing that a close relative has died in prison, apparently through their own actions, is in itself outside the range of most normal experience. Establishing basic information may be far from straightforward. The police must first satisfy themselves that there has been no foul play. The coroner must open and adjourn the inquest. Thus, added to the heightened features of bereavement associated with suicide, family and friends have to contend with the law and a bureaucracy that will be alien to most. It is by no means certain that the family unit will (or has been) running smoothly. Any or all of this adds to a very complex situation for some, which may further exacerbate or hinder bereavement. In some instances, news of the death will arouse little surprise, and perhaps even relief, that the individual – who may have had a very troubled life – is now 'at peace'. In others, the reaction will be profound disbelief, leading to suspicion and a conviction that staff within the system are in some way to blame for what has happened.

Each case will have its own particular features. In the authors' experience, each case needs to be handled according to its individual circumstances. Although those closely affected are likely to need to work through the full stages of bereavement, there is no standard formula for charting the precise progress. Reactions will be as varied as there are combinations of relatives and friends and complexities of relationships.

Breaking the news of a death is rarely easy and perhaps even less so when the death has been an apparent suicide. How news of the death is delivered is important to relatives. The precise mechanism will depend upon timing and geography, and in some instances it will need to be brokered by a third party such as the police. It is not always possible to contact the next-of-kin with ease; it is not unknown for a deceased to have identified the wrong individual as next-of-kin. There does not appear to be unanimity on the preferred approach to breaking the news, except to say that great sensitivity is called for and relatives have a legitimate need to know something about the circumstances surrounding the death. Reactions will vary from deep hostility (for a police/prison presence may itself be deeply resented) to appreciation.

At this early stage, it may not be possible to give too much detail – not through any desire deliberately to withhold information but simply because information known at this stage may be limited. The fuller narrative may necessarily await the internal Prison Service investigation, which is always carried out in cases of apparent suicide. There may anyway be limits on how much information can be absorbed by relatives at this early stage, where shock, if not disbelief, may be experienced. It is common for relatives to need to revisit this early information as they come to understand the fuller context over time. It is also important for relatives to be given *accurate* information, with a minimum of speculation. It is possible that, as enquiries are made, and the fuller narrative unfolds, earlier information may be superseded and sometimes contradicted. Experience indicates that relatives find changes in the narrative confusing, for it forms a natural basis for suspicion.

It is not unusual for the reactions of families to change over time as numbness and shock subside. Early favourable reactions to the authorities may turn into anger and a focus for blame. In the earlier section on responses to suicide generally, we noted the common reaction of personal guilt and anger; it would be surprising if such reactions were absent in this context too. A change from acceptance to hostility may surprise some staff, particularly where significant effort has been put into assistance and nurturing good relationships in the early stages; however, any unanticipated changes may be seen as a normal part of the bereavement process as relatives grapple with coming to terms with what has happened.

In addition to understanding the circumstances surrounding the death, relatives and friends need to be informed about the basic procedures that will occur following a death in custody – for example, their right to be represented at the post-mortem, and the role and function of the coroner's office. In addition to the responsibilities held by the authorities, a valuable role is provided by organisations such as Inquest and Death on Remand. Recent Prison Service developments to assist families in understanding the full narrative are described in the final section of this chapter.

It is widely recognised that the delay between the death and the completion of the coroner's inquest can be a source of great frustration to family and friends, and any such protracted delay may prolong the bereavement process. However, organising the inquest can be a very lengthy process: there may be many witnesses to be called to give evidence; an appropriate venue needs to be found; and a jury needs to be convened. It is in the complex cases where there are a great many issues for the coroner to consider that delays may be longest, which have the potential for added frustration.

Prisoners

Positive peer-group support is very important to prisoners' successful adaptation to the prison environment (as discussed in Chapter 6). Relationships, both formal and informal, can be powerful and intense in prison, as in any other type of closed institution.

For fellow prisoners who have become close friends over time and, in some cases, in adversity, the impact of an apparent suicide can be equally as powerful as in the outside community, eliciting all the range of responses: shock; guilt; blame; and self-scrutiny over whether anything could have been noticed or anything further done. It should not be surprising, therefore, for prisoners to undergo the full range of bereavement reactions, particularly where relationships had developed over a lengthy period. It is not uncommon for fellow prisoners to be wrestling with the knowledge that the deceased had expressed suicidal thoughts but these had been dismissed and categorised as run-of-the-mill discontent with prison and life problems. On occasions, prisoners have to live in the knowledge of having given advice to a fellow prisoner on the most effective means of suicide – advice that has been heeded.

A number of suicides have been prevented through sharing of accommodation, but sadly not all. Awakening to find one's cell mate dead is undoubtedly a chilling experience and is certainly out of the normal range of experience. Clearly, any prisoner who has been in this position needs support, although the possibility of foul play must also be examined as a matter of routine.

The introduction and expansion of formalised peer-support schemes offered by prison listeners was discussed in greater detail in Chapter 6. The majority of listeners work on Samaritan-supported schemes, which offer total confidentiality to fellow prisoners; thus, listeners are unable to disclose details of any discussion that has taken place. It is important to acknowledge that, occasionally, listeners may have to face the fact that they were among the last to spend time with a prisoner in crisis who has gone on to complete suicide. Such circumstances will inevitably result in powerful scrutiny of whether more might have been said or done to encourage the individual to seek help. Whether schemes are run on Samaritan or other principles, prisoners in this situation will themselves need support, not least because they may be called to give evidence to internal inquiries and/or the coroner's inquest. Indeed, listeners themselves are not immune to suicide: there have been a small number of self-inflicted deaths of practising listeners in recent years.

Staff

> Suicide is seldom neutral in its effects and, after the immediate family, it has impact upon the professionals involved and the local community.
>
> (Pritchard, 1995:144)

Although every suicide in prison may not be preventable, staff must operate as if they are (McHugh and Towl, 1997). Based on this approach, every self-inflicted death inevitably carries with it an element of failure.

Even within strict professional boundaries, relationships between staff and prisoners can be powerful and the impact of a prisoner's death may result in feelings of loss similar to those experienced following death in other circumstances. A great deal of support may have gone into working with the deceased prisoner: in day-to-day routine work; through personal officer schemes (where prisoners are assigned to an individual staff member for first-line support); through professional help from probation staff, psychiatrists, forensic psychologists or other specialists; or where there have been close working relationships with staff – where the prisoner has been a regular and trusted worker in workshops or education, for example. In such situations the cycle of shock, loss and guilt can be powerful among staff.

In the majority of cases, prisoners will not have been identified as being at elevated risk of suicide at the time of their death (as discussed in Chapter 4). Thus, a great deal of soul searching may take place on whether any signs or symptoms might have been missed, particularly where the individual has previously been managed under the current strategy for the management/prevention procedures or has had a history of self-injury. With the benefit of hindsight it is often possible to identify clues; it is important to keep these in the context of what could reasonably have been known at the time.

Staff who are first on the scene at a death may be profoundly affected. There will be a range of reactions depending upon the background and experience of the individual concerned. For some, this may be the first ever experience of a dead body. Conversely, because the majority of deaths occur at night and it is not uncommon for the same night staff to be first on the scene where there has been a previous death, there may well be some staff who, by virtue of their location and establishment postings, have attended the scene of many deaths during their professional lives. Either way, unless rigor mortis is clearly setting in, there is a requirement for immediate resuscitation in advance of arrival of the emergency services (as stipulated in Prison Service Order 2710 on the procedures to be adopted following a death in custody). As with any potentially traumatic incident, it is often the immediate physical sensations that cause a deep impact upon the senses: for example, the weight/feel of the body and the physical sensations in resuscitation. Death that has been achieved due to loss of blood, although rare, can be particularly disturbing for those in attendance.

Experience suggests that it is more common for staff to be affected than unaffected by an apparent suicide. However, a predominantly machismo culture often militates against the acknowledgement of adverse reactions, normal though they might be. The local establishment multidisciplinary Staff Care Team has an important role to play in ensuring that first-line support is offered to all staff who may be affected by a death in prison custody and in facilitating external specialist support for any individuals who are profoundly affected.

The prison establishment

As mentioned in the Overview to this chapter, over and above each prison establishment consisting of a collection of individual members of staff and prisoners (each of whom may be affected by the death of a prisoner in a distinct way), there is a sense in which the prison as a whole – as a community – is also affected by a death. Thus, the bereavement process can be applied to the establishment as a whole. Numbness, shock, self-scrutiny and soul searching, collective guilt and feelings of failure are common.

It is useful to place the governor-in-charge of the establishment in this group because there is a real sense in which they represent and carry responsibility for the whole establishment. One death presents its challenge; a sequence of deaths is a challenge of a different order. An individual governor may have had prior experience of deaths in prison custody, but the first such experience when in charge of an establishment may feel quite different.

Aside from the normal investigative processes that are initiated following a death (to be discussed presently), it is a time for self-scrutiny. Unlike most other serious incidents that happen in prison, death is irretrievable. However, the prison routine must go on. There will be heightened anxieties about those prisoners known to be at elevated risk of suicide and those for whom the occurrence of a completed suicide might give them the courage to make that final decision. A sense of balance is required; over-anxiety may be counterproductive.

A sequence of apparent suicides can affect establishments in different ways, and much will depend upon the individual circumstances surrounding the deaths. It can be particularly demoralising for those establishments that have put a great deal of effort into providing care for the suicidal; it will be a testing time where holding on to what is good is essential. We know that there is no simple relationship between what an individual prison invests in suicide prevention and any outcome in reduction in numbers of suicides. A sequence of suicides is often seized upon by the outside world as an indicator that a prison is in crisis. The evidence points to the contrary: numbers of suicides alone are a poor barometer of an establishment's health. It takes strong determination to persist with good practice when there may be powerful internal and external pressures to be seen to change. Sadly, the issue of suicide in prison is occasionally used as a sacrificial pawn to draw attention to the inadequacies of imprisonment as a main response to the problems of crime.

It is clear from the above discussion about the wide range of impacts following a death that there is some commonality between the experiences of families, staff and prisoners through the classic stages of bereavement. It is manifestly clear that all of the authorities involved in the aftermath of a death can do much to ease the pain for relatives and to provide assistance that should go some way toward alleviating – or at the very least avoid exacerbating – the process of bereavement. However, it is perhaps worth remembering that there are limits on what organisations may achieve. The causes of an individual suicide are invariably complex, and it is an intensely personal experience for those left behind. It is unrealistic to expect that the organisations involved can absorb the total pain and bitterness. Nonetheless, there are a number of practical ways in which the Prison Service can assist in the aftermath. In the final two sections of this chapter we outline some recent developments and indicate areas that would merit future attention.

Recent procedural developments

During 1998, the Prison Service issued revised guidance and instructions on procedures to be adopted following a death in custody (Prison Service Order 2710), including separating establishment procedures from the internal investigation that is always carried out where there has been an apparent suicide. Apart from generally drawing good practice together, the Prison Service Order (PSO) acts as a comprehensive compendium of the key stages and processes, including the following: immediate action on discovery of a body; reporting requirements; contact with the Prison Service's Press Office and media; support for staff and prisoners; follow-up support for the family involved; preparation for an internal investigation; contact with the coroner and the arrangements for the inquest (including an explanation of the inquest process); funeral arrangements; and disclosure of information to the family and their legal representatives. It is inevitable that such instructions can be refined and improved in the light of experience; similarly, not all situations can be catered for. Individual reactions may vary and be unpredictable.

The PSO distinguishes between mandatory action (expressed in italics in the order) and recommended good practice. This distinction sometimes appears puzzling to those outside the Prison Service where the concept of discretion may seem at odds with the nature of the task in hand. However, in reality it is impossible to prescribe for every circumstance. Not only do such instructions have to take account of differing needs according to the differing types of establishment, but also the particular circumstances of each individual death. The instructions make clear that death can only be pronounced by a qualified doctor, but acknowledge that it is unreasonable to expect that resuscitation be attempted where the fatal act took place long before and rigor mortis is clearly setting in. In short, individual judgements have to be made. Similarly, the instructions recommend good practice in contacting and informing next of kin, but the precise method will depend upon a number of factors, not least geography; a balance has to be struck between sensitivity and expediency. Offering the family a visit to the prison to see the place where death occurred and, perhaps, to hold some kind of memorial, have been found to be of great comfort to some families. The emphasis is upon giving relatives the choice, but in their own time.

In parallel with the independent inquiry conducted by the coroner, the Prison Service conducts an internal investigation into every apparent suicide. The two inquiries are conducted for different purposes, (the purpose of the coroner's inquest was described in an earlier section). Although the two inquiries overlap, the main purpose of the internal investigation is to establish the degree of compliance with policy and procedures and to see whether there are any lessons that may be learned and that may inform future development of suicide prevention strategies. The Prison Service has a duty to co-operate fully with the coroner; during the 1990s the practice developed of routinely providing the coroner with the report of the internal investigation as background to assist the inquest. During 1998, procedures for conducting the internal investigation were revised to a new standardised format so that each investigation is carried out by a team led by a trained senior investigating officer, who will be a senior governor from outside the establishment where the death occurred. In addition to an increased level of objectivity, this allows the Prison Service to identify lessons more effectively and consistently where they are to be learned.

A more recent development, introduced for deaths occurring after 1 April 1999, concerns procedures for the disclosure of information from reports of internal investigations into deaths. The former policy of the Prison Service was to treat reports of investigations into deaths as confidential and not available for routine disclosure. This policy came under criticism from a number of quarters, not the least of which was from families and their legal representatives who have found themselves disadvantaged at the coroner's inquest by having only limited access to the facts surrounding the death. The policy attracted criticism from the Parliamentary Commissioner for Administration (1999), who investigated several complaints arising from deaths in prison custody. The new policy that was introduced for April 1999 represents a welcome move towards greater openness by allowing disclosure of the investigation report, subject to the views of the coroner and, with some restrictions on security-sensitive or personal information, prior to the inquest to those whom the coroner identifies as properly interested parties. At the time of writing (mid-2000), the new policy is in its initial stages of implementation and it is too early to assess its impact. However, it is anticipated that the practice will assist families in better understanding the narrative of events, which in turn should assist them in their bereavement. At the very least, the change should help reduce suspicions about secretiveness and cover-up by the authorities.

Summary and conclusions

It will be clear from the discussions in this chapter that much of what is understood about the impact of a death in prison custody comes from deep personal experiences, which by nature are anecdotal and loosely drawn together. There are a number of areas where our knowledge and understanding is speculative that would benefit from further inquiry.

Little is known about the impact that a suicide has upon other prisoners and the likelihood of it precipitating further deaths. The phenomenon of apparent clusters remains poorly understood and is worthy of further exploration. The issues covered in the inquiry into deaths at Glenochil (Chiswick *et al.*, 1985) merit revisiting. There may be a sense in which a death generates a climate that legitimises the act of suicide at either an individual or an institutional level.

We know little about how exposure to suicides at work affects staff attitudes and their handling of suicide prevention. The outcome could equally be involvement or disengagement depending upon the nature of the experience. Similarly, little is known about the impact of experiences of suicide and self-injury in the personal lives of staff and whether that has any effect upon attitudes towards what is achievable within the prison context.

Current Prison Service responses to the aftermath of death do not, perhaps, pay sufficient sensitivity to differing cultural interpretations of death according to faith and background. We are not aware of significant problems, but this is an issue that should not be overlooked.

Finally, of prime importance are the experiences of the bereaved and what has proved most beneficial in providing assistance. The 1990s have seen significantly increased engagement and dialogue between the Prison Service and bereaved families and interest groups. It is important that the dialogue continues in an area where there will always be room for improvement.

9

Future directions

Martin McHugh, Graham Towl and Louisa Snow

Overview

The development of strategies for suicide awareness and prevention is a continuing process. In this chapter current developments on suicide awareness and prevention in prisons in England and Wales are outlined. A number of pointers are included to indicate where energies might usefully be focused in the future.

Reception and induction

As evidenced throughout earlier chapters, an almost universal finding is that the early period following a prisoner's arrival at an establishment is associated with elevated risk of suicidal behaviour, with 10 per cent of deaths occurring within the first 24 hours after arrival (Towl 1999). This presents particular difficulties for Local prisons and establishments with a remand function, where large numbers of individuals have to go through the process of reception during what is often a restricted time period and in what are, commonly, less than ideal conditions. Numbers and timings of arrivals to prison are beyond the direct control of the Prison Service, whose function is to receive all those who the courts have ordered should be held in prison custody.

Any changes that can improve the quality of the reception process, and the quality of information elicited about individual prisoners, will be a step in the right direction. During 1999, work was undertaken as part of the revision to Health Care Standard One (Reception Procedures) to develop a new healthcare screening procedure. Although all staff involved in the reception process have a role to play in the identification of prisoners at risk, the healthcare interview is a key opportunity for in-depth assessment.

A drawback of the existing screening tool (First Reception Health Care Screening F2169) is the requirement to gather a large range of health information about the prisoner immediately on arrival, irrespective of the degree of urgency of the information at this early stage. The screening procedure includes information on previous self-injury and attempted suicide and an assessment of the level of current risk of suicide. The new screening procedure tackles this problem by adopting a triage line of inquiry, focusing upon those critical factors that need to be elicited within the first few hours of arrival in custody, yielding markers that may need to be explored later during the induction period. This should enable greater concentration on vital information. Training will be necessary for staff in using the new screening tool. An important element of that will be advice on creating a climate that will encourage prisoners to disclose their worries and concerns. This is an important issue since the individual prisoner is a key source of information during the reception period.

One issue that is the subject of debate is the extent to which it is necessary for all prisoners to be seen by a doctor within 24 hours of arrival. Although there are various statutory requirements that must be undertaken on initial reception, all staff involved in the process are in a position to detect indicators that an individual is at elevated risk. It is important that the new reception procedures being tested are not seen in isolation from the induction period. Anecdotal evidence – to a certain extent supported by data on self-inflicted deaths – suggests that elevated risk may continue over the early days after arrival; in some cases risk seems to increase once the reality of the situation has dawned upon prisoners after an initial period of numbness and shock.

Eliciting, recording and communicating information about current and previous risk is crucial to an effective reception process. Recent years have seen improvements in co-ordination between the contracted-out escorting services and establishments receiving and discharging prisoners. Current instructions require escorting staff to open up an F2052SH if they have concerns about a prisoner. Where a prisoner has been identified as at elevated risk of suicide, the open F2052SH should accompany the prisoner on movement outside the prison.

A more effective system for communications between the Prison Service, the escort contractors and the police was introduced in January 1999 through a new Prisoner Escort Record (PER), which is completed on each prisoner movement. The previous system relied upon a special-risk-factor form (commonly known as the POL1) being filled out only on prisoners identified at special risk. Although this had the advantage of giving heightened saliency to those identified, the absence of a POL1 was interpreted as nil risk and thus the system was primed towards false negatives. The new PER form provides a substantial improvement; it includes risk indicators for a variety of behaviours, including risk of self-injury or suicidal behaviour, and is completed for each prisoner movement.

Although it is useful to distinguish between the reception process and the induction period, in practice there should be a smooth transition between the two. An important development would be to shift the emphasis away from the 'process', of which the introduction of a more effective screening tool is only one element. Reducing the risk of self-injury and suicide during this high-risk period is likely to be achieved through ensuring that regimes are improved. Many establishments provide special support for 'first-nighters'. Many establishments ensure that prisoner listeners/buddies are available during both reception and induction and that access is given to phone lines, including one to The Samaritans.

Although, as stated above, it is important to elicit information from the prisoner in relation to factors that may increase the risk of suicide, just as important is the giving of information to each prisoner, especially on reception. This point is rarely stressed in the literature but cannot be overemphasised. Information giving by staff serves to decrease the uncertainty in the prisoner's world, which should reduce anxiety. Clear, concise and relevant information, given early on arrival, underpins good practice in suicide awareness and may well have a positive impact upon the overall mental health of prisoners.

It is clear from the foregoing that improving the quality of reception and the induction period will be crucial in reducing the risk of suicide. A significant contribution will be made by the introduction of new Prison Service standards on reception and induction and the preparation of new Prison Service Orders on these topics.

Technological development

The use of IT in the recording and transfer of information about prisoners' histories of self-injury and any current level of risk of suicide is in its earliest stages. It is beyond the scope of this chapter to explore the issues in detail, but there are encouraging signs that the issue of 'joined-up communications' across the criminal justice agencies is at last beginning to receive the attention it deserves, particularly in joint operations between the Prison Service and the Probation Service.

Breakdown in communications is an issue that crops up regularly whenever inquiries are conducted into deaths within custodial settings. Devising compatible and reliable communication systems presents a formidable challenge, but it must be a step in the right direction. Two cautionary notes, however, apply: information has to be acted upon; and, whatever system is in operation, there will inevitably be reliance upon the individual prisoner as an authoritative source, particularly so in assessment of the level of suicide risk.

An important technological development, which is set for expansion during 2000 and beyond and which could impact significantly upon the numbers of prisoners moving between prison and the courts, is videoconferencing. This operates by the designation of part of the prison as an extension of the court through video and sound linkage, thereby obviating the need physically to transfer a prisoner to the relevant court. The system has been tested successfully through pilot schemes and it is hoped that it will be extended further. The system is proposed only for pre-trial hearings and not for trials and sentencing; but even so it is estimated that full-scale adoption could reduce court appearances by 40 per cent. It may have an impact upon risk of self-injury or suicide through fewer movements of prisoners and subsequent disruption, but also it offers substantial cost savings.

Cell design

Although the primary focus of suicide awareness strategies is upon staff–prisoner relationships, it is clear that cell design has a part to play in the reduction of risk of suicide. The majority of suicides involve hanging from cell window-bars. It is probable, although not entirely proven, that reducing the means for suicide may reduce the likelihood that a prisoner going through a temporary crisis, and acting on impulse, will complete suicide.

During the 1990s the Prison Service designed a modified cell window that dispenses with the normal ligature points. The window design was introduced in several prisons but on too small a scale to provide hard evidence as to its efficacy.

In the mid-1990s, sparked partly through ministerial interest, the scope for reducing potential ligature points was explored by Prison Service construction services and evolved into a design brief for what has become a standard cell design for future prisons. The concept involves a holistic design that carries a range of safety features beyond the original brief. They include: safer and easier staff searching; reduced likelihood of barricades; significantly reduced opportunities for ligature points; reduced opportunities for vandalism; and use of high-quality materials that create a more ambient environment. The design and fabric of the cell, sometimes unhelpfully referred to as a 'safe cell', were piloted in single and double form in a prison in South-East London. Its introduction retrospectively has been on a small scale because of the costs of retro-fitting existing cells. The design has, however, been incorporated into a whole new houseblock in a prison in the South-East of England and is being introduced into whole establishments in the building programme for new prisons. It will be interesting to see whether its introduction on such a scale has an impact upon levels of self-injury or suicidal behaviour.

There are a number of other initiatives that have been developed locally within prisons. CCTV is used in some establishments as part of general monitoring, although its efficacy is largely unexplored. The drawbacks are that it can reduce direct human contact; the monitors need to be watched continuously; and the system offers no guarantee that self-injury will be prevented, particularly since the time interval between observation and intervention may be substantial.

The use of seclusion in the management of suicidal prisoners is an area where the Prison Service has received justified criticism. The Office for National Statistics' study on psychiatric morbidity (1999) reported that between one-quarter and one-third of all prisoners who had attempted suicide in the previous 12 months had been held in 'strip' conditions.

Placement of prisoners in what are commonly referred to as 'strip cells' or 'stripped conditions' is a practice that has been discouraged and eliminated in many establishments. The Prison Service is committed to eliminating such practice entirely during the year 2000, and a Prison Service Order (PSI 27/00) was issued in March 2000 that advises on a range of alternatives. This is a crucial step in providing an appropriate standard of care, since there is some evidence that the use of 'strip cell' conditions is seen as punitive by prisoners and acts as a disincentive for true worries and concerns to be revealed (Dexter and Towl, 1995; Brannigan and Wellings, 2000). There will, of course, continue to be a need for the use of isolation where prisoners are behaving aggressively and the safety of staff and others is at risk. The difficulty arises where such prisoners begin to display suicidal tendencies, which may be overlooked. There are no easy answers in such situations.

Mental health services

The provision of adequate mental health services for prisoners has been a source of contention for many years. As described in Chapter 3 and mentioned in the previous section here, the Office for National Statistics' report on psychiatric morbidity (1998) identified high levels of mental health problems amongst prisoners. Even allowing for the lower incidence of mental health factors in prisoner suicides in comparison with the outside community, any improvement in mental health services is likely to have a positive impact on the reduction of risk of self-injury or suicide.

The latest development, which has the potential for great impact in this area, is the forging of the joint partnership between the Prison Service and the National Health Service under the framework announced in 1999 (Department of Health, 1999). It is beyond the scope of this chapter to go into detail but this alliance carries with it the potential for significantly enhanced services for prisoners, drawing upon local needs assessments that will in future include the prison formally as part of the community. It is to be hoped that the partnership will yield improved services to remand prisoners, although it must be acknowledged that the new arrangements for working will require a substantial timeframe of around five years to come to full fruition. An important step has been the inclusion of prison suicides within the Department of Health's *Framework for Mental Health* (1999).

Another development of note is a current initiative under the auspices of the World Health Organisation, which concerns the adoption of a set of principles and common standards for achieving improved mental health among both prisoners and staff in prisons in Europe (WHO, 1998). This initiative is of particular interest since it is predicated upon a definition of mental health that is much broader than the traditional narrow definition of mental illness. The argument is based upon evidence that suggests that if the general level of mental well-being in the population at large can be enhanced, this has a positive impact upon the extreme end of the mental illness spectrum. This approach is clearly worth exploring in the prison setting, and if it is adopted it is likely to have some impact upon the extent to which a prison establishment meets the criteria of a healthy and safe environment.

Future research

As described in earlier chapters, there has been a growth of research into suicide in prisons in recent years. There remains, however, much to be explored. For a number of reasons, much research has taken completed suicides as the logical starting point. Although this is an important area for continuing and improving investigations (in the development of better-quality studies using matched control or comparison groups, for example) the focus has, arguably, resulted in a neglect of other types of studies – on prisoners who have survived an attempt at suicide, for example. The net effect has been a growing body of knowledge about factors that elevate risk to the exclusion of factors that reduce risk or protect against suicide.

There are a number of important areas on which future researchers could focus. These are discussed more fully below, but in essence cover the following: the effects of prison regimes; access (or restricted access) to means of injury or suicide and its effects; and on broader environmental or community-based influences. Another important area for research is intervention. Future research could also usefully draw upon the distinct experiences, knowledge, skills and attitudes of individual prisoners, their families, prison staff and management, as well as organisations outside the establishment.

At the individual prisoner level, the developing knowledge-base would benefit from application of a range of methodologies, both quantitative and qualitative. For example, studies of prisoners who have survived an attempt at suicide may well be a rich source of learning. Liebling (1998) reminds us that 'those who have attempted suicide in prison possess a wealth of knowledge about the prison experience. We should listen very carefully to what they have to say' (p. 74). As intimated, a useful focus for future research would be on factors that protect against suicide and self-injury amongst groups of prisoners at heightened risk.

In terms of prison regimes, there has been little systematic study of the factors that account for differing levels of self-injury or suicide across similar types of establishment. Such research could usefully explore the extent to which individual prisons differ in culture and operation – differences that may well have an impact on overall rates of self-injury/suicide. Further, the impact of differential regimes (which afford different levels of access to resources for prisoners according to their behaviour) could be usefully explored.

With regard to the issue of access to means of injury and attempted suicide, there are a number of factors whose efficacy in reducing the risk of suicide could usefully be explored. Examples include: the utility of cell sharing (widely believed to be a protective factor); the impact of in-cell TV; and the impact of the improved cell design described earlier.

Finally, research is needed into the impact of initiatives such as prisoner listener/buddy schemes and increased access to outside organisations such as The Samaritans (notwithstanding the difficulties in measuring their impact, as outlined in Chapter 6). Also, research into the effect of group interventions is overdue. Although a number of initiatives have been developed at a local level, their efficacy has been largely unexplored.

An encouraging development is the setting up of a quarterly Research Forum, hosted by the Suicide Awareness Support Unit at Prison Service Headquarters, which acts as a network for people either involved in, or contemplating, research into suicide or self-injury within forensic settings both within and outside the Prison Service.

The Prison Service has recently linked up with the National Confidential Inquiry into Suicide and Homicide by People with Mental Illness and is funding a research project that examines the subsample of suicides that occur within prisons. The main focus of this project is upon involvement with, and level of provision of, mental health services.

Staff training

It is widely recognised that a key to the success of suicide awareness programmes is a sound underpinning of staff training. The current staff-training programme, which dates back to 1993, is being revised. There are three main elements to the revision, each of which is being implemented during 2000. First, the current modules are being condensed into a common core training package that can be delivered efficiently and speedily to all staff. The focus aims to avoid an overconcentration upon procedures, with more of an emphasis upon building up staff confidence in approaching and supporting the suicidal through practical demonstration of what can be done. Secondly, improvements will be introduced to the quality of training delivery by greater standardisation in the quality of training for trainers. Thirdly, a new training programme will be delivered as preparatory training for senior managers who have lead responsibility for managing the Suicide Awareness Team at establishment level.

Time and resources available for staff training will always be at a premium in an organisation as complex as the Prison Service. It is all the more essential that the limited time available is used effectively and with high quality.

HMCIP's Thematic Review 1999

Following publication of the Thematic Review in May 1999, the Prison Service set up a steering group to examine recommendations and see how they could inform the existing programme of work. Development is being taken forward in a number of areas.

The review recommended that new approaches be adopted in suicide prevention in the Local prisons where the problems are felt most acutely. It is expected that, following the example already adopted in a small number of prisons, full-time Suicide Intervention Co-ordinators will become the norm in Local prisons, with the task of driving forward local initiatives. The recommendation that the Prison Service should pay prisoners as Inmate Observation Aides in Local prisons, with a remit to act as the eyes and ears of staff in identifying prisoners at risk, has received little enthusiasm; it does not sit well with the current Samaritan-supported Listener schemes, which require confidentiality. However, it is an idea worth exploring and it is being tested out in a pilot project.

Other recommendations in the review are being carefully examined, including how the needs of women prisoners and young offenders might be better addressed. The proposal that the Prison Service should set up key performance indicators or targets in suicide prevention is being examined cautiously, for this is a sensitive area where the focus must be upon the positive.

Revisions to current instructions

The Prison Service is drawing together all extant instructions into a new format of standardised Prison Service Orders (PSOs). The new PSO (2700) on caring for prisoners at risk of self-harm and suicide is due for issue in 2000. It provides a useful opportunity to refine and clarify areas of concern, such as:

- ensuring that the designation 'shared cell' for prisoners identified at risk is fully understood operationally to distinguish between continuous company and overnight company;
- ensuring that procedures for the transfer between prisons, and to courts, of prisoners identified at elevated risk are clearly understood and adhered to;
- highlighting the importance of effective anti-bullying strategies and the link between levels of self-injury;
- providing examples of good practice.

Summary and conclusions

This chapter has outlined the major areas identified for development in suicide awareness and prevention in the next few years. It is an area where there is great scope for local initiative and enthusiasm within the overall multidisciplinary approach. Success in the twenty-first century will be influenced as much by what happens in society and within the criminal justice system as a whole as in prisons themselves. Whatever the future holds, there will always be a need for specific programmes to provide the care and support needed for those individuals who are in crisis and at an inflated risk of self-injury or suicide.

Endnotes

1 Borstal and detention orders refer to court sentences imposed on young offenders and are now superseded. Topp does not, understandably given the small sample size, provide a separate analysis of the data for those defined as young offenders.

2 Topp does not provide an operational definition of 'psychiatric treatment' or of 'in-patient' treatment in the study.

3 As with psychiatric treatment, Topp does not operationally define 'depressive episodes' or 'a tendency to depression'.

4 Topp does not detail the evidence that more than 50 per cent of deaths were '… on a sudden impulse …'. Nor does he provide further detail on his observation that the behaviours were part of a more general pattern of 'attention seeking'.

5 Topp mentions this in the context of discussing his results from prison-based studies. Little methodological detail is given of the NHS study.

6 The total number of cases was 300, but case files for five individuals were not available.

7 Values of $c2 = 4.83$, df = 1, $p < 0.04$, as reported by Dooley (1990).

8 Dooley uses the average daily population of remand prisoners as the basis on which to estimate their relative risk. In fact, for remand prisoners, ADP provides a very poor estimate of the number of individuals placed at risk in the prison environment. The remand population in the Prison Service changes at a much higher rate than the sentenced population. Thus, for remands, receptions (suitably corrected for double counting) provide a better, though still rather crude, estimate of the number of individuals placed at risk in the prison environment (see Dexter and Towl, 1995; Bogue and Power, 1995; Crighton and Towl, 1997).

9 The study adopted a broad definition of 'psychiatric history'.

10 Social Enquiry Reports (SERs) were, at the time of the research, the main form of social reports produced for the court by the relevant Probation Service. These would generally involve the Probation Officer making recommendations and/or suggested sentencing options, including possible community sentences.

11 Operationally defined as a self-reported rate of alcohol use greater than eight units per day.

12 There also appear to have been significant differences in terms of the nature of the substance abuse. Of the control group, 22 per cent reported cannabis

use alone, compared with 6 per cent of the subject group. The subject group were more likely to have used LSD and heroin.

13 The subject group were also more likely to report engaging in 'negative' activities as a means of relieving boredom (22 per cent vs. 6 per cent).

14 Prison-based healthcare staff are employed as primary care practitioners (essentially as general practitioners). Referral of those who intentionally self-injure to specialist mental-health services is often routine in such contexts.

15 Scotland does not have a system of coroner's courts. In most cases, the decision about whether a death was suicide is taken by the investigating police service.

16 See McHugh and Towl (1997) for a more detailed discussion of some of the definitional issues concerned.

17 Bulusu and Alderson (1984).

18 As recorded by the Prison Service Suicide Awareness Support Unit.

19 This was something that was alluded to in Topp (1979) and was addressed in detail by later researchers (Dexter and Towl, 1995; Bogue and Power, 1995).

20 The term per 100,000 average population appears to be calculated per 100,000 average daily prison population per annum.

21 The authors did not analyse sentenced and charged prisoners separately.

22 The authors do not define 'attempted suicide' or 'deliberate self-harm'.

23 A number of studies have been conducted into the levels of psychiatric disturbance in prisons. Most have used very broad definitions of such disorders (e.g. Barraclough and Hughes, 1987), suggesting levels of morbidity up to 90 per cent.

24 Early studies of prison suicide often calculated rates of suicide per 100,000 of average daily population (ADP). Such studies generally found that those on remand showed much higher rates of self-injury than those under sentence. However, this is grossly misleading since ADP is a very poor indicator of the number of remand prisoners exposed to the prison environment. When rates are calculated on the basis of receptions into prison, the significance of remand status as a risk marker is dramatically reduced or even absent.

25 Plutchik advocates a sophisticated vectoral model for such behaviours. Such a model implies that different variables may operate to differing extents in combination. He also argues that such a model helps to explain why apparently small events may go on to have large effects, by upsetting the dynamic balance within an individual.

26 'Amplifiers' is the term used by Plutchik for events that serve to increase the likelihood of aggressive behaviour resulting in violence, whilst 'attenuators' refers to events decreasing this likelihood. Other factors will, in turn, act to determine the expression of violence. Plutchik also notes that the interaction of both is likely to be vectoral and complex, rather than being additive in a simple manner.

27 Within ICD 10, schizotypal disorder is listed under schizophrenia, rather than under personality disorders as it is in DSM IV.

28 The term 'client' is used throughout to mean the offender under assessment. It is acknowledged that the identification of precisely who the client is in the forensic field may not always be immediately apparent.

29 Figures for remand receptions are corrected to allow for double counting. Figures for receptions refer to the period 1991–5. Prior to 1991, this information was not calculated by the Home Office.

30 Until 1989, national Prison Service data was collected for 14–16-year-olds and 17–20-year-olds. Therefore the ADP figures for these groups necessarily relate to the period 1990–5.

31 According to Weiss (1975), two basic forms of isolation exist: emotional isolation results from the absence of an intimate partner; and social isolation is a consequence of the absence of supportive friends and ties to a social network.

32 When considering the impact of imprisonment, it is important to bear in mind the distinction between pain and harm: pain may be understood as an immediate aversive condition that may or may not result in extended damage; harm, on the other hand, has lasting negative consequences (Goodstein and Wright, 1989: 241).

33 The exception, as stated in current Guidance, is the freedom to disclose any information that contravenes the Prevention of Terrorism (Temporary Provision) Act 1989 (HM Prison Service Instruction 032/1997).

34 A value of $p < 0.01$ indicates a statistically significant result – a difference that would not be expected by chance.

35 A value of $p < 0.05$ indicates a statistically significant result – a difference that would not be expected by chance.

36 'ns.' indicates that the differences between the groups are not statistically significant; these differences might be expected by chance.

37 A value for p less that 0.001 indicates a highly significant result – a difference that would not be expected by chance.

38 Different rules apply for deaths from natural causes that occur in police custody. There is no requirement within the 1988 Act that an inquest *must* be held in such circumstances, although it is stated that a jury must be present if an inquest does indeed take place (Dorries, 1999: 33).

39 A 'properly interested person' is one who 'has a genuine desire to participate in the determination of how, when and where the deceased came by his death': R. v. *South London Coroner ex parte Driscoll* [1993] 159 JP 45, cited in Dorries, 1999: 144).

40 'Accidental death' is, suggests Dorries, (1999: 214) widely confused with 'misadventure' (discussed in the next note). The former, as suggested in *Jervis on Coroners*, should be returned in cases where death occurs as an unintended result of a deliberate act, in cases of death following a road traffic accident, for example.

41 Dorries (1999: 214–215) suggests that there remains a logical distinction between the verdicts of accidental death and misadventure, such that the latter might be applied when a person deliberately undertakes a task that then goes wrong, thus causing a death. An example is when an adverse reaction to an administered drug causes death; the term 'accident' might imply that the wrong drug or dose was given, while 'misadventure' suggests that the drug was given intentionally but that misfortune supervened.

References

Albanese, J.S. (1983) Preventing inmate suicides: A case study. *Federal Probation*, 47, 65–9

Alessi, N.E., McManus, M., Brickman, A. *et al.* (1984) Suicidal behaviour among serious juvenile offenders. *American Journal of Psychiatry*, 141, 286–7

American Psychiatric Association (1994) *Diagnostic and Statistical Manual (Version 4)*. Washington DC: American Psychiatric Association

Arnold, L. (1995) *Women and Self-Injury: A Survey of 76 Women*. Bristol: Bristol Crisis Service for Women

Arnold, L. (1997) *Working With People Who Self-injure – a Training Package*. Bristol: Bristol Crisis Service for Women

Aronson, E. (1995) *The Social Animal* (7th edn). San Francisco: Freeman

Babiker, G. and Arnold, L. (1996) *The Language of Injury: Comprehending Self-Mutilation*. BPS Books: Leicester

Backett, S. (1987) Suicides in Scottish prisons. *British Journal of Psychiatry*, 151, 218–21

Bagley, C. (1968) The evaluation of a suicide prevention scheme by an ecological method. *Social Science and Medicine*, 2, 1–14

Banister, P.A., Smith, F.V., Heskin, K. J., and Bolton, N. (1973) Psychological correlates of long-term imprisonment: 1 Cognitive variables, *British Journal of Criminology*, 13, 312–323

Baron, R.S., Cutrona, C.E., Hicklin, D., Russell, D.W. and Lubaroff, D.M. (1990) Social support and immune function among spouses of cancer patients. *Journal of Personality and Social Psychology*, 59, 344–352

Barraclough, B., Jennings, C. and Moss, J. (1977) Suicide prevention by The Samaritans. *Lancet*, ii, 237–239

Barraclough, B.M. and Hughes, J. (1987) *Suicide: Clinical and Epidemiological Studies*. London: Croom Helm

Barraclough, B.M., Bunch, J. and Nelson, B. (1974) A hundred cases of suicide: clinical aspects. *British Journal of Psychiatry*, 170–2. Quoted in R. Jenkins, S. Griffiths and I. Wylie (eds) *The Prevention of Suicide*. Department of Health: London

Beck, A.T. (1967) *Depression: Clinical, Experimental and Theoretical Aspects*. New York: Harper Row

Beck, A.T., Kovacs, M. and Weissman, A.S. (1979) Assessment of suicidal intention: the scale for suicidal ideation. *Journal of Consulting and Clinical Psychology*, 47, 343–50

Biggam, F.H. and Power, K.G. (1997) Social support and psychological distress in a group of incarcerated young offenders. *International Journal of Offender Therapy and Comparative Criminology*, 41(3), 213–230

Biggar, K. (1996) Befriending in prison. In A. Liebling (ed.) *Deaths in Custody: Caring for People at Risk*. London: Whiting and Birch Ltd

Board of Prison Commissioners (1881) *Annual Report*. Quoted in Topp, D.O. (1979) Suicide in prison. *British Journal of Psychiatry*, 134, 24–7

Board of Prison Commissioners (1911) *Annual Report*. Quoted in Topp, D.O. (1979) Suicide in prison. *British Journal of Psychiatry*, 134, 24–7

Bogue, J. and Power. K, (1995) Suicide in Scottish Prisons 1976–1979. *British Journal of Forensic Psychiatry*, 6, 527–40

Bonta, J. and Gendreau, P. (1990) Re-examining the cruel and unusual punishment of prison life. *Law and Human Behaviour*, 14, 437–472

Botsis, A.J., Soldatos, C.R. and Stefani, C.N. (1997) *Suicide: Biopsychosocial Approaches*. Amsterdam: Elsevier

Bottoms, A.E. (1977) Reflections on the renaissance of dangerousness. *Howard Journal of Penology and Crime Prevention*, 16, 70–96

Bowden, P. (1996) in N. Walker (ed.) *Dangerous People*. London: Blackstone Press

Bowlby, J. and Parkes C.M. (1970) Separation and loss within the family. In E. J. Anthony and C. Koupernick (eds) *The Child and his Family*, vol 1. New York: Wiley Interscience

Boyd, J.H. and Weissman, M.M. (1982) Epidemiology. In E.S. Paykel (ed.) *Handbook of Affective Disorders*. Edinburgh: Churchill Livingstone

Brannigan, P. and Wellings, K. (2000) *The Use of Stripped Cell Conditions in the Care and Management of Suicidal Prisoners*. A report by the Health Promotion Research Unit. London School of Hygiene and Tropical Medicine, Keppel Street, London WC1E 7HT

Brockington, I.F., Kendell, R.E. and Leff, J.P. (1978) Definitions of schizophrenia: Concordance and prediction of outcome. *Psychological Medicine*, 8, 387–98

Brown, G.W., Andrews, B., Harris, T.O. and Bridge, L. (1986) Social support, self-esteem and depression. *Psychological Medicine*, 16, 813–831

Bulusu, L and Alderson, M. (1984) Suicides 1950–82. *Population Trends*, 35, 11–17

Cain, A.C. and Fast, I. (1972) Children's Disturbed Reactions to Parent Suicide: distortions of guild, communication and identification. In E.J. Dunne, J. McIntosh and K. Dunne-Martin (eds) *Survivors of Suicide*. Springfield, Ilinois: Charles C. Thomas.

Carolissen, M. (1996) The Wandsworth prisoners: befriending in prison from a listener point of view. In A. Liebling (ed.) (1996) *Deaths in Custody: Caring for People at Risk*. London: Whiting and Birch Ltd

Chapman, L.J. and Chapman, J.P. (1967) Genesis of popular but erroneous psycho-diagnostic observations. *Journal of Abnormal Psychology*, 72, 193–204

Chapman, L.J. and Chapman, J.P. (1969) Illusory correlations as an obstacle to the use of valid psychodiagnostic signs. *Journal of Abnormal Psychology*, 74, 271–80

Charlton, J., Kelly, S., Dunnell, K., Evans, B., Jenkins, R. and Wallis, R. (1992) Suicide deaths in England and Wales: trends in factors associated with suicide deaths. Reprinted in R. Jenkins, S. Griffiths and I. Wylie (eds) *The Prevention of Suicide*. Department of Health: London

Chisnall, L. (1999) *Working with women who self injure*. Presentation to the BPS Division of Criminological and Legal Psychology, Ninth Annual Conference, 27–29 September 1999, Churchill College, University of Cambridge

Chiswick, D., Spencer, A., Baldwin, P., Drummond, D., Henderson, A.D., Kreitman, N., Stark, R. and Younghohns, P. (1985) *Report of the Review of Suicide Precautions at HM Detention Centre and HM Young Offenders Institution, Glenochil*. Scottish Home and Health Department, HMSO: Edinburgh

Clemmer, D. (1940) *The Prison Community*. New York: Holt, Rinehart and Winston

Cohen, S. and Hoberman, H.M. (1983) Positive events and social supports as buffers of life-change stress. *Journal of Applied Social Psychology*, 13, 99–125

Cohen, S. and MacKay, G. (1984) Social support, stress and the buffering hypothesis: a theoretical analysis. In Baum. A., Singer, J.E. and Taylor, S.E. (eds), *Handbook of Psychology and Health*, 4, 253–267

Cohen, S. and Taylor, L. (1972) *Psychological Survival: The Experience of Long-term Imprisonment*. London: Penguin

Cohen, S. and Wills, T.A. (1985) Stress, social support and the buffering hypothesis. *Psychological Bulletin*, 98, 310–357

Coid, J. (1984). How many psychiatric patients in Prison? *British Journal of Psychiatry*, 145, 78–86

Coid, J., Wilkins, J., Coid, B. and Everitt, B. (1992) Self-mutilation in female remanded prisoners ii: a cluster analytic approach towards identification of a behavioural syndrome. *Criminal Behaviour and Mental Health*, 2, 1–14

Cookson, H.M. (1977). A survey of self-injury in a closed prison for women. *British Journal of Criminology*, 17(4), 332–347

Cooper, C. and Livingston, M. (1991) Depression and coping mechanisms in prisoners. *Work and Stress*, 4(2), 149–154

Copas, J.B. (1982) *Statistical Analysis for the Redevelopment of the Reconviction Prediction Score*. Unpublished paper, University of Warwick

Cox, T. (1978) *Stress*. London: Macmillan

Crighton, D.A. (1997) The psychology of suicide. In G.J. Towl (ed.) *Suicide and Self-Injury in Prisons, Issues in Criminological and Legal Psychology*, 28. Leicester: British Psychological Society

Crighton, D.A. and Towl, G.J. (1997) Self-inflicted deaths in England and Wales 1988–1990, and 1994–95. In G.J. Towl (ed.) *Suicide and Self-injury in Prisons, Issues in Criminological and Legal Psychology*, 28. Leicester: British Psychological Society

Cudby, T. (1997) *An exploratory study of the accuracy and attitudes of prison staff in performing risk assessments*, paper presented at the Division of Criminological and Legal Psychology Conference, University of Cambridge

Cullen, J.E. (1985) Prediction and treatment of self-injury by female young offenders. In D.P. Farrington and R. Tarling (eds) *Prediction in Criminology*. Albany, NY: State University of New York Press

Cutler, J., Bailey, J.E. and Dexter, P. (1997) Suicide awareness training for prison staff: an evaluation. In G.J. Towl (ed.) *Suicide and Self-Injury in Prisons*,

Issues in Criminological and Legal Psychology, 28. Leicester: British Psychological Society

Cutter, F. (1979) The relation of new Samaritan clients and volunteers to high-risk people in England and Wales (1965–1977). *Suicide and Life Threatening Behaviour*, 9(4): 245–50

Department of Health (1999) *National Service Framework for Mental Health: modern standards and service models*. Department of Health: London

Dexter, P. and Towl, G. (1995) An investigation into suicidal behaviours in prison. In N.K. Clark and G.M. Stephenson (eds) *Criminal Behaviour: Perceptions, Attributions and Rationality, Issues in Criminological and Legal Psychology*, 22, 45–53. Leicester: The British Psychological Society

Diekstra, R.F.W. and Hawton, K. (eds) (1987) *Suicide in Adolescence*. Dordrecht: Martinus Nijhoff Publishers

Dooley, E. (1990) Prison suicide in England and Wales, 1972–87. *British Journal of Psychiatry*, 156, 40–45

Dorries, C. (1999) *Coroner's Courts: a guide to law and practice*. Chichester: John Wiley & Sons

Duff , W. (1999) Changing a culture. *Prison Service Journal*, 124, 10–13

Dunn. R.G. and Morrish-Vinders, D. (1987) The psychological and social experiences of suicide survivors. *Omega*, 18, 175–215

Durkheim, E. (1888) *Suicide: A Study in Sociology*, translated by J.A. Spaulding and G. Simpson (1952). London: Routledge and Kegan Paul

Dyregrov, A. (1997) The process in psychological debriefings. *Journal of Traumatic Stress*, 10(4), 589–605

Eiser, J.R. (1980) *Cognitive Social Psychology*. McGraw Hill: London

Evans, J. (1989) Biases in human reasoning: Causes and consequences. In S.E. Newstead and J. St.B. T. Evans (eds) *Perspectives on Thinking and Reasoning – Essays in Honour of Peter Watson*. Hove, UK: Lawrence Erlbaum Associates

Farrington, D.P. (1993) The challenge of teenage anti-social behaviour, paper prepared for the Martach Castle Conference: *Youth in the Year 2000*

Farrington, D.P. and Tarling, R. (1985) Criminological prediction: an introduction. In D.P. Farrington and R. Tarling (eds) *Prediction in Criminology*. Albany: State University of New York Press

Foucault, M. (1979) *Discipline and Punish: the birth of the prison*. London: Penguin

Gelder, M., Gath, D., Mayou, R. and Cowen, P. (1996) *Oxford Textbook of Psychiatry* (3rd edn). Oxford: Oxford University Press

Goffman, E. (1961) *Asylums: essays on the social situation of mental patients and other inmates*. New York: Doubleday

Goldstein, I.L. (1993) *Training in organisations: needs assessment, development and evaluation*, 3rd edn. Pacific Grove, CA: Brooks and Cole

Goodstein, L. and Layton MacKenzie, D. (eds) (1989) *The American Prison: Issues in Research and Policy*. New York: Plenum Press

Goodstein, L. and Wright, K. (1989) Inmate Adjustment to Prison, in Goodstein, L. and Layton Mackenzie, D. (1989) (eds) *The American Prison: issues in research and policy*. New York and London: Plenum Press

Goring, C. (1913) *The English Convict*. London: Darling. Quoted in Topp, D.O. (1979) Suicide in prison. *British Journal of Psychiatry*, 134, 24–7

Gresham, M.S. (1971) *The Society of Captives: A study of maximum security division.* Princeton, NJ: Princeton University Press

Gunn, J., Maden, A. and Swinton, M. (1991) *Mentally Disordered Prisoners.* London: Home Office

Gunn, J., Robertson, G., Dell, S. and Way, C. (1978) *Psychiatric Aspects of Imprisonment.* London: Academic Press

Gunnell, D (1994) *The Potential for Preventing Suicide: A Review of the Literature on the Effectiveness of Interventions aimed at Preventing Suicide.* Health Care Evaluation Unit, Department of Epidemiology and Public Health Medicine: University of Bristol

Haddock, G. and Slade, P.D. (1996) *Cognitive-Behavioural Interventions with Psychotic Disorders.* London: Routledge

Hare, R.D. (1986) Twenty years of experience with the Cleckley Psychopath. In W.H. Reid, D. Dorr, J. Walker and J.W. Bonner (eds) *Unmasking the Psychopath: Antisocial Personality and Related Syndromes.* New York: Norton

Hatty, S.E. and Walker, J.R. (1986) *A National Study of Deaths in Australian Prisons.* Canberra: Australian Centre of Criminology

Hauser, M. (1987) Special Aspects of Grief after a Suicide. In E.J. Dunne, J. McIntosh and Dunne-Martin (eds) *The Aftermath of Suicide: understanding and counselling the survivors.* New York and London: W.W. Norton

Hawton, K. (1994) Causes and opportunities for prevention. In R. Jenkins, S. Griffiths and I. Wylie (eds) *The Prevention of Suicide.* London: HMSO

Hawton, K. and Fagg, J. (1992) Trends in deliberate self-poisoning and self-injury in Oxford, 1976–90. *British Medical Journal,* 304, 1409–11

Hawton, K., Fagg, J., Simkin, S. *et al.* (1997) Trends in deliberate self-harm in Oxford, 1985–1995. *British Journal of Psychiatry,* 171, 556–60

Haycock, J. (1989) Race and suicide in jails and prisons. *Journal of the National Medical Association,* 81, 405–11

Heskin, K. J., Smith, F.V., Banister, P.A. and Bolton, N. (1973) Psychological correlates of long-term imprisonment: II. Personality variables. *British Journal of Criminology,* 13, 323–330

HM Chief Inspector of Prisons for England and Wales (1990) *Review of Suicide and Self-Harm.* London: Home Office

HM Chief Inspector of Prisons for England and Wales (1999) *Suicide is Everyone's Concern: A Thematic Review.* London: The Stationery Office

HM Prison Service (1992) *Caring for Prisoners at Risk of Suicide and Self-injury: The way Forward.* London: Prison Service

HM Prison Service (1999) Death in Custody, *Prison Service Journal, July 1999,* No 124

HM Prison Service and National Health Service (1999) *The Future Organisation of Prison Health Care.* A joint report by the Prison Service and the National Health Service Executive Working Group: London

HMSO (1971) *Home Office Report on Death Certification and Coroners,* Cmnd. 4810. London: HMSO

Hobhouse and Brockway (1922) *English Prisons Today.* London: Longmans, Green and Co.

Holmes T.H. and Rahe, R.H. (1967) The Social Readjustment Rating Scale. *Journal of Psychosomatic Research,* 11, 213–218

Home Office (1984) *Suicide in Prisons:* Report by Her Majesty's Chief Inspector of Prisons. London: HMSO

Home Office (1986) *Report of the working group on suicide prevention*, London: Home Office

The Howard League (1999a) *Desperate Measures: prison suicides and their prevention*. London: The Howard League for Penal Reform

The Howard League (1999b) *Scratching the Surface: the hidden problem of self-harm in prisons*. London: The Howard League for Penal Reform

Illich, I. (1976) *Limits to Medicine*. London: Marion Boyars

Ivanoff, A. and Jong, S.J. (1991) The role of hopelessness and social desirability in predicting suicidal behaviour: a study of prison inmates. *Journal of Consulting and Clinical Psychology*, 59, 394–99

Jablensky, E. (1981) quoted in Kendell, R.E. (1994) Mood (affective) disorders. In R.E. Kendell and A.K. Zealey (eds), *Companion to Psychiatric Studies* (5th edn). Edinburgh: Churchill Livingstone

Jones, A. (1986) Self-mutilation in prison: a comparison of mutilators and non-mutilators. *Criminal Justice and Behaviour*, 13, 286–96

Jones, N.L. (1996) *An Empirical Study of Suicidal Behaviour in Prisons*, unpublished M.Sc. dissertation, University of London

Kendell, R.E. (1994) Mood (affective) disorders. In R.E. Kendell and A.K. Zealey (eds) *Companion to Psychiatric Studies* (5th edn.). Edinburgh: Churchill Livingstone

Kerkhof, A,J.F.M. and Bernasco, W. (1990). Suicidal behaviour in jails and prisons in the Netherlands: incidence, characteristics and prevention. *Suicide and Life Threatening Behaviour*, 20, 123–37

Klerman, G.L. and Weissman, M.M. (1989) Increasing rates of depression. *Journal of the American Medical Association*, 261, 2229–35

Krietman, N. (1976) The coal story: UK suicide rates 1960–71. *British Journal of Preventive and Social Medicine*, 30, 86–93

Kreitman, N. (ed.) (1977) *Parasuicide*. London: Wiley and Sons

Kreitman, N., Philip, A.E., Greer, S. *et al.* (1969) Parasuicide. *British Journal of Psychiatry*, 115, 746–7

Kubler-Ross (1970) *On Death and Dying*. London: Tavistock

Lang, W.A., Ramsey, R.E., Tanney, B.L. and Tierney, R.J. (1989) Caregiver attitudes in suicide prevention. In R.F.W. Diekstra *et al.* (eds) *Suicide and its Prevention*. Leiden: E.J. Brill

Lazarus, R.S. (1966) *Psychological Stress and the Coping Process*. New York: McGraw–Hill

Leenars, A. (1994) A conference report: attempted suicide in Europe. Quoted in Schmidtke, A. *et al.* (1996)

Lester, D. (1991) Physical abuse and physical punishment as precursors of suicidal behaviour. *Stress Medicine*, 7, 255–6. Quoted in M. Livingstone (1997)

Lester, D. (1994) The effectiveness of suicide prevention centres. *Suicide and Life Threatening Behaviour*, 23(3), 263–267

Liebling, A. (1991) *Suicide in Prisons*, unpublished PhD thesis, University of Cambridge

Liebling, A. (1992) *Suicides in Prisons*. London, Routledge

Liebling, A. (1998) Prison suicide and the nature of imprisonment. In A.

Liebling (ed.) *Deaths of Offenders: The Hidden Side of Justice*. Winchester: Waterside Press

Liebling, A. and Krarup, H. (1993) Suicide attempts and self-injury in male prisons, report for the Home Office Research and Planning Unit

Linehan, M.M., Goodstein, J.L., Nielsen, S.L. and Chiles, J.A. (1983) Reasons for staying alive when you are thinking of killing yourself. *Journal of Consulting and Clinical Psychology*, 57, 2: 276–86

Linghan, R. (1995) Mental Health and Risk Management. Symposium presented at the Institute for the Study of Delinquency Annual Conference, University of Nottingham

Livingstone, M. (1994) *Self-injurious behaviour in prisoners*, unpublished Ph.D. thesis, University of Leeds

Livingstone, M. (1997) A review of the literature on self-injurious behaviour amongst prisoners. In G.J. Towl (ed.) *Suicide and Self-Injury in Prisons, Issues in Criminological and Legal Psychology*, 28. Leicester: British Psychological Society

Longfield, M. (1999) The interface between the criminal justice system and the NHS. In G.J. Towl, M.J. McHugh and D. Jones (eds) *Suicide in Prisons: Research, Policy and Practice*. Brighton: Pavilion Publishing

Mathieson, T. (1965) *The Defences of the Weak: a Sociological Study of a Norwegian Correctional Institution*. London: Tavistock

McHugh, M.J. and Towl, G.J. (1997) Organisational Reactions and Reflections on Suicide and Self-Injury. In G.J Towl. (ed.) *Suicide and Self-Injury in Prisons, Issues in Criminological and Legal Psychology, 28*. Leicester: British Psychological Society

McIntosh, J. (1987) Survivor Family Relationships. Literature review in E.J. Dunne, J. McIntosh and K. Dunne-Martin (eds) *Survivors of Suicide*, Springfield, Illinois: Charles C. Thomas

McKay, H.S., Jayewardene, C.H.S. and Reedie, P.B. (1979) *Report on the Effects of Long-term Incarceration and a Proposed Strategy for Future Research*. Contract Report for the Ministry of the Solicitor General of Canada.

McNeil (1994) Hallucinations and violence. In J.Monahan and H.J. Steadman (eds) *Violence and Mental Disorder: Developments in Risk Assessment*. Chicago: Chicago University Press

Medlicott (1999) Prisoners as knowledgeable agents. *Prison Service Journal*, 124, 16–19

Menninger, K.A. (1938) *Man Against Himself*, New York: Harcourt Brace

Monahan, J. (1981) *Predicting Violent Behaviour: An assessment of clinical techniques*. Beverley Hills, CA: Sage

Monahan, J. and Steadman, H.J. (eds) (1994) *Violence and Mental Disorder: Developments in Risk Assessment*. Chicago: Chicago University Press

Morgan, G., Buckley, C. and Nowers, M. (1998) Face to face with the suicidal. *Advances in Psychiatric Treatment*, 4, 188–196

Morgan, H.G. (1979) *Death wishes? The Understanding and Management of Deliberate Self-harm*. New York: John Wiley and Sons

Moser, K.A., Fox, A.J. and Jones, D.R. (1984) Unemployment and mortality in the OPCS longitudinal study. *Lancet*, ii, 1324–28

Moser, K.A., Goldblatt, P., Fox A.J. and Jones, D.R. (1990) Unemployment and mortality. In P. Goldblatt (ed.) *Longitudinal Study 1971–81: Mortality and*

Social Organisation, OPCS LS series

Nagel, W.G. (1976) Environmental influences in prison violence. In A.K. Cohen, G.F. Cole and R.G. Bailey (eds) *Prison Violence.* Lexington, MA: Heath, Lexington Books

National Confidential Inquiry into Suicide and Homicide by People with Mental Illness (1999) *Safer Services: Summary.* Department of Health, PO Box 410, Wetherby, Leeds

Report of the National Steering Group on Deaths in Prisons: Eire 1999

Neal, D. (1996) Research, policy and practice: what progress? In A. Liebling (ed.) *Deaths in Custody: Caring for People at Risk.* London: Whiting and Birch

Needs, A.P.C. (1989) *The lifer assessment manual.* Unpublished Prison Service document

Nisbett, R. and Ross, L. (1980) *Human Inference: Strategies and Shortcomings of Social Judgement.* Engelwood Cliffs, NJ: W.H. Freeman

Office for National Statistics (1998) *Psychiatric Morbidity Among Prisoners in England and Wales.* London: The Stationery Office

Office for National Statistics (1999) *Non-Fatal Suicidal Behaviour among Prisoners.* Office for National Statistics, London: The Stationery Office

Oltmanns, T.F. and Maher, B.A. (eds) (1988) *Delusional Beliefs.* New York: J. Wiley and Sons Ltd

Parkes, C.M. (1972) *Bereavement: Studies of grief in adult life.* London and New York: Tavistock Publications

Parliamentary Commission for Administration, 7th Annual Report, Session 1998–9, presented to Parliament pursuant to section 10(4) of the Parliamentary Commission Act 1967, Ordered by the House of Commons to be printed 23 June 1999, HTTP: http://www.ombudsman.org.uk

Pattison, E.M. and Kahan, J. (1983) The Deliberate Self-Harm syndrome. *American Journal of Psychiatry,* 140, 867–72

Paykel, E.S. and Cooper, Z. (1992) Life events and social stress. In E.S. Paykel (ed.) *Handbook of Affective Disorders.* Edinburgh: Churchill Livingstone

Platt, S. and Kreitman, N. (1984) Unemployment and parasuicide in Edinburgh 1968–82. *British Medical Journal,* 289, 1029–32

Platt, S., Backett, S. and Kreitman, N. (1988) Social constructions or causal ascription: distinguishing suicide from undetermined deaths. *Social Psychiatry and Psychiatric Epidemiology,* 23, 217–22. K. Hawton, G. Morgan and A. Tylee (1994) (eds) *The Prevention of Suicide.* Department of Health: London

Plous, S. (1993) *The Psychology of Judgement and Decision Making.* New York: McGraw Hill

Plutchik, R. (1997) Suicide and violence: the two stage model of countervailing forces. In A.J. Botsis, C.R. Soldatos and C.N. Stefanis (eds) *Suicide: Biopsychosocial Approaches.* Amsterdam: Elsevier

Pokorny, A.D. (1983) Prediction of suicide in psychiatric patients. *Archives of General Psychiatry,* 40, 249–257

Power, K., McElroy, J. and Swanson, V. (1997) Coping abilities and prisoners: perception of suicidal risk management. *The Howard Journal,* 36(4): 378–92

Prien, E.P., Goldstein, I.L. and Macey, W.H. (1987) Multidomain job analysis: Procedures and applications in human resource management and development. *Training and Development Journal,* 41, 68–72

175

Prins, H. (1996) Risk assessment and management in criminal justice and psychiatry. *Journal of Forensic Psychiatry*, 7(1), 42–62

Prison Service Journal (1999) *Death in Custody*, July No. 124

Pritchard, C. (1995) *Suicide – The Ultimate Reaction? A Psycho-Social Study*. Buckingham: Open University Press

Reiger, D.A., Boyd, J.H., Burke, J.P. *et al.* (1988) One month prevalence of mental disorders in the United States. *Archives of General Psychiatry*, 45, 977–86

Ross, R.R. and McKay, H.B. (1979) *Self-mutilation*. Massachussetts: Lexington

Ross R. R., McKay, H.B., Palmer, W.R.T. and Kenny, C.J. (1978) Self-mutilation in adolescent female offenders. *Canadian Journal of Criminology*, 20, 375-92

Rossau, C.D. and Mortensen, P.B. (1997) Risk factors for suicide in patients with schizophrenia: nested case-control study. *British Journal of Psychiatry*, 171, 355–59

Royal College of Psychiatrists (1998) *Management of Imminent Violence; Clinical Practice Guidelines to support mental health services*. Occasional Paper 41. London: Royal College of Psychiatrists

Russell. D., Cutrona, C. E., Rose, J. and Yurko, K. (1984) Social and emotional loneliness: an examination of Weiss's typology of loneliness. *Journal of Personality and Social Psychology*, 46, 1313–21

Samaritans, The (2000) http://www.samaritans.org.iuk/sams.html/suuiuk.html

Sapsford, R.J. (1978) Life Sentence Prisoners: psychological change during sentence. *British Journal of Criminology*, 18, 128–145

Schmidtke, A., Bille-Braher, U., DeLeo, D. *et al.* (1996) Attempted suicide in Europe: rates, trends and sociodemographic characteristics of suicide attempters during the period 1989–1992. Results of the WHO/EURO multicentre study on parasuicide. *Acta Psychiatrica Scandinavia*, 93, 327–38

Shneidman, E.S. (1985) *Definition of Suicide*. New York: John Wiley and Sons

Shneidman, E.S. (1987) A psychological approach to suicide. In G.R. Vanden Bos and B.K. Bryant (eds) *Cataclysms, Crises and Catastrophes: Psychology in Action*. Washington, DC: American Psychological Association

Scott, P.D. (1977) Assessing Dangerousness in Criminals. *British Journal of Psychiatry*, 131, 127–42

Seale, C. (1998) *Constructing Death: the sociology of dying and bereavement*. Cambridge: Cambridge University Press

Shaver, P. and Rubenstein, C. (1980) Childhood attachment experience and adult loneliness. *Review of Personality and Social Psychology*, 1, 42–73

Shea, S.J. (1993). Personality characteristics of self-mutilating male prisoners. *Journal of Clinical Psychology*, 49, 576–85

Sheskin, A. and Wallace, S.E. (1976) Differing bereavements: suicide, natural and accidental death. *Omega*, Journal of Death and Dying, 7, 3, 299–42

SHOUT for women: self-harm overcome by understanding and tolerance, c/o PO Box 654, Bristol, BS99 1XG

Sletten, I.W., Everson, R.C. and Brown, M.L. (1973) Some results from an automated statewide comparison among attempted, committed, and non-suicidal patients. *Suicide and Life Threatening Behaviour*, 3, 191–7. Quoted in A.J. Botsis *et al.* (eds) (1997)

Smalley, H. (1911) report by the medical inspector in The Report by the Prison Comissioners. London: HMSO

Snow, L. (1997) A pilot study of self-injury amongst women prisoners. In G.J.Towl (1997) (ed.) *Suicide and Self-Injury in Prisons, Issues in Criminological and Legal Psychology*, 28. Leicester: British Psychological Society

Snow, L. (1998) A review of the role of peer group support in prisons, unpublished report, University of Kent

Snow, L. (2000) Suicide Prevention within New York City Department of Corrections Facilities. *British Journal of Forensic Practice*, 2(1), 36–41

Staudacher, C. (1988) *Beyond Grief: A Guide for Recovering from the Death of a Loved One*. London: Souvenir Press

Stern, V. (1998) *A Sin Against the Future*. London: Penguin

Stillion. J.M. and McDowell, E.E. (eds) (1996) *Suicide Across the Life Span*. Washington: Taylor & Francis

Suicide Awareness Bulletin (1999), No 2, HM Prison Service, Suicide Prevention Strategy Group, Abell House, London

Surtees, P.G. and Sashidharan, S.P. (1986) Psychiatric morbidity in two matched community samples: a comparison of rates and risks in Edinburgh and St. Louis. *Journal of Affective Disorders*, 10, 101–13

Sykes, G.M. (1958) *The Society of Captives*. Princeton, NJ: Princeton University Press

Sykes, G.M. and Messinger, S. (1960) The Inmate Social System. In R. Cloward (ed.) (1960) *Theoretical Studies in Social Organisation of the Prison*. USA: Social Sciences Research Council

Taylor, P.J. (1994) Schizophrenia and crime: distinctive patterns in association. In S.Hodgins (ed.) *Crime and Mental Disorder*. Beverley Hills, CA; Sage

Thornton, D. (1990) Depression, self-injury and attempted suicide amongst the YOI population. *DPS Report Series* I: 34, 47–55

Toch, H. (1992) *Living in Prison: The ecology of survival*. Washington, DC: American Psychological Association. (Originally published in 1977.)

Toch, H., and Adams, K. (1989). *Coping: Maladaptation in prisons*. New Brunswick, NJ: Transaction

Topp, D.O. (1979) Suicide in prison. *British Journal of Psychiatry*, 134, 24–7

Towl, G.J. (1990) Understanding the voices. *Nursing Times*, 86, 2

Towl, G.J. (1994) Ethical issues in forensic psychology. *Forensic Update*, DCLP(39). Leicester: British Psychological Society

Towl, G.J. (1996) Homicide and suicide, risk assessment in prisons, *The Psychologist*, September. British Psychological Society: Leicester

Towl, G.J. (ed.) (1997) *Suicide and Self-injury in Prisons, Issues in Criminological and Legal Psychology*, 28. Leicester: British Psychological Society

Towl, G.J. (1999a) Self-inflicted deaths in prisons in England and Wales from 1998 to 1996. *British Journal of Forensic Practice*, 1(2), 28–33

Towl, G.J. (1999b) Suicide in prisons in England and Wales, 1988–1996. In G.J. Towl, M.J. McHugh and D. Jones (eds) *Suicide in Prisons: Research, Policy and Practice*. Brighton: Pavilion Publishing

Towl, G.J. (2000) Reflections upon suicide in prisons. *British Journal of Forensic Practice*, 2, 1, 28–33

Towl, G.J. and Crighton, D.A. (1996) *The Handbook of Psychology for Forensic Practitioners*. Routledge: London

Towl, G.J. and Crighton, D.A. (1997) Risk assessment with offenders. *International Review of Psychiatry*, 9, 187–93

Towl, G.J. and Crighton, D.A. (1998) Suicide in prisons in England and Wales from 1988 to 1995. *Criminal Behaviour and Mental Health*, 8, 184–192

Towl, G.J. and Fisher, J. (1992) Education in prisons: ideology and change. *The Criminologist*, 16, 3

Towl, G.J. and Fleming, C. (1997) Self inflicted deaths of women prisoners. *Forensic Update*, 51, 5–8

Towl, G.J. and Hudson, D.I. (1997) Risk assessment and management. In G.J. Towl (ed.) *Suicide and Self-Injury in Prisons, Issues in Criminological and Legal Psychology*, 28. Leicester: British Psychological Society

Towl, G.J. and McHugh, M. (1999) Prison Service Policy: caring for the suicidal in prisons. In G.J. Towl, M. McHugh D. and Jones (eds) *Suicides in Prisons: research policy and practice*. Brighton: Pavillion Publishing

Turner, R.J. (1983) Direct, indirect and moderating effects of social support on psychological distress and associated conditions. In H.B. Kaplan. (ed.) *Psychosocial Stress: Trends in theory and research*. New York: Bruce and Stratton

Tversky, A. and Kahneman, D. (1974) Judgement under uncertainty: heuristics and biases. *Science*, 185, 1124–31

Van Egmond, D. and Diekstra, R.F.W. (1989) The predictablity of suicidal behaviour. In R.F.W. Diekstra, *et al.* (eds) *Suicide and Its Prevention*. Leiden: E.J. Brill

Walsh, B.W. and Rosen, P.M. (1988) *Self-mutilation: Theory, research and treatment*. New York: Guilford Press

Walter, T. (1994) *The Revival of Death*. London: Routledge.

Watts, F.N., Powell, E.G. and Austin, S.V. (1973) The modification of abnormal beliefs. *British Journal of Medical Psychology*, 46, 356–63

Weiss, R.S. (1975) *Marital Separation*. New York: Basic Books

Wertheimer, A. (1991) *A Special Scar: The Experience of People Bereaved by Suicide*. London: Routledge

Wicks, R. J. (1972) Suicide Prevention. *Federal Probation*, 36(3), 29–31

Wilkins, J. and Coid, J. (1991) Self-mutilation in female remanded prisoners: 1. An indicator of severe psychopathology. *Criminal Behaviour and Mental Health*, 1, 247–267

Wilkinson, R. (1996) *Unhealthy Societies, The afflictions of inequality*. London: Routledge

Williams, J.M.G. and Scott, J. (1988) Autobiographical memory in depression. *Psychological Medicine*, 18, 689–95

Wills, T. A. (1991) Social support and interpersonal relationships. In M.S. Clark (ed.) *Prosocial Behaviour*. Newbury Park, CA: Sage

Winkler, G.E. (1992). Assessing and responding to suicidal jail inmates. *Community Mental Health Journal*, 28, 317–326

Wool, R. J. and Dooley, E. (1987) A study of attempted suicides in prisons. *Medical Science and the Law*, 28: 297–310

World Health Organisation (1948) Official Report of the World Health Organisation 1948, 11:23. Quoted in *ICD, Manual of the International Statistical Classification of Diseases, Injuries and Causes of Death, 9th Revision*. Geneva: WHO

World Health Organisation (1955) *Report of the International Conference for the*

7th revision of the International list of diseases and causes of death. Unpublished document WHO/HS/7 Rev. Conf/17. Rev.1

World Health Organisation (1965) *Report of the International Conference for the 8th revision of the International list of diseases and causes of death.* Unpublished document WHO/HS/7 Rev. Conf/17. Rev.1

World Health Organisation (1977) *International Classification of Diseases: Manual of the international statistical classification of diseases, injuries and causes of death* (9th Revision). Geneva: WHO

World Health Organisation (1993) *International Classification of Diseases* (10th Revision). Geneva: WHO

World Health Organisation (1998) *Mental Health Promotion in Prisons*, WHO (Regional Office for Europe) Health in Prisons Project, HM Prison Service Health Care. HTTP: http://www.hipp-europe.org

Zamble, E. and Porporino, F. J. (1988) *Coping Behaviour, Adaptation in Prison Inmates*. New York: Springer-Verlag

Index